"Covering a wide range of territory in a reasonably condensed space, attorney Niose (president, American Humanist Assoc.) looks at the culture wars from the perspective of secular America. While confronting numerous commonly held misconceptions by believers about secularism (e.g., the religious Right implying that religious faith is part of patriotism), Niose admirably refrains from antireligious hostility, striving for equality rather than proving the superiority of his perspective. . . . This is a calm, informative, and positive portrait of the rapidly growing secular segment of the American population. Highly recommended for politically oriented readers of all religious persuasions."

—*Library Journal*

"This excellent book is simultaneously disturbing and reassuring. David Niose lays bare the whole dismal history of how the Religious Right hijacked America and betrayed the secular intentions of the Founding Fathers. Fortunately, as he also documents, decent Americans are now fighting back, and the book ends on an uplifting note of hope."

—Richard Dawkins, author of *The God Delusion*

"David Niose is a talented writer with keen insights into contemporary secularism. As a key leader in the secular movement, Niose is uniquely situated to help Americans understand this fast-growing phenomenon."

—Rob Boston, author of *Why the Religious Right is Wrong About Separation of Church and State*

"Dave Niose is a highly valued and respected leader in the secular movement."

—Wendy Kaminer, author of *Free for All and I'm Dysfunctional, You're Dysfunctional*

"Dave Niose writes clearly and concisely and advocates effectively for the secular tradition. I expect Secular Americans who read this book will feel more motivated to seek the visibility and respect they so richly deserve."

—Herb Silverman, president of the Secular Coalition for America

NONBELIEVER NATION

THE RISE *of* SECULAR AMERICANS

DAVID NIOSE

palgrave
macmillan

NONBELIEVER NATION
Copyright © David Niose, 2012.
All rights reserved.

First published in 2012 by PALGRAVE MACMILLAN® in the United
States—a division of St. Martin's Press LLC, 175 Fifth Avenue, New York, NY
10010.

Where this book is distributed in the UK, Europe and the rest of the world,
this is by Palgrave Macmillan, a division of Macmillan Publishers Limited,
registered in England, company number 785998, of Houndmills, Basingstoke,
Hampshire RG21 6XS.

Palgrave Macmillan is the global academic imprint of the above companies and
has companies and representatives throughout the world.

Palgrave® and Macmillan® are registered trademarks in the United States, the
United Kingdom, Europe and other countries.

ISBN 978-0-230-33895-1

Some names have been changed in this work to protect privacy.

Small segments of this work first appeared in David Niose's blog, *Our
Humanity Naturally:* "The Myth of Militant Atheism," "Mommy, Don't We
Love America?" and "On Being Post-Theological"

Library of Congress Cataloging-in-Publication Data
Niose, David.
  Nonbeliever nation : the rise of secular Americans / David Niose.
    pages   cm
  Includes index.
  ISBN 978-0-230-33895-1 (hardback)
  1. Secularism—United States. 2. Religion and politics—United States.
3. Culture conflict—United States. I. Title.
BL2760.N5632012
211'.60973—dc23

                                                        2011049323

A catalogue record of the book is available from the British Library.

Design by Letra Libre, Inc.

First edition: July 2012

10 9 8 7 6 5 4 3 2 1

Printed in the United States of America.

For Katy, who's given me much in which to believe.

CONTENTS

INTRODUCTION

THE DECLINE OF THE AMERICAN DIALOGUE

A CENTURY AGO, IN THE HISTORIC PRESIDENTIAL CAMPAIGN OF 1912, American voters saw a rare contest of four relevant candidates: the unpopular Republican incumbent, William Howard Taft; Democratic challenger Woodrow Wilson; former president Theodore Roosevelt, running on the Progressive (or "Bull Moose") ticket; and Socialist Party candidate Eugene Debs. The abundance of candidates was just one of many remarkable aspects of the campaign, for few American presidential elections have seen such dramatic twists and intrigue.

Roosevelt, who just four years earlier had selected Taft as his successor, now returned to presidential politics to challenge the incumbent for the Republican nomination, polarizing the party between two men who were a study in contrasts. Energetic and full of gusto, having embarked on an African safari after leaving the presidency in 1909, Roosevelt campaigned with zeal and progressive rhetoric. He was popular among Republican voters and won the vast majority of state primaries, including even Taft's home state of Ohio. Taft, meanwhile, the heaviest man to ever occupy the White House, conveyed none of Roosevelt's vigor and charisma nor his populist spirit. He carried only one primary state.

In 1912, however, primary elections were not as critical as they are today. Only about a dozen states had presidential primaries back then, so most of the delegates needed for the nomination were instead selected by party insiders. Unlike today, when the national convention is usually just a coronation ceremony where the only suspense might be the selection of the nominee's running mate, a century ago the conventions were frequently an arena for heavyweight politicking and backroom deals, where multiple ballots would often be needed to finally decide the ticket. Thus, having been beaten badly in the primaries, Taft was nevertheless able to use his influence with party regulars at the GOP convention in Chicago to secure the nomination. This was much to the chagrin of Roosevelt who, not a gracious loser, alleged improprieties and stormed out of the hall with his delegates, subsequently forming the Progressive Party with himself at the top of the ticket.

The scene was nearly as wild at the Democratic convention in Baltimore, where the party took a grueling 46 ballots before finally selecting its nominee. House Speaker Champ Clark appeared to be the early favorite, but his ties to the corrupt Tammany Hall political machine eventually led party stalwart William Jennings Bryan—who himself had been the Democratic presidential nominee three times previously (losing the general election each time)—to throw his support to Wilson, thereby leading others to do the same. Wilson, the erudite, moralistic former president of Princeton University and governor of New Jersey, was perceived as a moderate reformer with integrity.

Adding a unique new angle to the campaign would be Eugene Debs, the passionate socialist who argued that he was the only true progressive in the race, accusing Roosevelt of demagoguery and calling all three of his opponents pawns of large business interests. Debs received almost a million votes in the general election, an impressive 6 percent of the total, representing an all-time high-water mark for any Socialist Party candidate.[1]

The raucous nomination battles of 1912 were just a prelude to the general campaign. A few weeks before the November election, Roosevelt was shot in the chest by a deranged saloonkeeper before giving a speech in Milwaukee. Consistent with his tough-guy image, Roosevelt denied immediate medical care and went on to deliver a lengthy speech despite the bullet lodged inside him. The Taft campaign, meanwhile, would suffer a blow of its own when Taft's running mate, the sitting vice president James Sherman, died of natural causes just a week before the election, a fatality that was ominously foretelling of the Taft administration's own impending demise.

With the Republicans split, Wilson was able to coast to an easy victory despite a modest vote total. Receiving just over 42 percent of the popular vote, Wilson nevertheless carried the vast majority of states and received 435 electoral votes to just 88 for Roosevelt and 8 for Taft. With only 3.4 million votes, Taft's total was well under Roosevelt's 4.1 million and closer to that of the Socialist candidate Debs than to Wilson.

Looking back at the presidential candidates of a century ago, we discover unsettling truths about today's America. Wilson, probably the most religious of the four, had this to say when asked about Charles Darwin's theory of evolution by natural selection: "Of course, like every other man of intelligence and education I do believe in organic evolution. It surprises me that at this late date such questions should be raised."[2] Roosevelt was also a vocal admirer of Darwin's work, calling the British naturalist "the great Darwin."[3] In a later memoir, referring to his love of nature, Roosevelt said, "Thank Heaven I sat at the feet of Darwin and Huxley."[4] (Thomas Huxley was known as "Darwin's bulldog" for his aggressive defense of the theory of evolution.) While Roosevelt expressed sentiments that would make him a lonely man in the modern GOP, Taft was a genuine religious skeptic. "I do not believe in the divinity of Christ," he wrote in an 1899 letter, "and there are many other of the postulates of the orthodox creed to which I cannot subscribe."[5] And finally, Debs, the socialist, was decidedly secular, highly critical of organized religion and the use of religion as a political tool, saying, "I don't know of any crime that the oppressors and their hirelings have not proven by the Bible."[6]

When compared to today, these statements of long-dead public figures reveal the travesty of contemporary American politics and public dialogue. Typically, when we examine history from the vantage point of a hundred years, many of the predominant attitudes from that earlier time will seem antiquated; we may see beliefs that reflected a lack of knowledge that has since been gained, or perhaps prejudices that we now know to be plainly wrong. When we take a closer look at the candidates of 1912, however, we find that in important ways the process of antiquation seems to have worked in reverse—that the political generation of a hundred years ago, though lacking the benefit of a century of scientific advancement, nevertheless displayed considerable evidence of intellectual maturity that is woefully lacking today.

The ignoble demise of the American public dialogue becomes glaringly apparent when we contrast the views of the four men who ran for president in 1912 to the modern political landscape. Today, a full century after the era of Roosevelt and Wilson, we routinely see presidential candidates assure voters that they are doubtful of the theory of evolution, pandering to a large segment of the electorate that believes the world is just a few thousand years old. Rick Perry, for example, governor of the second-most-populous state in the nation, lucidly conveys America's intellectual decline by expressing his views on evolution this way: "God may have done it in the blink of the eye or he may have done it over this long period of time, I don't know." Evolution "is a theory that's out there," Perry explained, but it "has some gaps in it."[7] The Texas chief executive is by no means an anomaly, as other major political figures, such as Sarah Palin, Michele Bachmann, and Mike Huckabee, have made a point of emphasizing their refusal to accept evolution theory, and even former president George W. Bush favored teaching creationism, disguised as so-called intelligent design, in public schools.

It's no secret that a major cause of this regression is the Religious Right, the loose-knit but powerful movement that has been changing the dynamics of American politics for over three decades. Guised as representing "traditional family values," the Religious Right is driven by a small minority that is extreme in its views, well funded, organized, and fueled by a fear of modernity that unfortunately resonates on a mass level. It exploded onto the scene in 1980, when the inaptly named "Moral Majority" flexed its political muscle to help elect Ronald Reagan, and it has increased in power with virtually every election cycle since, to the point that it now commands almost complete control of one major party and greatly influences the other.

From the standpoint of those interested in rational public policy, what is perhaps most troubling is that the public and the media have become largely desensitized to the Religious Right. When concerns were raised

in 2011 about some extreme fundamentalist views associated with candidates Michele Bachmann and Rick Perry, for example, *Washington Post*
and *Newsweek* religion writer Lisa Miller dismissed them in a column,
saying, "Some on the left seem suspicious that a firm belief in Jesus equals
a desire to take over the world."[8] Hence, whereas even a century ago many
believed that biblical literalism and religious conservatism were unlikely to
remain potent forces in politics, over the last 30 years the Religious Right
has shown such predictions to be dead wrong. Extreme religious conservatives, men and women who would have seemed backward even a hundred
years ago, are now viewed by well-informed mainstream journalists as a
normal part of America's political landscape. Today, even many adults are
too young to remember the country before the likes of Jerry Falwell, Pat
Robertson, and James Dobson. As a result, they are unfazed by the political influence of religious fundamentalists.

It would be an oversimplification to suggest that all of America's woes
since the late 1970s are due to the rise of the Religious Right, but it would
be just as erroneous to downplay the harm caused by politically mobilized
religious fundamentalism. The Religious Right is a uniquely American
phenomenon, and its rise correlates with undesirable social phenomena
that are also uniquely American, from high rates of violent crime and teen
pregnancy to low rates of scientific literacy. Defiant anti-intellectualism has
become mainstream, resulting in disastrous public policy and the decay of
some of America's most cherished values—rational discourse, pragmatism,
and pluralism, to name just a few. When a significant segment of the politically engaged population stands firmly opposed to science, reason, and
critical thinking, intelligent debate and policy making become impossible.

This book, as the title suggests, is not just about the Religious Right, but the
growing resistance to it. Effective opposition to the Religious Right has
been slow to crystallize in the wasteland of modern American politics, but
now that it is emerging, it represents real hope. That opposition is made
possible by the rise of the long-overlooked population of Americans who
reject outright the notion that religiosity is a prerequisite to patriotism or
sound public policy.

Until recently, because conventional wisdom presupposed that the
public demanded the exaltation of religion, the most visible opponents of

the Religious Right emphasized their own religiosity. They argued, for example, that religious conservatives do not speak for all religious citizens, often stressing that liberals can also be religious. While of course true, this emphasis proved inadequate and sometimes even counterproductive. When liberals and moderates joined the Religious Right in the enthusiastic acclamation of religion, they marginalized nonbelievers and unwittingly played directly into the hand of religious conservatives, implicitly conceding that a nonreligious worldview is wrong and un-American. This, in turn, only validated the Religious Right's righteous claims that, as the most fervently religious segment of the population, they represent real American values.

As a result, far from having gained ground against the Religious Right, liberals and moderates have been fighting a losing battle for over three decades, as is evidenced by the steady increase in power of religious conservatives since the late 1970s. With a few notable exceptions (such as the success of the LGBT—lesbian, gay, bisexual, transgender—movement), the Religious Right has seen few major setbacks in its relentless effort to reshape the American public policy debate. Those opposed to the Religious Right have been getting beaten badly, and the sooner that this reality is accepted the sooner a better strategy can be found.

In fact, many are already utilizing a better strategy—a grassroots, identity-oriented approach that confronts the Religious Right head-on. In recent years, a movement of unapologetic Secular Americans has emerged, determined to return politicized religious fundamentalism to its pre-Reagan level of influence. The pages ahead will document the rise of that movement and the hope that it offers, examining who these Americans are, what they believe, and the issues and events that have created the so-called "culture wars." Secular Americans—though long ignored by the general public, the media, and politicians—in recent years have quickly become the Religious Right's biggest threat. Call them skeptics, humanists, atheists, agnostics, or just plain nonreligious, they are coming into the mainstream, and their success will pull the pedestal out from underneath the Religious Right, rebutting its claim to the moral high ground and pushing its extreme policy positions back to the fringes.

Much has changed in America, for better and worse, in the century since the 1912 election. As Americans went to the polls that year, few would have imagined that in the decades ahead the country would split the atom, send men to the moon, and become the globally dominant military and economic power. Few would have predicted the progress, even if imperfect, that America has made toward racial equality, women's rights, and gay rights. Unfortunately, however, not all the change has been positive. Despite its achievements, America now sits in the early years of the twenty-first century as a highly dysfunctional and seriously troubled society, and many of its problems—from the immature level of its internal dialogue to the misguided direction of its public policy—can be traced directly or indirectly to the impact of the Religious Right and, perhaps even more importantly, to the marginalization of the secular demographic.

As such, the rise of Secular Americans is not happening a moment too soon. If America does not learn to recognize and respect nonbelievers and religious skeptics as a valued segment of the population, bleak times will surely await the country and the rest of the world. Over three decades ago, when religious conservatives became a major political force, the country embarked on a terrible, long descent—one that continues today and will not be reversed without a renewed appreciation of reason, critical thinking, and the forward-looking values promoted by Secular Americans. This is not to suggest that religion itself must be made irrelevant, but only that effective opposition is needed to the politically mobilized fundamentalist element. That effective opposition, lacking for decades, is now taking root in a transformative movement fueled by Americans who will no longer allow personal secularity to be stigmatized. Given the state of affairs after several decades of Religious Right dominance, we should all be hoping that Secular Americans win their place at the table.

ONE

THE WEDDING INVITATION

THE WEDDING INVITATION ITSELF WASN'T A SURPRISE, BUT ITS content was.

I hadn't seen Maria since we both graduated from college five years earlier. I met her during our junior year in an elective sociology class, where we sat next to each other and quickly became friends. As often happens among college crowds, she and her other friends started hanging around with my buddies and me, and we all spent lots of time together, staying up late chatting, as only college kids with too much free time can, about everything—life, love, politics, truth, religion, God. Neither Maria nor I had majored in philosophy, but in real life every college student sooner or later becomes a late-night philosopher. Along with our friends, we would be sitting around watching stupid pet tricks on Letterman or listening to Pink Floyd, when inevitably someone would start speculating about something deep.

More often than not, the opinions would be nothing too profound, but Maria's comments were always intelligent and articulate. She was born into a Catholic family but by then was a nonbeliever and secular humanist who had no room for any of the superstition or doctrine of traditional religion. In fact, while unsympathetic in her assessment of all revelation-based religion—Christianity, Islam, and Judaism—she was especially tough on

the Catholic Church, which she considered a grossly outdated relic over-
seen by a paternalistic, misogynistic hierarchy. She loathed the church's
positions on birth control and abortion rights, considered its views toward
sex repressive, thought the whole celibacy thing was absurd, and blamed
the church for the anti-Semitism that eventually gave rise to the Holocaust. To call her a disaffected Catholic would be an understatement.

After graduation, we went our separate ways but managed to stay in
touch with one or two phone calls a year. So I was not surprised to find,
when I opened my mail one day in 1989, an invitation to Maria's wedding. Since I knew she had been dating someone seriously, the invitation
was certainly no shocker, but what bewildered me was what the invitation
said: the wedding would take place at the Immaculate Conception Roman
Catholic Church in Maria's hometown. Knowing her as I did, it made no
sense that Maria would turn to the Catholic Church to seal vows of love
and commitment with her life partner. As I mulled it over, I concluded
that Maria had probably gone back to her family's church to get married
because that's what her family, especially her parents, expected. Coming
from a big Catholic family that hadn't seen any of its members have a wedding (or at least a *first* wedding) anywhere else but the hometown Catholic
church, she probably couldn't break with tradition.

It turns out that I was right. It would be several more years before I
would be able to have a conversation with Maria and her husband about it,
but when that conversation finally happened, over dinner one night when
I was visiting, Maria explained the whole ordeal to me. "The Catholic
Church is the last place I wanted to get married," she said. "But I really felt
we had no choice. In our family, especially with Mom and Dad paying for
the wedding, there was no way it was going to take place anywhere else. It
wasn't even a topic that was open for discussion."

The rest of the night was a lot like being back in college. We all sat
around and chatted about life, love, politics, truth, and religion, the only
difference being the years of added life experience. She was still a secular
humanist, still a wonderful person, and now married to a great guy. I was
happy for her.

Maria's story is a common one, and it illustrates a dilemma that many young,
secular people face in our society. Family pressure and cultural expectations

often force nonbelieving or halfheartedly believing participants into religious ceremonies that convey validity and legitimacy upon institutions for which they have little admiration and sometimes even contempt.

In Maria's case, the chain will end there. Despite the fact that her family pressured her into having her wedding at the Immaculate Conception Church, she and her husband are raising their children without traditional religion. Though there was some controversy when the wider family learned that the kids weren't getting baptized or going to church, they eventually accepted the couple's decision to raise a secular family.

Maria and her family have joined the ranks of the Secular Americans, a growing group of individuals who affirmatively choose to live without religion or, at the very least, without theistic religion. Secular Americans have existed as long as the country itself, but only in recent years have they begun to stand together as a unit and demand recognition, respect, and equality. Whereas in the past someone in Maria's position would have been more likely to yield to family pressure by indifferently shuffling the kids through the milestones of a Catholic upbringing—baptism, Sunday school, First Communion, Confirmation, and so forth—today a growing segment of the population sees the value of rejecting such gestures outright, of standing firm as openly secular.

THE SECULAR AMERICAN DEMOGRAPHIC

Before discussing who the Secular Americans are, what they want, and what they are doing to get it, a few words about terminology are in order. The word *secular* simply means "without religion." Some dictionaries will use the definition "worldly or temporal, rather than religious or spiritual." In civics class, we usually learn that "secular government" is a basic characteristic of most modern democracies. That doesn't mean that a secular government must be antireligion, but only that government should be neutral on religion and not controlled by clerics or based on religious law. Some modern democracies, such as Great Britain, technically mix church and state (the British monarch is also head of the Church of England, the nation's established church), but aside from such exceptions, we usually associate modern democracies with secular government. Secular democracies support religious tolerance and freedom of conscience, and for this reason they are almost universally seen, at least in the developed world, as enlightened and desirable.

Unlike secular government, to be "personally secular" means that an individual is *personally* without religion. Thus, while most Americans support the general notion of secular government, a smaller number are personally secular, living as individuals without theistic religion. These Secular Americans identify in various ways. A very small percentage of them openly identify as atheists, meaning they do not believe in the existence of any gods. A similarly small percentage identify as agnostic, which is commonly defined as a view that nothing can be known about the existence of a god. Agnostics often say that they don't believe there is a god, but they don't necessarily have an affirmative belief that there isn't one either, because they simply concede that they don't know. Generally speaking, however, most agnostics are functionally atheists, because they have no affirmative belief in a divinity and they typically have little use for organized religion.[1]

Other Secular Americans, again a small percentage, prefer to be called humanists. Unlike atheism and agnosticism, both of which address only the single issue of the existence of a divinity, humanism is a broad philosophy that includes affirmative values and ethical principles without relying on belief in a supernatural deity. Humanism is sometimes divided into two categories: secular humanism and religious humanism. The difference between the two has nothing to do with their views on the existence of a god (both secular and religious humanism are not theistic), but they may have significantly different practices. Secular humanists generally have no need for any kind of religious structure, such as membership in a church, whereas religious humanists usually find value in belonging to some kind of religious institution, whether it be a Unitarian-Universalist church or fellowship, a congregation of Humanistic Judaism, an Ethical Culture group, or some other religious entity. Thus, religious humanists are a puzzling category to some, as they are nonbelievers who nevertheless consider themselves "religious." But since the word *secular* can also mean "without theism," religious humanists can still be considered Secular Americans.[2]

Finally, there is another segment of the population that also fits under the Secular American umbrella, and this is by far the largest: those who are without religion or without theism but do not identify as atheist, agnostic, or humanist. These Secular Americans will often answer "none" when asked for religious identity, or many will even continue to identify with the religious category of their upbringing despite having long ago rejected the tenets of that religion. Many are simply apathetic to the question of whether deities exist, seeing the issue as unknowable and irrelevant to daily life, and still others may even acknowledge some kind of vague belief akin to Deism. What is similar about these individuals is that they typically approach daily life without supernatural beliefs, don't rely on an interventionist god, and have little use for traditional theology.

Calculating the number of Secular Americans is difficult because, like many questions relating to religious categorization, the answer depends on whether we define the term according to religious belief, religious identity, or religious practice. We can see this dynamic by considering other religious categories, such as the Catholic demographic. Currently, about fifty-seven million Americans, or 25.1 percent of the adult population, identify as Catholic.[3] There are, however, many Catholics who are less than devout in their belief, often to the point of rejecting most or all of church doctrine. Many never attend mass, for example, and many routinely use birth control even though the church considers contraception not just a sin, but a mortal sin. It is not at all unusual to hear ordinary "Catholics" say that they question the authority of bishops and cardinals, have serious doubts about life after death, and even doubt the divinity of Jesus. The point is not to suggest that Catholics are more uncertain than others with respect to their core religious convictions, as surely inconsistencies and outright contradictory views can be found among the adherents of most religions; rather, the point is that precise categorization is an impossible exercise.

We see these same kinds of inconsistencies when we try to quantify the Secular American demographic. The most glaring inconsistency is found when we compare findings on religious belief and religious identity. According to the American Religious Identification Survey, just over 81 percent of Americans affirmatively claim a belief in a divinity (69.5 percent claim a belief in a personal God; 12.1 percent in a "higher power"), leaving almost one in five (18.4 percent) who do not affirm such a belief.[4] Of that 18.4 percent, about one-third (6.1 percent) refused to answer the question, with the remaining two-thirds stating that they disbelieved, felt there is no way to know, or were unsure. Even if all of those who refused to answer are in fact believers (which is highly doubtful, since it is more likely that the stigma attached to nonbelief would often be the reason for refusal), we are still left with over 12 percent who are implicitly atheist or agnostic based on their answers (either stating disbelief or conceding uncertainty or lack of knowledge).

Most interesting, however, is that these belief numbers differ markedly from the reported numbers on identity. Even though almost one in five Americans do not affirmatively report a belief in a divinity, and more than one in ten can undoubtedly be defined as nonbelievers, only 1.6 percent actually identify as atheist or agnostic![5] Even if some of the aforementioned 18.4 percent would not be accurately categorized as atheist or agnostic, the inconsistency between secular belief and identity is undeniable. This inconsistency is no doubt attributable to the stigma surrounding atheist identity in America. For complex reasons that will be discussed later, Americans have a grossly distorted view of nonbelievers, causing many to remain "in the closet."

For the purpose of quantifying the Secular American demographic, a modest estimate could use the range of 12 to 18 percent just described, depending on whether one chooses to include those who refused to answer. This range is almost certainly conservative when we consider that 20.2 percent of Americans reported either "none" (15 percent) or "don't know" (5.2 percent) when asked for religious identity. The "none" category has doubled since 1990, one of the only categories of religious identification to show significant growth during that time period, and among younger people it is even more prominent (22 percent).[6]

Although one could argue that some who reported "none" might nevertheless be devout believers, it can simultaneously be argued that many who report religious identity are essentially secular in their views and practices. The most obvious indicator in this regard is church attendance, which shows that less than half the population attends religious services on a regular basis.[7] Moreover, given the various social and cultural pressures that encourage over-reporting of religiosity (the stigma attached to nonbelief, the general societal association of religion with morality, and family pressures to identify with the religion of our upbringing), it would be reasonable to infer that the 12 to 18 percent figure is probably conservative.

We should also acknowledge that these kinds of studies are unable to reflect the complex layers of nuance and subtle variation in individual religious beliefs. It is almost insulting to suggest that a person's religion can be quickly categorized under a neat label with millions of others. We do it, of course, because we need some categorization to effectively examine such a topic, but we should be mindful of the inherent limitations.

For example, is a person who is "spiritual but not religious" a Secular American? Can someone who believes in an afterlife, but is otherwise not religious and not theistic, be called a Secular American? These are some of the gray areas that make categorization difficult. Just as someone who practices birth control and doesn't believe Jesus was a god might still identify as Catholic, many would argue that some beliefs that are less than ardently naturalistic should not automatically disqualify someone from the Secular American group. Some people sympathize with a secular worldview and rationally conclude that it is both right and good, but they nonetheless have undeniable inclinations to believe in some supernatural concepts. Religious identification and nonidentification can require deeply personal "soul searching" (if you'll excuse the term). Each of us must find our own center of gravity, our own comfort zone for identity, and many will conclude that they don't fit into any neat category.

For these reasons, any numbers estimating the size of the secular demographic are going to be generalizations that fail to fully capture the country's religious diversity. But even the conservative estimate of Secular Americans—15 percent—represents almost fifty million people, a noteworthy demographic bloc. This is a group that outnumbers the combined populations of American Methodists (about eleven million), Lutherans (nine million), Pentecostals (eight million), Presbyterians (five million), Jews (three million), Episcopalians (three million), Mormons (three million), and Muslims (1.4 million).[8] All of these religious groups together would not outnumber a conservative estimate of America's secular population!

HISTORICALLY OVERLOOKED

It is remarkable that this enormous demographic category has been overlooked for so long. Being personally secular is nothing new in America;

religious skeptics have been a part of the country since its earliest days. Thomas Paine (1737–1809), the founding era's great agitator, whose pamphlet *Common Sense* helped raise anti-British sentiment and launch the American Revolution, later wrote another treatise, called *The Age of Reason*, intended to stir antireligious action. He was unambiguous in his views on religion: "I do not believe in the creed professed by the Jewish church, by the Roman church, by the Greek church, by the Turkish church, by the Protestant church, nor by any church that I know of. My own mind is my own church."[9] Other important early Americans—Benjamin Franklin, George Washington, Thomas Jefferson, James Madison, and others—were religious dissenters of varying degrees as well, and they will be discussed in some detail later.

But throughout history, most American religious skeptics have not been particularly vocal. In fact, many twentieth-century humanists tried hard to avoid calling attention to their rejection of theism, preferring instead to assimilate into the wider culture without being seen as religious nonconformists. This tendency can be traced to John Dewey (1859–1952), considered one of America's most important philosophers and sometimes referred to as the grandfather of modern humanism. Dewey was a naturalist, without theistic beliefs, but he nevertheless cloaked his humanist views in religious language. Like many early twentieth-century thinkers, he saw humanism as the religion of the future, but despite his rejection of theism he frequently used terms such as "God" and "the divine" and "faith." Dewey made it clear, at least on an intellectual level to those who were interested, that his "God" was not the divinity of traditional religion. In his work *A Common Faith*, he described "the idea of God" as "one of ideal possibilities." He went on: "But this idea of God . . . is also connected with all the natural forces and conditions—including man and human association—that promote the growth of the ideal and that further its realization." This leads to his conclusion: "It is the active relation between ideal and actual to which I would give the name 'God.'"[10]

Got that? So, if you follow Dewey's brand of humanism, you can talk to your neighbor about the importance of God without the neighbor ever finding out that you're a nonbeliever! By speaking of "God" in this way, with a wink and a nod, it is possible to fly under the radar and not be noticed for your religious skepticism.

Dewey and other early modern humanists had good reasons for taking this approach. At the time, religion seemed to be fading away, while humanism clearly appeared to be the wave of the future, so humanists of that era thought they needed to simply wait patiently for the rest of society to catch up. Organized humanism was less of a movement than a club—a club with many of the elite intellectuals of that time as members. The job of organized humanism in those days was basically twofold: first, to provide a place for humanists to interact, share ideas, bestow awards for achievements and good deeds, and so forth, and second, to advocate for issues of importance to humanists, so long as those issues had little overt connection to religious disbelief. In all of this, there were few efforts made to promote humanist identity or any other secular identity on a mass level, nor was there any serious effort to convince the general public that rejecting theism was acceptable.

As it turns out, traditional religion certainly did not "fade away" as many had predicted—in fact, quite the opposite happened. The use of religious language by Dewey and his contemporaries actually served to validate the most conservative of religious positions. Few ordinary evangelicals or Catholics, for example, would have been aware that references to "God" by Dewey and others meant a "relation between ideal and actual"; instead, they would see such language as a reference to the God of the Bible. To them, America seemed a very godly country. By giving a vague, naturalistic meaning to a plainly theistic word, Dewey not only encouraged several generations of intellectuals and nonbelievers to be mild about challenging traditional conservative religion, but he also unwittingly created a public atmosphere of near unanimity on the importance of theism. If virtually everyone was using "God" language, then it becomes difficult to argue with claims from religious conservatives that only fringe characters reject religion and theism outright. In hindsight, we can see the disastrous consequences of this thinking. With open secularity marginalized and hidden from the mainstream, the ground was fertile for the political mobilization of religious conservatives.

This validation of traditional religion, to the point of exaggerating the American consensus regarding its importance, resulted in the marginalization of disbelief and religious skepticism, even though many Americans are in fact nonreligious. In modern America less than half the population goes to church on a regular basis, yet conventional wisdom rarely acknowledges this lackadaisical attitude toward religion. All we hear in the media and from politicians is the false claim that America is a deeply religious country, which of course implies that nonbelievers are less than exemplary Americans. Yet even in religious families, there are usually members who simply prefer to stay home on Sundays rather than go to church, an uncle or aunt who will tell you candidly that he or she thinks organized religion is a farce. Those skeptics historically have kept to themselves, and, if asked for religious identity, they would normally respond with whatever the family's religious tradition is—Baptist, Greek Orthodox, Lutheran, and so forth. (This is perhaps easiest for many secular Jews, whose ethnic identity can be used as a religious identity, making the statement "I'm Jewish" natural even for a Jewish atheist.)

As we'll see, this tendency of skeptics to maintain traditional religious identity is one of the focal points of today's secular movement. Few Secular Americans have much interest in trying to "convert" believers into nonbelievers, but there is interest across the movement in convincing all nonbelievers to openly identify as secular. Indeed, one reason for optimism within the secular movement is that there is significant room for growth without convincing any religious believers to convert. Right now, there are millions of nonreligious individuals who identify with the religion of their upbringing by default. As these people realize that their religious identification means something, that traditional identity actually validates politicians who believe that the world is six thousand years old whereas secular identity empowers those who would support rational public policy, the importance of honest secular identity will become more apparent.

Growing up in a typical working-class Catholic family, in which some were devout believers who followed church doctrine closely while others were more secular in their outlook, I thought just about everyone in the family seemed pretty decent. Certainly the vocal religious skeptics seemed no less moral and ethical than the others. Uncle Charlie would rant about how the church was a self-perpetuating, corrupt institution that thrived on people's fears and vulnerabilities, but then he would go outside and mow Grandma's lawn for her, and he would be the first to help you fix your car or lend a hand if you needed help. As with many Catholic families, even some of the churchgoers didn't always seem to take religious doctrine all that seriously. Casual conversations about the use of birth control, which was (and still is) forbidden by church doctrine, were not uncommon, with little weight given to the Vatican's opinions on such matters. Many in the family, it seemed, thought the death penalty was a good idea that, if anything, was not used often enough, despite the church's position to the contrary.

Interestingly, however, it seemed unimaginable that anyone in the family would not identify as Catholic. Even those who seemed to loathe the church's hierarchy, doubt most of its teachings, and never attend mass would nevertheless answer "Catholic" to any inquiry about religion. This tendency to maintain traditional religious identity is still common across America today, but increasingly there is a realization that it can be problematic. Historically, few considered that such traditional identification was playing into the hand of religious conservatives, enabling politically active fundamentalists by creating a sense that devout religiosity was more widespread than it really was. The rise of the Religious Right over the last three decades, however, has prompted much rethinking.

THE RELIGIOUS RIGHT EMERGES

With the Religious Right now having been a powerful political force for over three decades, many Americans know nothing different. Until Jimmy Carter ran for president in 1976, however, no serious presidential candidate had ever claimed to be "born again," and relatively few candidates for high office emphasized their faith. But in the wake of the Watergate scandal, with Americans soured by the corruption and dishonesty of the Nixon administration, Carter's wholesome religiosity seemed like a breath of fresh air to many, and he rode that theme into the White House. Secular Americans, people like Uncle Charlie, didn't think much of Carter's religiosity and assumed that this mix of religion with politics was a unique, strange phenomenon that would quickly pass.

Boy, were they wrong! Carter only lasted for one term, partly because, despite his deep religious faith, many engaged and mobilized religious fundamentalists opposed his reelection bid in 1980. Led by a new organization called the Moral Majority, which was founded by notorious evangelical preacher Jerry Falwell, religious conservatives flexed their political muscle like never before to bring down the Carter presidency and elect the Republican candidate, Ronald Reagan. (The irony of Falwell and his religious followers opposing the devout Carter and backing the divorced Hollywood actor Reagan is hard to miss, but one gets accustomed to irony when observing the Religious Right.) Falwell, who died in 2007, was a magnet for controversy, and his positions were often far outside the mainstream of American opinion. He was critical of Martin Luther King, Jr., he featured segregationist politicians on his *Old Time Gospel Hour* program, he loathed the Supreme Court's *Brown v. Board of Education* decision that desegregated public schools, and he opposed sanctions against the repressive South African apartheid regime. Like many evangelical preachers, he was virulently antigay, and he even blamed the September 11 terrorist attacks on America's tolerance for gays and lesbians.[11]

Even when the Moral Majority surprised everybody with its show of strength in 1980, few observers thought politically conservative Christianity would be a longstanding factor in American politics. Many agreed with Norman Lear's assessment of Falwell's group: "The Moral Majority is neither the moral point of view, nor the majority."[12] Few believed that politically engaged fundamentalists, a seemingly fringe population with views based on selective interpretations of ancient theology, would be shaping American politics and policy on a long-term basis.

Once again, almost everyone underestimated the Religious Right. Not only did right-wing Christians maintain their strength, but through impressive organization, fundraising, and strategizing, they seemed to increase their influence with each election cycle. Although the Moral Majority faded in influence and eventually dismantled in 1989, the Christian Coalition, a well-funded group founded by another fundamentalist evangelical preacher, Pat Robertson, filled the void. Like Falwell, Robertson's career was a chronology of controversies, often arising from his intolerant statements. Antifeminist, antigay, anti-Muslim, anti-Hindu, and anti-ACLU, Robertson, like Falwell, frequently interpreted disastrous events, such as the destruction of New Orleans by Hurricane Katrina in 2005, as God's wrath for American immorality. The Christian Coalition remained a major force in politics throughout the 1990s and into the next decade, bragging that it distributed over seventy million "voter guides" in the 2000 election cycle to inform people about "pro-family" issues.[13]

With the rise of the Moral Majority and the Christian Coalition, numerous other activist Christian groups have also appeared. Focus on the Family, for example, claims its mission is "to cooperate with the Holy Spirit in sharing the Gospel of Jesus Christ with as many people as possible by nurturing and defending the God-ordained institution of the family and promoting biblical truths worldwide."[14] Though this could be mistakenly viewed as merely theological, it is in fact a political statement. The group's founder, James Dobson, like many evangelical leaders, has access to high-ranking politicians and is very much politically engaged, even personally meeting and advising President George W. Bush. With annual budgets in the range of $150 million, Focus on the Family and other religious organizations like it have exerted enormous political influence in recent decades.

These major national groups, along with an explosion of grassroots political activity, have changed the nature and dialogue of American politics. There can be no question that these groups and their fervent members have overtaken the Republican Party at the national level and in most states, and they have also caused Democrats to become keenly aware of religion and faith. In much of the country, candidates of both parties now outwardly profess their faith, often expressly declaring a relationship with Jesus, taking the Bible literally, rejecting evolution, and opposing "liberal" ideas such as environmental protection and government social programs. Also, oddly, these fundamentalist followers of Jesus, perhaps history's most famous pacifist, often argue that enormous military budgets are a reflection of the "Christian" position. As I said, there is no shortage of irony.

There was a time when even Republicans were quite secular, rarely mentioning religion or God. Sure, any politician might have occasionally spouted "God Bless America!" but before the Religious Right there was rarely a sense that such statements were mandatory. In fact, before the rise of the Religious Right, the socially conservative agenda was not a centerpiece of the Republican Party. Major GOP leaders such as Nelson Rockefeller, US vice president from 1974 to 1977 and governor of New York from 1959 to 1973, and Barry Goldwater, the party's 1964 presidential nominee and a conservative stalwart for four decades, supported abortion rights.

Rockefeller was quoted as saying, "I do not believe it right for one group to impose its vision of morality on an entire society."[15] It's hard to imagine any GOP leader making such a statement today. Goldwater, like many in his party, had a generally libertarian view on social issues and was so frustrated by the Religious Right that he said the GOP had been taken over by a "bunch of kooks" shortly before he retired in the late 1980s.[16]

Those "kooks," however, did a remarkable job. Even those of us who are sharply opposed to the Religious Right must be in awe of what it has accomplished, even as we cringe at almost every item on its agenda. There's a lesson to be learned.

PREDICTIONS OF DECLINE

Until just a few years ago, most Secular Americans probably would have agreed with the sentiment expressed by historian and author Howard Zinn when I interviewed him about religion in 2003. "When we solve fundamental problems of peace and justice," he told me, "religion will fade in importance."[17] This view, that religion will eventually fade away as society moves forward, was prevalent throughout the twentieth century. "Religion is something left over from the infancy of our intelligence; it will fade away as we adopt reason and science as our guidelines," Bertrand Russell (1872–1970), one of the leading philosophers and critics of religion of the last century, is often quoted as saying.[18]

Even much earlier, similar predictions of the demise of traditional religion were not hard to find. Thomas Jefferson, writing to his friend Dr. Benjamin Waterhouse in 1822, predicted the rapid decline of the key supernatural beliefs, such as the Trinity, underlying the major Christian religions: "I rejoice that in this blessed country of free inquiry and belief, which has surrendered its creed and conscience to neither kings nor priests, the genuine doctrine of one only God is reviving, and I trust that there is not a young man now living in the United States, who will not die an Unitarian."[19] Over half a century later, in a much less subtle fashion, philosopher Friedrich Nietzsche (1844–1900) would address the issue, proclaiming, "God is dead. God is still dead. We have killed him."[20]

Nietzsche was speaking metaphorically, as he was referring not to the physical or biological death of a being, but to the death of the idea of God.

Today, over a century after Nietzsche's death, however, the idea of God is certainly not dead. Similarly, Jefferson was also plainly wrong, as Unitarianism remains a fairly small denomination on the American religious landscape while the more conservative, superstition-filled religions have grown.

It is noteworthy that while many intellectuals and activists have historically seen religion as outdated, most have had little interest in taking affirmative steps to hasten its demise. Zinn, for example, who was very active in the civil rights movement, cited churches as essential to that effort, even though he was himself an atheist. He had no interest in direct secular activism but instead believed that economic progress would lead to a world in which religion becomes less relevant.

Thus, as the Religious Right grew in influence during the 1980s and early 1990s, the idea of secular activism did not immediately take root. Few saw the notion of an identity-oriented secular movement as a potent antidote to the Religious Right. For a variety of reasons, Secular Americans simply did not coalesce into anything resembling a movement. Some, like Zinn, continued to feel that economic and social justice issues were primary, while others were simply resigned to the fact of religion's influence in society and saw little sense in taking a visible stand in favor of secularity. Still others incorrectly assumed that secular activism equates to religion bashing, despite their own personal religious skepticism.

This last point is worth addressing because it is an issue that continues to arise from time to time. The vast majority of Americans, religious and secular, have great distaste for anyone who engages in attacking the deeply held personal convictions of others, particularly when those convictions are not infringing on anyone else's rights. Most of us realize that life is hard, and if you have found a religious view that brings you personal peace of mind and helps you maintain a healthy outlook, that's probably a good thing. Whether you worship Jesus, Allah, Vishnu, or no god at all, and whether you pray all the time, once a week, or never, few of your neighbors, religious or secular, are going to care. Your religious views only become relevant to me when they encroach into my life, and vice versa. When you insist that government should be used as a means of promoting your religious views, then of course I become concerned and your religion becomes relevant to me. And when you claim that your religion is the primary basis for your public policy positions (such as, for example, when you try to stop my kid's school from teaching evolution), then your religion becomes relevant to me. With few exceptions, these are the only times you will find most Secular Americans criticizing the religious views of others.

Secular activism is not about bashing religion but about defending the rights of those who choose secularity as a personal identity and worldview. It's about letting other Americans know that a secular demographic exists and that Secular Americans are as good and decent as everyone else. Though some Secular Americans enjoy debating theology and philosophy, secular activism is not about changing the religious views of others; instead, it encourages those who are secular to "come out," stand up for their rights, push back against the fundamentalist agenda, and join the movement to normalize secularity in American culture.

In this sense, modern secular activism, emerging only in the last decade, has taken a page from the LGBT playbook, which produced remarkable results through identity-oriented activism. For too long Secular Americans accepted marginalization, sitting silently while the Religious Right made belief in God synonymous with morality and argued that nonbelieving Americans were an insignificant minority that could be ignored. Everyone knew some individuals who were nonreligious, but few of those individuals asserted their secularity as an important part of their personal identity. To the media, professional pundits, and certainly politicians, there was no category of nonbelieving Americans that corresponded to the Religious Right. Now, after over three decades of watching the Religious Right expand, many Secular Americans have come to realize the importance of identity politics. Seeing that apathy feeds the Religious Right, nonbelievers are increasingly finding value in identifying openly and organizing.

SECULAR AMERICANS SLOWLY EMERGE

Like most Secular Americans, at first I didn't do much in response to the growth of the Religious Right. Throughout the 1980s and 1990s, I was focused on college and pursuing my career as a lawyer. I followed politics, so I was certainly aware of the Religious Right, and like many, I grew increasingly uneasy about it as the years went by. I found it especially troubling that, by the 1990s, even Democratic candidates seemed to be emphasizing their faith more frequently, almost out of necessity.

It's probably safe to say that most Secular Americans spent the 1980s and 1990s hoping that the Religious Right would fade into history; instead, they watched as it grew into a behemoth. Even the 1992 election of Bill Clinton, who was often portrayed in the media as a liberal, wasn't really a setback for the Religious Right, since Clinton was quite vocal about his own faith and therefore validated the idea of faith-based politics for Democrats as well as Republicans. Clinton's vocal religiosity created national unanimity on the importance of faith, and this implicitly legitimized the motives, if not the specific agenda, of the Religious Right. Clinton even introduced Charitable Choice, a program for governmental funding of religious organizations' charity work, a forerunner to George W. Bush's Faith-Based Initiatives program, which resulted in millions of tax dollars being diverted to churches in what many consider to be a blatant church-state violation. This, combined with the fact that the GOP was becoming wholly subservient to the Religious Right, gave Secular Americans little reassurance during the 1990s.

But for many Secular Americans, including me, the real wake-up call was the presidency of George W. Bush. With Bush, we now had a president who seemed to celebrate anti-intellectualism, who didn't just pander to the Religious Right but belonged to it. Around the time Bush took office in 2001, I began to realize how the Religious Right worked. The Religious Right didn't influence the political environment by winning debates against Secular Americans; it did so by marginalizing them, by keeping Secular Americans entirely removed from public dialogue. It had created an atmosphere in which the media and politicians never even thought about Secular Americans as a legitimate demographic. The Religious Right so successfully executed its plan that all candidates, even those who opposed it on specific issues such as abortion, were often afraid to run without extolling the virtues of faith. Certainly, no viable candidate would criticize the religious views of opponents, and no savvy politician would want to be associated with nonbelievers.

Like many others around the same time, I finally realized that the Religious Right was not going to simply fade away, and that the only way to seriously challenge its power would be for the collective voice of all atheists, agnostics, secular Jews, lapsed Catholics, and other nonbelievers to defend and promote secular values. So rather than going to work for the ACLU, Planned Parenthood, or rational political candidates, I joined the effort to fight for the rights of the long-neglected Secular American demographic. This reflected a recognition that many of America's problems are not superficial—not matters that can be quickly remedied by electing the other party next time or by winning a battle over a piece of legislation—but deep cultural flaws that in some ways transcend politics. Anti-intellectualism, the disappearing middle class, the sorry state of participatory democracy, the low level of the public dialogue—all of these problems (and many others) trace back, directly or indirectly, to the exaltation of religion and the marginalization of nonbelievers. The rise of the Secular American demographic would be a means of bringing about real, lasting positive change.

Over the course of the last decade, many Secular Americans have gotten tired of being ignored and marginalized while watching activist religious conservatives claim moral superiority. They realize it is time to change the societal presumption that religion and morality are synonymous. As such, the last ten years have seen the rumblings of a seismic shift, an awakening among secular individuals and organizations. Secular Americans from various backgrounds are discovering their common bonds and working together to communicate with the public and win acceptance. Secular groups that had never made a serious effort to assert their rights have made a conscious decision to change strategy. National advertising campaigns have been launched, books about secularity have entered the mainstream, politicians are "coming out" as personally secular, misinformation is being corrected, and new legal strategies are being utilized. And perhaps most importantly, for the first time in history, millions upon millions of Americans are openly and publicly identifying as secular—some simply as nonreligious and others as humanist, atheist, or agnostic—in online social media and elsewhere.

The ramifications of this emergence are huge. By demonstrating that secular beliefs and identity reflect a legitimate worldview, an approach to life that deserves no scorn or marginalization, Secular Americans and their allies are turning up the heat in the culture wars and seriously chipping away at the credibility of the Religious Right. At a minimum, the rise of Secular Americans threatens (or promises, depending on how one looks at it) to return the influence of the Religious Right to pre-Reagan levels.

A close look at the numbers reveals that Secular Americans are already a formidable voting bloc that politicians ignore at their own peril. For example, according to data from Pew Research, those who "never" attend church made up 16 percent of the electorate in 2008. Those who are religiously "unaffiliated" were 12 percent. (For a frame of reference, the "evangelical/born again" segment of the electorate was 23 percent.) Both the "never" and "unaffiliated" numbers were higher in 2008 than in the two previous elections, each growing a percentage or two in both 2004 and 2008.[21]

Secular voters, like conservative religious voters, tend to vote in a somewhat predictable pattern according to social issues, including reproductive rights, church-state separation, and LGBT rights. Whereas religious conservatives tend to flock to the candidate or party supporting socially conservative positions, secular voters tend to support the more progressive position on such issues. That often translates to religious conservatives voting for Republican candidates and secular voters for Democrats, though of course there are significant minorities voting in the other direction within each group. Some Secular Americans may have libertarian economic views, for example, leading them to vote for a GOP candidate espousing less government regulation and lower taxes even though that candidate may also support socially conservative positions that run contrary to usual secular sympathies. Similarly, there are certainly some religious conservatives who are also loyal Democrats.

Interestingly, however, the voting patterns of secular voters are more sharply defined than almost any other religious category. Religiously "unaffiliated" voters, for example, favored Obama by a margin of 75 percent to 23 percent over John McCain in 2008, a much higher pro-Obama ratio than all the major Christian groups. (Catholics were 54/45 for Obama; Protestants, both mainline and evangelical, were even lower.) The only religious category more heavily in favor of Obama than "unaffiliated" was Jewish (78/21), but the Jewish vote was only 2 percent of the overall electorate, much smaller than the secular bloc. In the two previous elections, the "unaffiliateds" also favored the Democratic candidates heavily, more than almost all other religious groups—no doubt a response to the Religious Right's dominance of the GOP. Leaving aside religious affiliation and turning to church attendance, those who "never" attend church were the strongest Obama supporters (67/30), with the ratio in favor of Obama declining steadily as frequency of church attendance increases (from "a few times a year" up to "weekly or more"). By the time we get to weekly church attendance, the vote for Obama is down to 43/55.[22]

The strong favoritism of secular voters toward Democratic candidates has led some to believe that Democrats need not worry about winning the secular vote, confidently assuming it is a foregone conclusion. But any candidate making such an assumption does so at his or her own risk. Just as Republican operatives know that they cannot assume that the religious conservative electorate will be motivated to turn out in large numbers for a particular candidate, Democratic candidates risk alienating base secular voters if they fail to demonstrate sufficient secular credentials. There can be little doubt, for example, that most Secular Americans see Obama as being more sympathetic to their views than his predecessor, but Obama's continuation of Bush's practice of funneling millions of tax dollars to religious groups for social programs has disappointed many. The turnout of Secular Americans and the degree of their support for Democrats are surely questions that will decide many elections for the foreseeable future, the issue being no less significant than the enthusiasm of religious conservatives for the GOP.

As with religious conservatives, the level of commitment of secular voters to a candidate and a party, translating to actual voter turnout and support for a particular party or candidate, will fluctuate depending on the specifics of an election. What we're finding today, as opposed to a decade ago, is that Secular Americans are more visible, better organized, more united than ever, and expecting that their opinions and values will be given consideration.

The continuing rise of Secular Americans has ramifications that go far into the future, affecting all facets of public life, including questions of war and peace, foreign policy, economic policy, education, church and state, the role of government, and innumerable others. As the nation with the world's largest economy and most powerful military machine slowly begins to accept its secular citizens, most of the rest of the world will breathe a sigh of relief.

And the impact of the secular emergence goes well beyond politics, into the personal and social realms that define America as a society. Because of the rise of the secular movement, fewer young people will be dealing with the difficult compromise that Maria faced—going back to a church she disdained to be married. As we'll see, more young adults today see their secular identity as a defining part of their character, and they are more likely to stand firm in their secular worldview as they enter the adult world and make important life decisions. Whereas in the past Secular Americans tended to keep their nonreligious outlook to themselves, today's social and technological landscape allows for an unprecedented feeling of community, and secularity is flourishing as a result. There's little doubt in my mind that if Maria were today just five years removed from college and preparing to get married, she would be doing so on her terms.

TWO

A RELIGIOUS PEOPLE?

AMERICAN POLITICIANS MAY NOT AGREE ON MUCH, BUT THERE is one point on which they are virtually unanimous: America is a very religious country.

Though we usually associate the Religious Right with the Republican Party, even Democrats are quick to declare that deep religious faith binds the country together. "It is a truism that we Americans are a religious people," declared Barack Obama in a 2006 article in *Time* magazine.[1] Former vice president Al Gore, no longer even a candidate for public office, made a similar assessment in a November 2008 interview. "We are a very spiritual, religious people," he surmised.[2] Repeated so frequently, this notion that America is a deeply religious country has become an unquestioned part of the country's self-image, an axiom that commentators repeat reflexively: "Of course, America is a very religious country . . ."

This self-image deserves some scrutiny because it both validates the Religious Right to some degree and contributes to the marginalization of Secular Americans. The political agenda of religious conservatives gets much traction from the belief that America's religiosity is a primary, defining characteristic of the nation and its people. There is a sense of exceptionalism and superiority in this view, which often presumes without question that being a "religious people" makes for a better society, that America's economic and military greatness is a reward for its piety or part of a divine plan. As such, it is instructive to examine these claims, to consider not just the nature and extent of America's religiosity, but whether that supposed piety translates to desirable social outcomes.

SURPRISING NUMBERS ON RELIGION AND SECULARITY

Over the last dozen years, the US homicide rate has averaged about 5.5 per 100,000—significantly higher than almost all other industrialized countries.[3] Neighboring Canada, for example, has a homicide rate of about 1.8 per 100,000 over the same period, and even that is high relative to other developed countries.[4] The homicide rate in France is 1.37 per 100,000; the United Kingdom, 1.35; the Netherlands, 1.02; and Germany, 0.84.[5]

And countries with low homicide rates are certainly not godlier than the United States. In fact, quite the contrary is the case: industrialized countries with the lowest violent crime rates tend to be much less religious. Gallup polling conducted from 2006 to 2008 asked people from around the world whether religion is important in their daily lives,[6] and most of the countries with the lowest rates of religiosity—for example, Japan, France, Norway, Denmark, Sweden, the Czech Republic, and numerous others—have among the lowest homicide rates, much lower than the religious United States.[7]

This phenomenon has been reported widely around the world and is even recognized by academic research within the United States. In the British publication *The Times* in 2005, for example, religion correspondent Ruth Gledhill explained the results of a study reported that year in the American *Journal of Religion and Society*[8]: "In general, higher rates of belief in and worship of a creator correlate with higher rates of homicide, juvenile and early adult mortality, STD infection rates, teen pregnancy and abortion in the prosperous democracies." She continued: "The United States is almost always the most dysfunctional . . . sometimes spectacularly so."[9] Citing that same 2005 study and three others, Phil Zuckerman of Pitzer College reported in *Sociology Compass* in 2009, "Murder rates are actually lower in more secular nations and higher in more religious nations where belief in God is deep and widespread."[10] The author of the *Journal of Religion and Society* study, Gregory S. Paul, found that there is a strong correlation between violence and religiosity. Within generally secular

Western Europe, for example, relatively religious Portugal has higher homicide rates than its more secular neighbors. Looking at rates of juvenile mortality, gonorrhea and syphilis, and abortion around the world, Paul concluded that conventional wisdom about religion's role in solving social and personal ills is largely unfounded:

> Indeed, the data examined in this study demonstrates that only the more secular, pro-evolution democracies have, for the first time in history, come closest to achieving the practical "cultures of life" that feature low rates of lethal crime, juvenile-adult mortality, sex related dysfunction, and even abortion. The least theistic secular developed democracies such as Japan, France, and Scandinavia have been most successful in these regards. The non-religious, pro-evolution democracies contradict the dictum that a society cannot enjoy good conditions unless most citizens ardently believe in a moral creator.[11]

Looking at criteria such as belief in God, church attendance, biblical literalism, and prayer practices, Paul showed that the United States is the only developed nation that retains levels of religiosity found in less-developed societies. In compiling data on various social problems, he reported that "in almost all regards the highly secular democracies consistently enjoy low rates of social dysfunction while pro-religious and anti-evolution America performs poorly."[12]

Taking the analysis further in another study, Gary F. Jensen of Vanderbilt University, an expert in criminology, found a strong correlation between high homicide rates and certain religious beliefs. He reported that a general belief in a divinity is probably fairly benign, as are practices such as church attendance and prayer, but that certain forms of religiosity, such as the passionate evangelical belief in absolute good and evil, may lead to socially undesirable outcomes.[13] To his credit, Jensen acknowledged the complexities inherent in the issues of violence and other social dysfunctions, and he hesitated to draw hasty conclusions about the causal connection between religion and violence, while nevertheless raising reasonable hypotheses: "If there is only one appropriate way for a spouse to behave with dualist 'macho' conceptions of the male as the lord of the household, then challenges to such authority may elicit passionate attempts to reestablish 'moral order.'"[14] Of course, conservative religion frequently promotes exactly such concepts, with intense emphasis on absolute good and evil and right and wrong, strict authoritarian views, and obedience and conformity.

Religious societies also fare poorly when measured by another barometer of social progress—that of academic excellence. More secular societies typically fill the top ranks in math and science testing, while the United States usually ranks unimpressively, often near the bottom, despite spending more per pupil than almost all other countries. US teens' math scores ranked twenty-fifth out of 34 countries in a 2009 assessment, for example.[15] If America has a reputation for being both religious and anti-intellectual, it is reasonable to infer that there is a relationship between the two.

Religious conservatives might respond to the aforementioned statistics by saying that it is only religion that keeps the numbers from being worse in American society. If not for our deep faith and religiosity, the argument goes, violent crime would be even more rampant, our children would perform even worse academically, and our teens would be pushing even more baby carriages. The only problem with this argument is that the facts show otherwise. Inside the United States, a list of states with the highest rates of social dysfunction is like a tour of the Bible Belt.[16] Zuckerman's statistical analysis, citing Census Bureau information and other data, reports as follows: "And within America, states with the highest murder rates tend to be highly religious, such as Louisiana and Alabama, but the states with the lowest murder rates tend to be among the least religious in the country, such as Vermont and Oregon."[17] The numbers get no better when we look at most other social ills, where we find the more religious states with higher rates of poverty, obesity, infant mortality, STDs, and teen pregnancy, and the lowest rates of college education.[18]

Looked at from a political perspective, bearing in mind that so-called red states that lean Republican also tend to be religiously conservative, the findings are interesting. Consistent with the numerous reports cited by Zuckerman is an analysis by *Smart Politics* in 2009, which found red states that voted for John McCain in 2008 (which are typically the strongholds of the Religious Right[19]) having rates of both violent crime and property crime that were higher than the less-religious blue states that voted for Barack Obama. The violent crime rate was 5.8 percent higher in red states, according to the report, and the property crime rate was 8 percent higher.[20] Similarly, another study in 2009 found that the states with more conservative religious beliefs had higher rates of teenagers giving birth. Another study reported that 19 of the 20 states with the highest teen birth rates voted for George W. Bush in 2004, and 17 of the 20 voted for McCain in 2008; conversely, 9 of the 10 states with the lowest teen birth rates were decidedly blue.[21] Those more religious states also tend to produce poorer academic test results than the more secular states.[22]

In response to such volumes of unflattering data, the best one can say in defense of religion is that correlation doesn't necessarily equal causation, that religiosity is not the cause of these socially undesirable outcomes.

Maybe not, but one must question why Americans continue to point to religiosity as an important virtue that unquestionably makes society better. American media and politicians consistently promote the idea of religion being inherently virtuous, while ignoring Secular Americans and vilifying secularity. Great consideration is given to whether or not religious conservatives would favor or disfavor a particular legislative proposal, but politicians never say, "This proposed bill will certainly have the support of secular citizens." This is exactly what Secular Americans are seeking to change.

UNDERSTANDING THE SECULAR AMERICAN POSITION

While it would be irresponsible to hastily conclude that correlation equals causation, it would be equally inappropriate to suggest that the pattern is irrelevant, especially when the correlation between religion and undesirable social outcomes is so consistent and overwhelming. One thing that the data does prove conclusively is that while the verdict is out on whether religion actually causes social ills, it is now clear that secularity *does not* cause them. As such, Secular Americans are now one step closer to removing the stigma surrounding secularity and gaining a place at the table in public policy making and dialogue. In fact, far from finding that a lack of religion should give rise to any concern, we often find the contrary. As Zuckerman reports, "Numerous studies reveal that atheists and secular people most certainly maintain strong values, beliefs, and opinions. But more significantly, when we actually compare the values and beliefs of atheists and secular people to those of religious people, the former are markedly less nationalistic, less prejudiced, less anti-Semitic, less racist, less dogmatic, less ethnocentric, less close-minded, and less authoritarian."[23]

These same studies also indicate that secular individuals are more likely to support gender equality and women's rights, that Secular Americans were much more likely to have opposed the 2003 American invasion of Iraq (with only 38 percent favoring the invasion compared to 68 percent of evangelical Protestants), and that Secular Americans are the least likely to support governmental use of torture.[24]

Despite all of this, few would attempt to argue that religion is the root cause of all of America's social dysfunctions. As far as most Secular Americans are concerned, it is sufficient to simply establish that America's deep religious character is doing little to prevent many of the social ills that we seek to minimize in modern society. Appreciation of religion is one thing, but the exaltation of it as an indicator of America's superior virtue is simply absurd. Compared with the rest of the developed world, Americans often appear violent and criminal, ignorant and anti-intellectual, and sexually uninformed and immature—all of this while we simultaneously hold ourselves out as pious, exemplary, upright, and being in a position to dictate moral standards to the rest of the world.

The belief that Americans are "a religious people" is one of the key reasons that politicians typically ignore the Secular American demographic. Another is the fact that many nonbelieving Americans choose not to identify openly as secular because of popular attitudes that vilify nonreligious people, particularly atheists, as bad and undesirable. Atheists, in particular, are traditionally so unpopular in America that a 2006 University of Minnesota study found them to be not only the most disliked and distrusted minority, but also the group into which Americans would least like to see their children marry, ranking behind Muslims, gays, and recent immigrants.[25] A friend within the secular movement told me a story that demonstrates the shocking irrationality of such biases. One family member, upon learning that my friend was an atheist, announced that she would not let her child spend private time with him anymore and that, in fact, she would be more likely to let the child share time with a pedophile. "The child molester can take my daughter's body," she told my friend, "but an atheist can destroy her soul." Such is the appalling logic against which some secular individuals find themselves.

LITTLE VIRTUE, LOTS OF HYPOCRISY

A religiously charged society is clearly no guarantee of virtue, and nowhere is this more evident than in the realm of politics. In a democracy, where political grandstanding is a regular occurrence, religion can become a useful tool for the candidate seeking to exude a certain moral aura. Even a casual observer of American politics, however, would quickly conclude that a visibly religious political arena is no indicator of highly moral leadership.

Hypocrisy, not virtue, is the predictable product of a political environment that exalts religiosity. Politicians of all parties and persuasions are susceptible to moral shortcomings, of course, but those career-ending scandals of politicians who vocally espouse "family values" and emphasize deep personal religiosity always seem the most grandiose. Take, for example, Mark Sanford, the former governor of South Carolina, who was considered potential presidential material until he disappeared from his state for several days in 2009. He didn't bother telling his staff where he was, but implied that he might be hiking the Appalachian Trail. Instead, it turned out that he was an entire continent away in Buenos Aires, Argentina, with his mistress. Having misled his family, the press, and his own staff, Sanford lied when confronted by a reporter who cornered him in an airport on the way home from his South American dalliance, telling the reporter he had been alone for the previous few days. Shortly thereafter, he confessed publicly to his tryst. As one would expect from a Bible Belt politician facing a sex scandal, the father of four invoked scripture as he faced the public and the press, adding, "I've been a person of faith all my life. There are moral absolutes."[26]

Such an affair and family crisis, even in the life of an elected official, would be of little importance in most circumstances, but as Secular Americans stand on the outside of public affairs, listening as politicians like Sanford adulate "a religious people" while either ignoring or vilifying secularity, such events become quite relevant. It's bad enough that Sanford

and others like him falsely craft their public images as being morally upright in order to get elected, but it's even worse that they do so in ways
that stigmatize secularity. For years, Sanford promoted the correlation of
religiosity and moral superiority, implying that secularity raises questions
of moral shortcoming. This is the clear message conveyed consistently by
the Religious Right, and Secular Americans would be remiss to ignore the
obvious counterargument: Sanford is evidence that religiosity means little
in terms of morality.

Unfortunately, the only thing unique about Sanford's adultery was the
five-thousand-mile journey that accompanied it. Aside from the frequent
flyer miles, Sanford's affair was otherwise akin to those of other moralistic,
vocally religious politicians. Take, for example, Senator David Vitter of
Louisiana, a family-values Republican who was revealed to be a frequent
customer of Deborah Jeane Palfrey, the so-called DC Madam. What is
most noteworthy is not so much the lurid details of a high-powered politician cheating on his wife and pursuing a reckless lifestyle of sexual escapades with prostitutes, but Vitter's shameless invocation of religion that
immediately followed the disclosure. In his first public comments, Vitter
went right to God talk: "This was a very serious sin in my past for which I
am, of course, completely responsible," he told the press and his constituents, adding that he "asked for and received forgiveness from God and my
wife." Not letting the divine relationship out of the discussion, the senator
went on to declare, "Out of respect for my family, I will keep my discussion
of the matter there—with God and them."[27] Vitter's record as a legisla-
tor, of course, gives no hint of his innate hedonism but instead parallels
the agenda of the Religious Right. On several occasions, for example, he
introduced bills to promote prayers by government bodies, one time as a
direct response to a court ruling that government-sponsored prayers were
unconstitutional. He has also supported government funding of Christian
groups, proposed a constitutional amendment to ban same-sex marriage,
and supported Christian-backed abstinence-only sex education. Vitter is
quick to decry "Massachusetts values" and the "Hollywood Left," which
might explain his opposition to the Franken Amendment, a bill to forbid
federal contractors from denying access to courts for victims of sexual assault. Before passage of the amendment, women assaulted in the employ of
federal contractors could be precluded from suing their assailants in court

due to arbitration clauses in their employment contracts. To cap Vitter's career summary, it's noteworthy that the deeply religious and adulterous senator was on record in 1999, the same year his phone number was recorded in the DC Madam's book, as saying that Bill Clinton should resign the presidency because of the Monica Lewinsky scandal, yet of course Vitter never resigned after disclosure of his habit of frequenting prostitutes. In fact, in 2010 he was reelected easily after campaigning, without blushing, as a family-values candidate.

Again, such tales do not mean that there is something inherently problematic with religion, but certainly they raise the question of whether marginalization of secularity is appropriate. Of the 535 representatives and senators in Washington DC, only one, Representative Pete Stark, a Bay-area California Democrat, serves openly as an atheist. Surely it couldn't be possible that the moral standards of our political culture would *decline* if more openly secular candidates were elected, but in today's America, few are considered viable.

No discussion of politics, sex, religion, and hypocrisy would be complete without mention of Newt Gingrich, the former House speaker, who has been in government since before the rise of the Religious Right. Gingrich first ran for Congress in 1974 and was elected in 1978 as a Republican representing a suburban Atlanta district. Those who knew him in the early days have remarked that the young Gingrich wanted no God language in his speeches. Lee Howell, a press secretary in Gingrich's 1974 campaign who was interviewed by *Mother Jones* magazine in 1984, had this to say about writing a speech for Gingrich: "I come from a Southern Protestant background, and Southern Protestants quote the Bible. Newt had me take out all the references to God, because he was not very religious—and isn't very religious. He went to church in order to get a nap on Sunday morning. He became a deacon because of who he was, not what he believed. He did not like us to use God in his speeches; he didn't want people to think he was using God, because he said that would be hypocritical. He said, 'I'm not a very strong believer.'" By the time of the *Mother Jones* article in 1984, however, Gingrich was already using references to God regularly in speeches.[28]

One could speculate, perhaps, that in the ten-year interim Gingrich had undergone some kind of religious awakening, but there is more reason to believe the awakening was political in nature. By 1984, the emergence of the Religious Right juggernaut, particularly in the South, was far too obvious to be overlooked by any politician, let alone one as opportunistic as Gingrich, whose scruples didn't prevent him from adapting to the new God-fearing environment. And as the Religious Right continued to grow over the next three decades, Gingrich increasingly sounded like a true believer.

Yet despite his religious rhetoric, Gingrich's personal life reflects anything but a life of pious morality and, in fact, is legendary for just the opposite—serial adultery, ruthlessness, and brazen hypocrisy. Gingrich, who is eager to advocate for "Christian values" and seems to hold himself out as an authority on that subject, was cheating on his first wife when he delivered divorce paperwork to her while she was hospitalized and recuperating from cancer surgery, and he was cheating on his second wife while he badgered President Clinton for sexual misconduct.

Having converted in 2009 to Catholicism, the religion of his third wife, Gingrich has tried to reinvent himself by arguing that his sexual escapades were caused not by his lack of ethics, but by his work ethic. Interviewed in 2011 on the Christian Broadcasting Network, Gingrich explained, "There's no question at times of my life, partially driven by how passionately I felt about this country, that I worked far too hard and things happened in my life that were not appropriate."[29] Hence, it was patriotism that was driving Gingrich's libido—love of country that somehow translated to love of extramarital carnal pleasure. It takes a talented and audacious politician to even attempt such a pitch, to make such a statement with a straight face, but the former House speaker hurled it at his believing audience like a major leaguer.

In fact, Gingrich soon thereafter went on a speaking tour that brought him to numerous religious venues, where, as reported in the online journal *Politico*, he was quick to warn the faithful about Secular Americans. "I have two grandchildren," he is reported as telling a crowd at the Cornerstone Church in San Antonio, Texas. "Maggie is 11, Robert is 9. I am convinced that if we do not decisively win the struggle over the nature of America, by the time they're my age they will be in a secular atheist country, potentially one dominated by radical Islamists and with no understanding of what it once meant to be an American."[30] Despite the extremism of this statement, it's hard not to appreciate its humor as well, for it is difficult to see how "secular atheists" could lead to a country dominated by "radical Islamists," unless perhaps in Bible Belt politics the two groups are seen as one.

The humor compounds itself, however, in the response of the attendees to Gingrich's speech. One audience member told the *Politico* reporter, "I was really impressed with his sincere faith. He didn't brag, but you can tell he's a man of God."[31] Yes indeed, so long as we keep Secular Americans marginalized, the nation can continue to be led by men of God such as Gingrich.

The misuse of religion—and the simultaneous unfair marginalization of secularity—is frequently an element in sex scandals involving closeted gay public figures. Commonly, we see individuals at the center of these affairs who have advocated against gay rights, and frequently the antigay zeal is accompanied by righteous religious rhetoric. This emphasis on religion and values makes these scandals most relevant to Secular Americans, as such rhetoric perpetuates the notion that secular (and gay and lesbian) individuals are lacking in morality.

One of the highest-profile hypocritical gay sex scandals was that of Senator Larry Craig of Idaho. Convicted in 2007 in connection with an arrest for attempting to solicit gay sex in an airport men's room, Craig had previously compiled a legislative record of opposing gay rights, even voting against the inclusion of sexual orientation within a hate-crime statute. Religiously fueled grandstanding was also evident in the case of vocal antigay activist George Rekers, a Southern Baptist minister who employed a gay escort hired from rentboy.com to accompany him on a two-week European vacation. For this sin, Rekers subsequently resigned from the National Association for Research & Therapy of Homosexuality. Pastor Eddie Long, a Georgia minister who has denounced homosexuality and preached for "sexual reorientation" and advocated for a constitutional amendment to deny marriage rights to same-sex couples, was sued by several young men who alleged that Long had used his pastoral influence to coerce them into sexual relationships. The suits were reportedly settled out of court in 2011.

When it comes to gay scandals revealing religious hypocrisy, however, the most spectacular example is Ted Haggard, who was one of America's most prominent religious leaders, president of the National Association of Evangelicals, until it was alleged in 2006 that for years he had been paying for gay sex and using crystal meth, all the while preaching against secularism. Though he initially denied the allegations, he eventually admitted most of them.[32] Haggard had built a fourteen-thousand-member megachurch from scratch in suburban Denver, and he had risen to become one of the most influential preachers in the country, even participating in weekly telephone exchanges with the White House. By promoting the notion that morality was to be pursued via the conservative Christian path, both explicitly and implicitly demonizing Secular Americans, Haggard was a darling of the Religious Right.

When Secular Americans criticize Haggard, the criticism is not for the fact that he was in the closet about his bisexuality, nor is it even for the adulterous nature of his affair. These issues are personal and not the public's business. From the standpoint of Secular Americans, even the hypocrisy of criticizing homosexuality while simultaneously engaging in intimate same-sex relationships is only of minimal relevance. The real issue jumping out at the secular community is that conservative Christianity sends a clear message that the nontheistic, nonreligious worldview is inherently evil. Sitting on the sidelines largely disliked, vilified, and seen as unqualified for public office, simultaneously watching their sharpest critics swim in hypocrisy, Secular Americans can understandably find the situation almost surreal.

The Religious Right never backs down in the face of scandals, hypocrisy, or mountains of evidence demonstrating that secularity is a positive force. There are stories like Haggard's, with preachers acting in most unholy ways, occurring almost daily across America, yet fundamentalist religious leaders persist in claiming that theirs is the only path to true morality, that Secular Americans cannot extol values that are just as valid as those of other Americans. Nonbelievers, however, don't expect to change the minds of religious conservatives; they instead hope to convince the more rational members of the public that the exaltation of religion and vilification of secularity is mistaken, that the continued marginalization of Secular Americans is against the public interest.

THE MARKETING OF SALVATION

Haggard is part of another uniquely American phenomenon that has directly paralleled the rise of the Religious Right in recent decades: megachurches. At first glance, the growth of megachurches would seem to be strong evidence supporting the argument that America is indeed a very religious society, for they stand as examples of the mass appeal of religion in many parts of the country. A closer look at the facts, however, shows that the truth is more complex.

Sometimes called "big box" churches, megachurches are defined as Protestant congregations with a regular weekly service attendance of over two thousand, and they are known for their slick, polished presentations; their professional, business-like approach to marketing and servicing congregants; and often their mall-like atmosphere. *Forbes* magazine reported that only 10 megachurches existed in the United States in 1970, a number that grew to 250 by 1990, and 740 by 2003.[33] Today, according to the Hartford Institute for Religion Research, there are at least 1,200 megachurches with as many as twelve million members.[34] "Welcome to the world of megachurches," reported *Forbes*, "where pastors often act as chief executives and use business tactics to grow their congregations." These churches, taking advantage of their tax-exempt status, are "entrepreneurial," according to the magazine, operating television and music studios, publishing houses, sophisticated information technologies, food courts, and a host of other nontraditional services. At the helm of such churches are leaders, almost always men, who, far from living a monk-like religious life of humble poverty and contemplation, are often reaping the rewards of a successful business enterprise.

Today's megachurches reflect the true Americanization of organized religion, a convergence of consumer culture and theology. They exploit America's consumption mentality to present salvation as the ultimate commodity that can be acquired like a new pair of jeans. Like smart retailers, megachurch pastors know that presentation, atmosphere, and emotional connection are all critically important to the successful marketing of their product, just as they are for a trendy upscale mall.

What we find when we look closer at the facts, however, is that the impressive growth of megachurches does not reflect a growth in overall religiosity in America. Despite the sharp increase in megachurches, church attendance in America has remained fairly steady for decades.[35] The rise of megachurches, which tend to be conservative theologically (and therefore politically by implication) and most frequently evangelical or Baptist, has been accompanied by a sharp decline in attendance for mainline Protestant and Catholic congregations. This no doubt helps explain the atmosphere of polarization so prominent in America, with the religious gravitating toward a conservative and politically charged theology that is a far cry from the message of mainline churches, while the more secular move away from religion altogether. Stuck in the middle are traditional Protestant and Catholic churches that cannot compete with their entrepreneurial competitors on one side and the lure of secularity on the other. As megachurches thrive, the traditional churches more often sit empty, relics of a bygone era.

NOT SO RELIGIOUS

If we look closer at the numbers, we find that there is reason to question the conventional wisdom that Americans are "a religious people." While it is true that the United States is more religious than most other developed countries, it is also true that America is much more secular than many countries. America's secularity becomes quite apparent as soon as we consider other societies that are unquestionably more religious.

One example of a truly religious country would be Somalia, a fact that Aisha Ibrahim Duhulow discovered in the most horrific way. In October 2008, the young Somalian girl, only 13 according to Amnesty International, was partially buried into the ground in a stadium in the port city of Kismayu, then stoned to death by a group of about 50 men in front of a crowd of approximately one thousand spectators. Her crime was reported as adultery, and the sentence was carried out pursuant to Islamic law. Her age was first reported as being 23 (as if that would justify the punishment) but was later verified by Amnesty International to have been only 13. Her father reported that she had been raped by three men and was not guilty of adultery, but this defense ultimately proved ineffective.[36]

A Western country like the United States stands little chance of invoking Islamic law, but we should be mindful that the Bible also calls for a similar punishment for adultery. Both Deuteronomy 22:22 and Leviticus 20:10 call for death for adulterers. Thus, it is only our willingness to reject biblical law, our insistence on adhering to modern secular standards of civility, that separates us from Somalian justice. Moreover, though it's rarely discussed publicly, there are many fundamentalists who take the Bible seriously and would not hesitate to return to biblical standards. Since Leviticus 20:13 punishes homosexuality with death, many conservative Christians, even if not going so far as to support capital punishment against gays, point to that Bible passage to justify their opposition to gay rights. And while imposing the death penalty for homosexuality through the American legal system is not plausible, some antigay Christian activists have worked zealously to encourage such penalties in other societies. After a group of American pastors visited Uganda in 2009 for a seminar entitled Exposing the Homosexual Agenda, a law was proposed in that country to impose the death penalty for homosexuality. Scott Lively, an American pastor who spoke at the seminar and runs an antigay group, described the proponents of the death penalty for homosexuality as "good Christians, better Christians than there are here in the States." He told ABC News, "They care about each other. And I think the reason they're pushing so hard on this law is that they don't want to see what happened to our country happen over there."[37]

Secular Americans, and of course LGBT Americans, should be thankful that such "good Christians" aren't running America—yet.

WHO'S MILITANT?

In 2011 in Pakistan, another very religious country, nine bullets fired from close range ended the life of Salman Taseer, making the regional governor yet another high-profile victim of religious violence. Taseer had the audacity to publicly question Pakistan's blasphemy laws, and for this transgression he paid with his life. Taseer, of course, joins a long list of numerous other high-profile victims of militant religion, such as Dr. George Tiller, the Kansas abortion doctor killed by a devout Christian assassin in 2009, and Theo van Gogh, the Dutch filmmaker whose provocative movie about Islam resulted in his being brutally murdered in 2004.

With militant religiosity so well documented, it is especially puzzling that the American media and public still perpetuate the cliché of so-called militant atheism. We hear the disparaging term *militant atheist* used frequently, but while millions of atheists can indeed be found in America, it would be difficult to find even one who could accurately be described as violently militant. In all of American history, it is doubtful that any person has ever been killed in the name of atheism; in fact, it would be difficult to find evidence that any American has ever even been harmed in the name of atheism. It just does not happen, because the notion of "militant atheism" is entirely a product of antisecular propaganda.

When the media and others refer to a "militant atheist," the object of that slander is usually a nonbeliever who had the nerve to openly question religious authority or vocally express his or her views about religion. This reflects a double standard that nonbelievers endure. Religious individuals and groups frequently declare, sometimes subtly and sometimes not, that you are a sinner and that you will suffer in hell for eternity if you do not adopt their beliefs, but they will almost never be labeled "militant" by the media or the public. Instead, such individuals are typically called "devout" or perhaps "evangelical." No doubt this double standard stems from the predominant notion that tells us that Americans are "a religious people." The lesson is clear: if you're not a fervent believer, shut up about it.

This at least partially explains why the secular demographic has gone unnoticed for so long in American society. The general disfavor exhibited toward open religious skepticism is so strong that many Secular Americans have found it easier to simply lie low, often identifying by default with a religion that they don't believe and don't practice. Analyze the labels and numbers all you want, but the inescapable conclusion is that millions of Americans are in the closet about their religious skepticism. This closeted secularity, in turn, only serves to validate and legitimize the Religious Right, because it suggests that there is something wrong with a nonreligious worldview. By keeping Secular Americans off the playing field, the Religious Right can claim the moral high ground and influence public policy to a greater degree than their numbers would normally allow.

Secular Americans are not trying to argue superiority—only equality. Seeing senseless religious violence and undesirable living conditions in religious societies, one could indeed argue that, in the words of the late Christopher Hitchens, "religion poisons everything," but relatively few Secular

Americans would advocate for such a broad thesis. Rather, most would be content with a simple recognition that secularity does *not* poison everything, that a personally secular worldview deserves respect, and that public policy and government actions should not be shaped by religious claims of superior morality. Secular Americans do not want favoritism—only equality and government neutrality. As we'll see in the next chapter, acceptance of secularity would not be a radical departure from America's true heritage; rather, it would only require the setting aside of false paradigms that have been successfully promoted in modern times by religious conservatives.

THREE

A SECULAR HERITAGE

IN A PUBLIC DISCUSSION IN 2011 ABOUT THE POSTING OF THE Ten Commandments in schools in Giles County, Virginia, school officials defended the biblical displays by claiming that they are intended as historical, not religious.[1] This "historical" argument is a common tactic of those who wish to inject religion into American public life. Displays that are religiously motivated are almost always considered unconstitutional, so proponents of religious expression must instead find some ostensible "secular intent" for their actions, and "acknowledging history" serves that purpose well.

Of course, the real motive behind such actions is usually to promote the religious views of those supporting the displays, the "historical" argument being merely a disingenuous means of satisfying legal scrutiny. It is rare indeed that we find any respected historians arguing for the erection of Ten Commandments monuments in schools, courthouses, or public squares. The Giles County displays had been posted about a dozen years earlier, not to teach about history or heritage but in response to a perceived "alarming moral breakdown" nationally. Quoted in the *Washington Post,* the principal of one of the county's elementary schools explained why he wanted the biblical passage displayed in his school, saying, "The commandments have been a compass for our lives."[2]

Historical, indeed.

A CHRISTIAN NATION?

In some ways, it's a good sign that the Religious Right still finds it necessary to argue that religious expressions are "historical" or "an acknowledgment of heritage," because such arguments show that even religious conservatives realize that blatant governmental religious expression is illegal. Increasingly, however, some in the Religious Right are speaking more boldly, claiming that America is a "Christian nation" and that the concept of separation of church and state should be questioned. For example, Representative Michele Bachmann is on record telling a group of students that constitutional church-state separation is "a myth,"[3] a suggestion that would have seemed ludicrous a generation ago but is now commonplace.

The "Christian nation" idea is popular not just at the outer regions of fundamentalism, but with high-profile figures. Sarah Palin, the 2008 GOP vice presidential nominee, said it would be "mind-boggling" to suggest that America is not a Christian nation.[4] Indeed, far from being a fringe belief, redefining America as a Christian nation has strong backing on Capitol Hill through the Congressional Prayer Caucus (CPC), a group of over a hundred lawmakers who share a commitment to promoting religion through government. An example of CPC activity would be its support for a bill called the "Public Prayer Protection Act," which would have removed all church-state cases involving prayer by public officials from federal court jurisdiction, thereby allowing each state to determine its own parameters for governmental expressions of religiosity. The CPC also makes frequent efforts to promote the "In God We Trust" motto and the "under God" wording of the Pledge of Allegiance.[5] Often dispensing with the façade of a purported "historical purpose," this group and its supporters see overt religious expression as not just constitutionally permissible, but desirable.

Those who call America a "Christian nation" predictably tend to be conservative Christians who welcome an interpretation of history that validates their worldview. While the tendency to intermingle religion with patriotism is increasingly common, any objective assessment of the facts quickly shows that America has never been a "Christian nation." To paraphrase the late senator Daniel Patrick Moynihan, Palin, Bachmann, and their companions are entitled to their own opinions about American history, but not their own facts.

Unfortunately, Americans are poorly schooled in history and civics, thereby making it easier for Christian revisionists to rewrite history. Chapter 2 showed the correlation between more religious societies and relatively low academic test scores, and here we see how that anti-intellectualism becomes self-perpetuating. According to a recent *Newsweek* report, 29 percent of Americans couldn't name the vice president, 44 percent did not know that the first ten constitutional amendments constitute the Bill of Rights, and two-thirds could not identify America's economic system as capitalistic or market-based.[6] A 2011 Marist Institute for Public Opinion survey revealed that only 58 percent of Americans know that the nation declared its independence in 1776, and 24 percent did not know that Great Britain was the country from which independence was declared.[7] With the public this misinformed, religiously motivated politicians and activists have little difficulty selling the "Christian nation" lie, especially when the pitch is made to those who want to hear it.

On the question of whether the Founding Fathers intended to form a "Christian nation," we have some strong indicators of their true sentiments. One of the most frequently cited sources is Thomas Jefferson's famous 1802 letter to a group of Baptists in Danbury, Connecticut, wherein he assured them the following: "Believing with you that religion is a matter which lies solely between man and his God, that he owes account to none other for his faith or his worship, that the legislative powers of government reach actions only, and not opinions, I contemplate with sovereign reverence that act of the whole American people which declared that their legislature should 'make no law respecting an establishment of religion, or prohibiting the free exercise thereof,' thus building a wall of separation between church and State."[8] Jefferson's "wall of separation" metaphor—actually first penned over a century earlier by Roger Williams, the religious dissenter who founded Providence Plantations in what later became Rhode Island after being exiled from Massachusetts—became a bedrock principle of American constitutional law, recognizing that religion and government are wholly distinct domains.

In recent years, however, the Religious Right has argued that this metaphor was merely the personal opinion of Jefferson and does not represent the view of the founders. Thus, in order to determine once and for all whether the founders intended the United States as a "Christian nation," we would want direct evidence from the founders themselves, ideally a direct statement saying something like, "The United States of America is founded as a Christian nation" or "The United States of America is not founded as a Christian nation."

As it turns out, there is such evidence. Unlike Jefferson's letter to the Baptists, this document is not just a personal correspondence from one of the founders, but an official public document, the Treaty of Tripoli, that was passed unanimously by the United States Senate in 1797, during the administration of John Adams, the nation's second president. Article 11 of the treaty reads as follows: "As the government of the United States of America is not, in any sense, founded on the Christian religion; as it has in itself no character of enmity against the laws, religion, or tranquility, of Mussulmen; and, as the said States never entered into any war, or act of hostility against any Mahometan nation, it is declared by the parties, that no pretext, arising from religious opinions, shall ever produce an interruption of the harmony existing between the two countries."[9] It is noteworthy that unanimous Senate votes were quite rare in the early days of the Republic. Of 339 votes that had taken place up to that time, this was only the third that was unanimous.[10] After being read aloud in the Senate chamber and approved, the bill was signed by Adams. It was also published in newspapers across the country, with no known vocal dissent or objection. There can be no credible claim that the language went unnoticed, as the entire treaty is under nine hundred words, in just 12 articles.[11] This leaves no doubt that, in the early days of the Republic, there was clear consensus that the American government was secular, that in no sense were we a "Christian nation."

THE GOD-FREE CONSTITUTION

In fact, the Treaty of Tripoli simply restates what the United States Constitution expresses—that the founders created a secular government with no religious bias of any kind. As the fundamental law of the land, the Constitution is the ultimate authority on all such questions, and the Constitution says nothing about Christianity or God.

In the Constitution, ratified in 1788, the ultimate source of authority is cited in the first three words: "We the people . . ." There is no reference to Jesus, or even to a more general notion of God or higher authority. James Madison and the other drafters discussed and debated each clause of the Constitution in great detail, including the possibility of referencing God, so the omission was certainly not an oversight. In fact, religion is mentioned only once in the original Constitution, and it is a negative reference to keep it at a distance from government. Article 6 reads in part that "no religious Test shall ever be required as a Qualification to any Office or public Trust under the United States."[12]

The secular intent of the founders can also be seen in Article 2, which sets forth the language of the presidential oath: "I do solemnly swear (or affirm) that I will faithfully execute the Office of President of the United States, and will to the best of my Ability, preserve, protect and defend the Constitution of the United States."[13] All the requirements pertaining to the oath highlight the secular mind-set of the framers. Even the act of *swearing* the oath, which is often seen as religious, is made optional, as the constitutional language allows the oath-taker to *affirm* instead. There is no requirement that the oath be taken with a hand on a Bible or holy text of any kind, which could easily have been required if the framers had wanted to even mildly express religious intent. Note also that there is no "so help me God" at the end of the presidential oath. Considering that the oath was written in the late eighteenth century when traditional religion was still extremely influential and when a divine reference would have been expected by the standards of the day, this is a remarkable omission by the constitutional drafters, a clear indication that there was no desire to connect the new nation to religion, let alone to Christianity in particular. Instead, the God-free Constitution demonstrates that the founders intentionally constructed the country upon a secular foundation.

As if to underscore that the secular nature of the presidential oath was not a fluke, in 1789, Congress, meeting in its first session, drafted a congressional oath that was also decidedly free of religion. Though there was some debate about possibly including religious language in the congressional oath, the nation's first lawmakers instead decided on strictly secular language. It was signed into law by George Washington on June 1, 1789, making it the very first law passed by the new United States government. Chapter 1, section 1 of the acts of the first Congress of the United States declares that the congressional oath shall be, "I, A.B., do solemnly swear or affirm (as the case may be) that I will support the Constitution of the United States." Like the presidential oath, there is again no Bible and no "so help me God," and again there is an option of affirming instead of swearing. This would hardly reflect the handiwork of a Congress that was seeking to construct a Christian nation.

Despite this clear constitutional and early statutory evidence, the Religious Right still argues that the founders intended to establish a "Christian nation." In doing so, it grasps at any factoid that can be construed as remotely implying religiosity. For example, Article 1, Section 7 of the Constitution, a clause that discusses how a bill can become law even if it is not signed by the president, provides that "if any Bill shall not be returned by the President within ten Days (Sundays excepted) after it shall have been presented to him, the Same shall be a Law, in like Manner as if he had signed it."[14] Religious Right commentators seriously point to this "Sundays excepted" language as indicating that the founders intended to create a Christian nation.[15] Of course, as a simple matter of tradition and ordinary practice, the founders did not conduct business on Sundays, so it should not be surprising that they excluded Sundays from the ten-day period in question, but to the Religious Right, this exception is compelling evidence of intent to construct a Christian nation, notwithstanding the mountains of evidence to the contrary. To make its claim even more comical, not finding any reference to God within the text of the Constitution, it therefore points to the date at the end of the document which reads, "in the year of our Lord," the English translation of the common Latin *anno Domini*—AD—which of course is still frequently used for dates. This was a standard way of dating official documents in the eighteenth century and still is today—even documents issued by secular institutions. (My law school diploma, for example, issued by a private secular university, is dated "in the year of our Lord.") Nevertheless, on this the Religious Right rests its case that America is a Christian nation.

Providing further evidence of the secular intent of the founders is the Bill of Rights, ratified in 1791, which consists of the first ten amendments to the Constitution. Like the Constitution itself, the Bill of Rights is completely God-free. In the first sentence of the First Amendment we find language directly addressing the issue of religion: "Congress shall make no law respecting an establishment of religion, or prohibiting the free exercise thereof . . ."

THE RELIGIOUS RIGHT'S HISTORIAN

In light of the clear secularity of both the Constitution and the Bill of Rights, only a rhetorical gymnast could keep a straight face while seriously arguing that America is a Christian nation, and the Religious Right's gold medalist in this event is David Barton.

Even though he has no academic credentials as a historian, Barton has become a favorite historical authority for conservative Christians. Cited by politicians such as Newt Gingrich, Mike Huckabee, and Michele Bachmann, Barton is an evangelical minister who graduated from Oral Roberts University as a religious education major, but he has astonishingly become an eminent historian in the eyes of the Religious Right. His organization, WallBuilders, is dedicated to "educating the nation concerning the Godly foundation of our country." It does so by "presenting America's forgotten history and heroes, with an emphasis on the moral, religious, and constitutional foundation on which America was built—a foundation which, in recent years, has been seriously attacked and undermined."[16] Huckabee, himself an ordained minister and once a presidential aspirant, is so enthusiastic about Barton's Christian narrative of history that he said all Americans should be "forced at gunpoint" to listen to it.[17] He expresses these sentiments because Barton's interpretation of history tells the Christian Right exactly what it wants to hear: America is a Christian nation, founded by Christian men who didn't believe in real church-state separation, and therefore its institutions and laws should generally reflect a pro-Christian bias. For years, Barton has traveled the country promoting America's "Christian heritage," usually to religious audiences, using cherry-picked quotes from American historical figures, sometimes of questionable validity and often taken out of context, as supporting evidence. One such quote, for example, purported to be from James Madison arguing that America should be governed according to the Ten Commandments, caught the eye of a Madison expert, Robert S. Alley, professor emeritus from the University of Richmond. Since Madison is known as a strong supporter of church-state separation, the quote used by Barton seemed inconsistent with the Madison known to historians. As it turned out, no support could be found for the quote, and Alley concluded that it was probably false. Barton eventually categorized the quote as "unconfirmed" on his website, along with about a dozen others. In *Church & State* magazine, Alley made his opinion clear. "It's one thing to get up and make a speech and allude to something that isn't there," he said, "but when you have somebody parading a document in a book and that turns out to be an outright lie, it's more than dangerous." He added, "The danger is that people will find credibility in what he does largely because he represents himself in that mode. He's a double fraud."[18] Numerous professional historians have now criticized Barton's work.

Despite being held in low esteem among historians, Barton cannot be quickly dismissed so long as his Religious Right constituents laud him as an expert and a courageous speaker of truth. Even after professional embarrassments that would have caused others to avoid the spotlight, Barton continues to appear on national television promoting his unique brand of history. "He's rediscovering the spiritual roots of this nation," said Sam Brownback, the governor and former senator from Kansas. "His research provides the philosophical underpinning for a lot of the Republican effort in the country today—bringing God back into the public square," Brownback added.[19] Pat Robertson, expressing the sentiments of many on the Religious Right, said of Barton, "I admire him tremendously for his breadth of information."[20] Michele Bachmann, always eager to find converts whether political or religious, proposed holding history classes for members of Congress with Barton as teacher.

A survey of Barton's work, almost all of which is available via the WallBuilders website, shows why the Christian Right is so enamored. With book and video titles such as *The Myth of Separation; America's Godly Heritage; The Influence of the Bible on America; Eight Steps for Thinking Biblically; Vote! A Christian Civic Responsibility; Science, the Bible and Global Warming;* and many others, Barton and WallBuilders are a rich resource for religious conservatives. Using carefully selected statements by Thomas Paine, for example, Barton argues for the teaching of creationism in schools, suggesting that the founders would want science to be taught theologically if they were alive today. An antisecular agenda permeates all of his work.

When Barton interacts with mainstream media, he is careful to moderate his message. Interviewed on the *Daily Show* with Jon Stewart, for example, he insisted that his calling America a "Christian nation" simply meant that America is "a nation whose institutions and cultures have been shaped by the institution of Christianity."[21] Although there is room for debate over just how much America has been influenced by Christianity, this definition is otherwise not very controversial, since even the most ardent Secular American would acknowledge that Christianity has, to some degree, shaped American institutions and culture.

Addressing his faithful audience of conservative Christians, however, Barton reveals a different agenda, which envisions a Christian America where religious minorities are second-class citizens. When Muslim Keith Ellison was elected to Congress from Minnesota and took his oath of office on a Koran, Barton wrote a lengthy piece casting clouds of suspicion over Ellison and generously quoting other critics who argued that Ellison should not be allowed to serve. Said one critic quoted by Barton, the conservative radio host Dennis Prager, "Insofar as a member of Congress taking an oath to serve America and uphold its values is concerned, America is interested in only one book: the Bible. If you are incapable of taking an oath on that book, don't serve in Congress." Barton used Ellison's election as an opportunity to discuss in detail the wrongdoings and human rights abuses of Muslims going back hundreds of years. He ended the piece by suggesting that good Christians should attempt to convert Ellison to Christianity.[22] Barton was also highly critical of an invitation to a Hindu priest to give an invocation to Congress in 2007, saying, "The prayer will be completely outside the American paradigm, flying in the face of the American motto 'One Nation Under God.'"[23]

But while Barton places Hindus, Muslims, and other non-Christians as second-class citizens, he reserves third class exclusively for Secular Americans. In the same article about Congressman Ellison, Barton pointed out, "America, while concerned about Ellison and the potential dangers of Islam, should be more concerned about secularists. The reality is that Members of Congress who refuse to swear an oath on any religious book represent a greater threat to American faith and culture than do those who swear on the Koran."[24]

Although the specifics of Barton's agenda are somewhat vague, the general theme of antisecularism is undeniable. On all issues, he is either unwilling or unable to understand the concerns of Secular Americans, instead staying singularly focused on promoting the conservative Christian position. In the aforementioned interview with Jon Stewart, for example, Barton made the odd claim that those who oppose governmental religious expressions, such as the "under God" wording in the Pledge of Allegiance, are doing so because they are claiming that "there's never been a religious influence on American history." This statement reflects a basic misunderstanding of the issue. When Secular Americans object to "under God" in the pledge or to the national motto In God We Trust, they do so because those statements, taken literally, are unambiguous religious truth claims. Such statements do not simply suggest that America has a religious heritage; they instead declare as a matter of truth that America is *under a god* and that *all Americans actually trust in a god.* (In fact, since both the pledge and motto utilize the singular, upper-case version of "God," they obviously endorse monotheistic religion over others.) As such, those who do not want their public schools telling children every morning that the nation is "under God" are not attempting to deny the historical influence of religion, but to stop the governmental practice of asserting a specific religious truth claim. If Barton were as honest as his claimed Christian morals require, he would admit that his advocacy of the pledge wording and the national motto has less to do with acknowledging religious heritage than promoting a specific religious view.

Former senator Arlen Specter, who switched parties from Republican to Democrat while in office and who, as a moderate, was frequently criticized by religious conservatives, got it right when he said that Barton's "pseudoscholarship would hardly be worth discussing, let alone disproving, were it not for the fact that it is taken so very seriously by so many people."[25] As we see from the way Barton is exalted by not just Bible Belt preachers but even politicians at the highest levels—even presidential aspirants—his work is not just intellectually flawed but outright dangerous. After three decades of ascendance, the Religious Right is now in a position to rewrite history and law through the distorted pseudoscholarship of a theologian.

THE DYSFUNCTIONAL CHRISTIAN FAMILY

While Barton's vision of a "return" to the Christian America of the founders is a fairy tale, we should nevertheless consider what it would mean to revert to the religious standards of early America.

It would be a gross exaggeration to suppose, as the Religious Right often does, that a broad, harmonious Christian tenet characterized the American founding era. The founders were themselves guilty of extreme prejudices against certain strands of Christianity, most notably Catholicism. John Adams referred to Catholicism (often called "Popery" in his day) as "nonsense and delusion" and "dangerous in society" and a "detestable system of fraud, violence and usurpation." The Catholic faith reduced people to "a state of sordid ignorance" and "cruel, shameful, and deplorable servitude." As such, Adams was pleased that, in his home region of Massachusetts, Catholics were "as rare as a comet or an earthquake."[26]

And Adams was by no means unique, for anti-Catholicism was the norm among the founders. Jefferson loathed "Jesuitism" as "a retrograde step from light towards darkness." John Jay, the first chief justice of the Supreme Court, was well known for despising Catholicism. In drafting language for the New York Constitution, he proposed tolerance for everyone *except* Catholics who refuse to renounce papal authority.[27]

With such prevailing attitudes, it's little wonder that Catholics constituted only about 1.6 percent of the population of the American colonies at the time of the revolution.[28] It wasn't until the great immigration waves of the nineteenth century that Catholics began arriving in America in large numbers. This influx resulted in a severe anti-Catholic backlash. Riots erupted in many American cities over the increasing presence and influence of Catholic immigrants. In one, later called the Philadelphia Bible Riots of 1844, rumors that Catholics wanted to remove the Bible from public schools sparked riots and resulted in the destruction of several churches. An entire political party, the American Party (better known as the "Know-Nothings"), rose to prominence in the 1850s, with former president Millard Fillmore as its torchbearer, on a platform that was brazenly anti-immigrant and anti-Catholic.

The rumor that Catholics wanted to remove Bibles from schools was not entirely unfounded. It was common in those days for Catholic school children to be disciplined, often physically, for refusing to read or pray from the King James (Protestant) Bible, which was the version typically used in public schools. This mistreatment of Catholic children caused many Catholics in that era to support the idea of separation of church and state, and it also fueled the movement to open Catholic schools around much of the country as a way of insulating Catholic children from unfair treatment in public schools.

With this background, we can better understand the Religious Right's bold and fraudulent pronouncements that America has fallen away from its "Christian heritage." This heritage of Christian solidarity is largely fictitious, as religious intolerance and disharmony were the norm for the better part of our history. We can also understand the apparent unity we see today between conservative Catholics and conservative Protestants as something that deviates from the historical relationship between the two. No longer able to fight about whose Bible will be used or whose prayers will be said publicly, they instead join forces to fight those who prefer that no public prayers be said at all. Standing together primarily to condemn secularism, even revising history to fit their agenda, there can be little doubt that doctrinal disputes and prejudices between the two factions would quickly arise if the common secular enemy were removed.

THE REAL "JUDEO-CHRISTIAN HERITAGE"

Sometimes, probably in an effort to appear more inclusive, conservative politicians avoid the "Christian nation" language and instead refer to our "Judeo-Christian heritage." In proposing a bill that would require the architect of the new Capitol Visitors Center in Washington to "prominently" display the motto In God We Trust and the Pledge of Allegiance to the Flag, including the "under God" passage, former representative Marilyn Musgrave, a Colorado Republican, cited the need to include "Judeo-Christian content" in government buildings.[29] Senator Jim DeMint, a South Carolina Republican, acknowledged that America reflects many religious viewpoints but asserted that "this does not mean that the Judeo-Christian values and principles that built America should be dismantled to accommodate cultures with different values."[30]

Musgrave and DeMint might be surprised to learn that the term "Judeo-Christian" was unknown to the Founding Fathers. Usage of the term, which today connotes a singular set of beliefs and values held in common by both Judaism and Christianity, dates back less than a hundred years, to the 1920s, when some began to use the term as a way of fighting anti-Semitism. (Some rare earlier instances of the term can be found, but they usually referred to Jewish converts to Christianity.)

In today's political semantics, the term serves a practical purpose for the Religious Right of uniting Jews and Christians under the same tent for the promotion of religion, yet it nevertheless represents the worst kind of deceptive, revisionist rhetoric. Indeed, from a historical standpoint, the notion of a proud "Judeo-Christian heritage," suggesting that Judaism and Christianity have a long history of common ground, would be laughable if it weren't such an affront to the truth. Christian-Jewish history is overwhelmingly defined by atrocities and hatred by the former toward the latter, and it is nothing less than shameful to gloss over this chronology by pretending that some kind of harmonious "Judeo-Christian heritage" has ever existed.

Anti-Semitism, like all hate-based thinking, is an ugly subject that few gentle souls would care to examine at length. Nevertheless, when the Religious Right suggests that America was founded on "Judeo-Christian" values, as if synergy has defined the historical relationship between Judaism and Christianity, as if the United States is somehow a product of a joint venture of the two religions, an informed observer can only wonder whether any argument can be more Orwellian. Only a complete whitewash of history could support such absurdity. In fact, official governmental discrimination against Jews was common in the colonies, and even after the new nation was founded, Jews were barred from holding office in many of the states. Maryland, for example, didn't allow Jews to hold public office until 1826, after several unsuccessful efforts against bitter opposition. New Hampshire, the last state to remove such prohibitions, didn't do so until 1877.[31]

Such details taken directly from American history demonstrate that the term "Judeo-Christian tradition" is at best a deceptive gimmick, but closer consideration of the longer historical relationship between Christianity and Judaism shows that political usage of the term can be even more egregious. By suggesting that the interactions between Christianity and Judaism somehow amount to a long, majestic heritage, the Religious Right is sidestepping the inconvenient truth. Let's consider some of the troubling facts about the real "Judeo-Christian tradition."

The history of Christianity, whether Catholic or Protestant, is largely a history of anti-Semitism. On the Protestant side, which is the side with the deepest and strongest roots in American culture, Martin Luther, the man who launched the Protestant Reformation, made his thoughts about Jews horrifically clear in his writings. Luther's *On the Jews and Their Lies*, published in 1543, declared that Jews were a "base, whoring people . . . no people of God" and "a defiled bride, yes an incorrigible whore and an evil slut."[32] Luther also wrote that Jews are "full of the devil's feces . . . which they wallow in like swine."[33] These quick references are mere samplings of Luther's lengthy rants against Jews.

John Calvin, another Reformation theologian whose work influenced the Puritans of New England and many others, was also venomous toward Jews. "Their [the Jews] rotten and unbending stiffneckedness deserves that they be oppressed unendingly and without measure or end and that they die in their misery without the pity of anyone," he declared, exemplifying majoritarian Christian attitudes toward Jews.[34]

It is just as misleading to suggest that the "Judeo-Christian tradition" within Catholicism is any less anti-Semitic. Christians began persecuting Jews soon after rising to political power in the Roman Empire in the fourth century, passing laws making it illegal to convert to Judaism and for Jews and Christians to intermarry, destroying synagogues, and much worse. Saint Augustine, considered the leading intellectual authority of the early church, called Jews "cursed" and blamed them for killing Christ. The Crusades brought mass murders of Jews that would serve as precedent for the atrocities of the twentieth century. Prejudice against Jews has been systemic through most of Christian history, especially in medieval times, which brought ghettos, the Inquisition, accusations of blood libels, forced conversions, and much outright slaughter.[35]

In the thirteenth century, various church councils, at Narbonne and elsewhere, presaging a similar move by the Nazis seven centuries later, ordered all Jews to wear a special marker. These instances, terrible as they are, barely skim the surface, as the history of Catholic hostility toward Jews could fill volumes—and has. While isolated instances of tolerance can be found, the overall history is one of oppression of Jews at the hands of the Christian—usually Catholic—majority.

Such is a brief history of the real "Judeo-Christian heritage."

There can be no question that the anti-Semitism that resulted in the Holocaust had deep roots within European culture, roots intertwined tightly with the Christian theology that completely dominated Europe for almost two thousand years. With such a "heritage," it's little wonder that a strong current of anti-Semitism ran through both European and American culture until modern times, and still has not completely disappeared today; neither is it at all surprising that talk of "Judeo-Christian values" was never part of the vernacular on either continent until well into the twentieth century.

Musgrave and DeMint might still argue that their "Judeo-Christian" rhetoric is justified because both religions have common theological roots. Jesus was, after all, a Jew, and both religions are "Abrahamic"—that is, both accept the books of Moses as being holy text. Those common roots, however, meant nothing over the course of the first two millennia of Christianity, when the Christian religion exerted enormous control over the social and political atmosphere of Europe. To most Europeans over that time period, the notion of embracing Jews as brothers and celebrating "Judeo-Christian values" would have been seen as absolutely preposterous, but this relationship is today a vitally important aspect of the Religious Right's definition of America. By adding the term "Judeo" to their definition of America's heritage, they not only give the appearance of being tolerant and broad-minded (or at least not anti-Semitic), but they also have plausible deniability when they are accused of trying to specifically promote Christianity. Other motivating factors—from opposing Islam to paving the way for the return of Jesus—also result in fundamentalist Christians frequently advocating positions that complement the notion of "Judeo-Christian" commonality.[36]

This raises yet another important point. If religious conservatives wish to embrace the common Abrahamic connection between Judaism and Christianity, obliviously fancying that there is a long history of cooperation and brotherhood, then we must also include the third branch of the Abrahamic tradition—Islam. Muslims, like their Jewish and Christian cousins, see their religion as also descending from Abraham and, in fact, recognize most of the claimed prophets of the Bible. If Musgrave and company insist on exalting "Judeo-Christian values," one must wonder why they don't instead refer to "Judeo-Christian-Islamic values."

AMERICA'S SECULAR FOUNDATION

Historians agree that the Founding Fathers were greatly influenced by the thinkers of the Enlightenment, men such as Thomas Hobbes (1588–1679), John Locke (1632–1704), David Hume (1711–1776), and Jean Jacques Rousseau (1712–1778). So it is baffling that today's Religious Right can even attempt to argue that the founders, being men of the Enlightenment, intended to form a Christian nation. Such an argument necessarily ignores the very nature of the Enlightenment and can only have weight in an atmosphere oblivious to basic facts of history and philosophy.

Widely divergent philosophers and viewpoints can be found under the umbrella of Enlightenment thought. For example, we find philosophers such as Hobbes, who urged authoritarianism, and Locke, who emphasized personal liberty and property rights. The Enlightenment is not noteworthy for extolling one consistent philosophical view; instead, its consistency can be found in certain methods and values that are common among Enlightenment thinkers. Virtually all Enlightenment philosophers, regardless of the particular conclusions that they may have reached, embraced reason, empiricism, and science as underlying principles.

It was these characteristics that made the period unique, and the Enlightenment today is often called the "Age of Reason" or the "Age of Science." Prior to the Enlightenment, throughout the Middle Ages and even during the Renaissance, the church had been the dominant force in society, but with the Enlightenment we see some degree of open skepticism of religion for the first time. Deism, a movement that rejected most organized religion and believed that the world was the work of a nonintervening Creator, became influential during the seventeenth century. It was the first inkling of a rational challenge to Christianity. Deism was radical for its time, an era when extreme religious conservatism, even with witch hangings, was still generally predominant. In the late eighteenth century, Deism would greatly influence America's founding generation. Jefferson, Franklin, and other founders expressed religious views that were strongly deistic, and Thomas Paine's *The Age of Reason* was a polemic that argued primarily that Deism should replace all revelation-based religion.

The Enlightenment was the philosophical foundation upon which America was built, and it is the starting point of a rich secular heritage. While there were some patriots, such as Patrick Henry, who would by today's standards probably be accurately described as religious fundamentalists, the majority of the Founding Fathers were religiously very liberal for their time and envisioned the new country as an experiment in secular democracy. We see this with the God-free Constitution and Bill of Rights that they produced and the obvious disdain that they had for the intermingling of church and state. It is noteworthy that, despite roots in Christian European culture that expected church-state intermingling, the new nation immediately set out on a path toward secular government. For example, while in the earliest days of the Republic many states had officially established religion (the Congregational Church was the established church in Connecticut, Massachusetts, and New Hampshire, for instance), all of the states voluntarily disestablished their state-supported churches not long after the federal Constitution was adopted.

Arguments that the founders would today be conservative Christians, or that they sought to create a "Christian nation," are refuted by the words of the founders themselves. Shortly before his death in 1790, Benjamin Franklin wrote, "As to Jesus of Nazareth, my Opinion of whom you particularly desire, I think the System of Morals and his Religion as he left them to us, the best the World ever saw, or is likely to see; but I apprehend it has received various corrupting Changes, and I have with most of the present Dissenters in England, some Doubts as to his Divinity: tho' it is a Question I do not dogmatise upon, having never studied it, and think it needless to busy myself with it now, when I expect soon an Opportunity of knowing the Truth with less Trouble."[37] Also in 1790, George Washington wrote to a Hebrew congregation the following: "All possess alike liberty of conscience and immunities of citizenship . . .

[T]he Government of the United States, which gives to bigotry no sanction, to persecution no assistance, requires only that they who live under its protection should demean themselves as good citizens in giving it on all occasions their effectual support."[38] To a Quaker group in 1789, Washington wrote, "I assure you very explicitly, that in my opinion the conscientious scruples of all men should be treated with delicacy and tenderness."[39] Such words are even more significant in the context of the times, when warm sentiments toward Jews and Quakers were hardly the norm in Western societies and a more narrow view of tolerance might have been expected. Washington was known to never take Communion, reflecting his deistic tendency to avoid supernatural ritual, and what few religious gestures he made seemed only enough to conform to social, military, and political expectations of the times. Contrary to popular myth, there is no reliable evidence that Washington—or for that matter any other president until about eight decades later—added "so help me God" to the oath of office at his inauguration.[40]

Washington's oft-cited proclamation calling for "thanksgiving and prayer" was made only twice during his eight years in office. Washington's successor, John Adams, issued such proclamations but later wrote that he regretted doing so. The third president, Thomas Jefferson, issued none during the eight years he was in office, making it clear that he viewed such gestures as improper for a secular government. Jefferson's successor, James Madison, yielded to political pressure and proclaimed days of thanksgiving but subsequently wrote that doing so was a mistake.[41] Importantly, after Madison, none of the next eleven presidents issued presidential proclamations of prayer until Lincoln, who did so in 1863 in the midst of the bloodbath of the Civil War.[42]

Over time, not surprisingly, the founder's secular governmental structure, based on high-minded principles, became watered down. Once the Constitution was enacted and elections began occurring, the nation was on a trajectory that was defined not so much by principle, but practical politics. With the government increasingly under the guidance of expedient politicians, not principled theorists and intellectuals, the electoral value of religious expression became relevant. In a democracy, where careers rely on the outcome of popularity contests, it can be toxic to oppose the religion of the vast majority.

THAT WAS THEN, THIS IS NOW

Compare the strong secular tradition reflected in the early years of the Republic—with only occasional religious proclamations issued in the earliest days and then a period of five decades when there were none—to today's hyper-religious environment in which the Religious Right demands an annual National Day of Prayer and goes apoplectic if the event is celebrated in a low-key manner. When President Obama in 2009 decided to acknowledge the annual event via a simple written proclamation and without a public ceremony, Fox News ran the headline "Obama's Decision to Observe National Day of Prayer Privately Draws Public Criticism."[43] The story showed that the Religious Right was on the attack over Obama's low-key approach to governmental religiosity. "We are disappointed in the lack of participation by the Obama administration," said Shirley Dobson, chairwoman of the National Day of Prayer Committee. "At this time in our country's history, we would hope our president would recognize more fully the importance of prayer." Andrea Lafferty of the Traditional Values Coalition had similar sentiments when Obama did the same thing in 2010. "I can't remember a time when America was more in need of God's blessing, but the president doesn't see it," she said.[44] Similarly, when Obama refrained from mentioning God in his Thanksgiving address to the nation in 2011, major news outlets gave headlines to criticism from Religious Right leaders who were reportedly "angry" and "riled" and "outraged."[45]

Americans have grown so accustomed to the Religious Right that we no longer realize how bizarre it is that powerful religious interests regularly influence our media and policy makers in this way. While there have been occasional right-wing preachers who have held some political sway over the course of American history, it would have been unimaginable that fringe fundamentalist religious leaders could have publicly badgered, say, Harry S. Truman, Dwight D. Eisenhower, or John F. Kennedy, for not holding a high-profile ceremony to publicly proclaim the importance of prayer, for "merely" issuing a written proclamation instead. It is bad enough that these religious fundamentalists are doing this, successfully convincing conservative religious voters that Obama has actually done something wrong, but it's even worse that much of the public is unperturbed about it, even unaware of it.

When concerns such as these are raised about governmental religiosity, the Religious Right will often argue that Secular Americans are trying to make government antireligious. In fact, however, a fair assessment of history would reveal that the structure of American government was not intended to be either proreligion or antireligion, but simply neutral on religion. What we find with the Religious Right is that it sees *neutrality* as *hostility*, because anything less than overt favoritism toward conservative Christianity is interpreted as adversarial.

The secular tradition in America is a strong one and, ultimately, one that should not be construed as hostile to religion. To be sure, there are genuinely antireligious sentiments that can be found throughout American history, even among the founders. Despite attempts by some to portray Jefferson a defender of traditional Christianity, anyone with knowledge of Jefferson knows otherwise. "And the day will come when the mystical generation of Jesus, by the supreme being as his father in the womb of a virgin will be classed with the fable of the generation of Minerva in the brain of Jupiter," he wrote in a letter to John Adams in 1823.[46] He told his nephew in 1787 to "question with boldness even the existence of God," and he clearly considered reason and science, not superstition and supernaturalism, to be his guides.[47]

Such a statement, and those of Franklin and Washington mentioned previously, would never be mistaken for a Jerry Falwell or Pat Robertson sermon, and these are the words of men who lived long before the modern scientific advances that have made traditional Christian supernatural beliefs and doctrines even less plausible. One can only imagine what the framers would think of Christian theology in light of the knowledge of astronomy, physics, evolution, genetics, and other scientific advances that have accumulated since their time. The Founding Fathers were relatively skeptical of religion with, compared to today's vast pool of scientific knowledge, relatively little basis for being so. Galileo had been persecuted for arguing against a geocentric universe only a century before their lifetime, and Darwin's breakthrough discoveries on natural selection were still half a century away.

POST-FOUNDING SECULAR TRADITION

After the founding generation, the secular tradition in America continued. Though Abraham Lincoln is often portrayed as a religious man, he was known to be a religious skeptic. Perhaps the man who knew him best, his law partner of many years, William Herndon, described the sixteenth president's religious beliefs in a letter less than a year after Lincoln's assassination. He wrote, "Mr. Lincoln's religion is too well known to me to allow of even a shadow of a doubt; he is or was a Theist & a Rationalist, denying all extraordinary–supernatural inspiration or revelation." He went on to say, "At one time in his life, to say the least, he was an elevated Pantheist, doubting the immortality of the soul as the Christian world understands that term. I love Mr. Lincoln dearly, almost worship him, but that can't blind me. He's the purest politician I ever saw, and the justest man."[48]

One of the most important proponents of America's strong secular heritage was Robert G. Ingersoll (1833–1899), known as the Great Agnostic, who is often cited as the greatest orator of his era. Though not a household name today, Ingersoll was a prominent attorney and influential at the highest levels in politics (ironically, he was a staunch Republican) but was most famous for his eloquent attacks on religion and defense of skepticism. Paying audiences would fill halls to hear him speak, which he would often do for hours without notes, advocating rational thinking and humanistic views. He was unambiguous in his criticism of religion: "If by any possibility the existence of a power superior to, and independent of, nature should be demonstrated, there will be time enough to kneel. Until then let us stand erect."[49]

Secular Americans also played an important part in the women's suffrage movement. Elizabeth Cady Stanton (1815–1902), the great social activist and suffragist, was an outspoken critic of religion and its role in oppressing women and obstructing social progress in general. In her book, *The Woman's Bible*, a bestseller in the 1890s, she said, "I do not believe that any man ever saw or talked with God, I do not believe that God inspired the Mosaic code, or told the historians what they say he did about woman, for all the religions on the face of the earth degrade her, and so long as woman accepts the position that they assign her, her emancipation is impossible."[50] Stanton was unrelenting in her criticism of religion, and her place in history may have suffered because of that. "Jehovah has never taken a very active part in the suffrage movement," she wrote to Susan B. Anthony in 1878.[51] Anthony (1820–1906), who like Stanton was an agnostic but was less vocal in her criticism of religion, was a leading figure with Stanton in the suffrage movement for much of the nineteenth century. She has become better known than Stanton in modern popular culture, her face now adorning coins and her role in the women's movement often receiving more attention in school curricula. Many feel that this is because, unlike Stanton, her work for women's rights was not as frequently accompanied by harsh criticism of religion.

A TROUBLING RELIGIOUS TRADITION

Although America does indeed have a noteworthy religious heritage, that tradition has frequently been cringe-worthy and nothing that should instill pride. If you're feeling nostalgic for America's religious heritage, you could look back to the days when our forefathers were more religious. Mary Dyer, a Quaker woman, experienced firsthand the devout religiosity of early Bostonians in 1660, when she was publicly hanged for her religious beliefs. To citizens of modern secular democracies, where pluralism is an important value, such executions of Christians by Christians, over what today seem like extremely minor doctrinal differences, are puzzling. In those times, however, theocracy ruled in Massachusetts Bay Colony and Puritan leaders set forth biblical standards of justice with vicious piety. The Quaker hangings of the mid-seventeenth century are to be distinguished from the better-known witch trials of the 1690s, which were yet another example of America's rich religious heritage. We should all be grateful that America is not nearly as religious as it once was.

Conservatives often misrepresent America's religious history as being synonymous with religious freedom, with piety portrayed as a phenomenon to be remembered with nothing but fondness, when in fact such reminiscing is a gross distortion. Puritans settling in New England had little interest in religious freedom, or even a general freedom of conscience, but rather they sought to escape Europe so that they could construct a severely intolerant, oppressive religious society of their liking. While they had faced some degree of discrimination in Europe, it is noteworthy that many left the relatively tolerant environment of the Netherlands to settle in America, partly because they felt that freedom and tolerance were corrupting influences. The Puritans loathed pluralism, and that's why they wanted their own remote settlement in the New

World. In deciding to leave the Netherlands, Puritan leader William Bradford wrote that he wanted to shield the community's children from being "drawn away by evil examples into extravagance and dangerous courses" and that he envisioned the American settlement as a "great hope . . . for the propagating and advancing the Gospel of the kingdom of Christ."[52] As we see from the execution of Quakers and others after the Puritans settled in America, that Christian vision resulted in an extreme, fearful, and brutal theocracy.

From these facts, the Religious Right constructs a mythical notion of the early colonists being lovers of freedom and tolerance, the farcical idea that religion has been nothing but a positive force in America from the start.

If you are inclined to express gratitude to divinities, you should thank God that modern America isn't such a religious country after all. Sure, we have preachers like Terry Jones, the fundamentalist pastor from Florida who expressed a mixture of ignorance and intolerance by publicly burning a Koran in 2011, but we don't have a culture akin to that of Afghanistan, which reacted to Jones's actions with violent riots that killed at least 20 people. Of course sociologists, anthropologists, psychologists, and other cultural commentators can analyze such events in a way that portrays religion as something less than the primary factor in causing such violence, and such analyses might even have some degree of validity; but still, even the most ardent religious apologist must concede that religion is an important factor at some level, hardly benign.

As further evidence of America's religious heritage, the Religious Right may correctly point to various energetic popular religious revivals that have from time to time swept America, such as the Great Awakenings that took place in the nineteenth century. It is indeed true that these religious awakenings were noteworthy episodes in the American narrative, evidence of a real religious heritage. Again, however, like the intolerance of the Puritans and the anti-Catholicism of the founding generation, these events are in many ways embarrassments. The Great Awakenings were highlighted by followers immersed in postmillennial hysteria and convinced that the Second Coming was imminent, only to be proven wrong by actual events. One could reasonably question whether this is an aspect of our heritage that we would want to emphasize, for such gullible and irrational actions hardly seem to be worthy of pride.

COMPARE AND CONTRAST

Compare this perplexing religious heritage to the secular heritage that was simultaneously developing, with figures such as Ingersoll, Stanton, Anthony, and others. Mark Twain (1835–1910) was another important critic of religion from the same era. Even during his lifetime, he was vocally satirical of piety and organized religion, but he saved some of his harshest criticism for posthumous release. In his autobiography, which he requested be withheld from publication for one hundred years after his death, he was perfectly blunt in his assessment of Christianity: "There is one notable thing about our Christianity: bad, bloody, merciless, money-grabbing, and predatory. . . . Ours is a terrible religion. The fleets of the world could swim in spacious comfort in the innocent blood it has spilled."[53] Clarence Darrow (1857–1938) was perhaps the most famous lawyer of the twentieth century, having represented Tennessee schoolteacher John Scopes in the famous Monkey Trial that put the issue of evolution onto the public stage. He was also a nonbeliever, and of course there were many others.

Despite the rise of the Religious Right in the political sphere, America's secular tradition has continued in many other areas of the culture. In fact, arts and entertainment are abundant with secular individuals and themes that are widely acclaimed. Consider the popularity of comics and social commentators such as George Carlin (1937–2008) and Bill Maher, for example, who in many ways built their careers around the art of criticizing religion. Or consider the popularity of irreverent films such as Maher's *Religulous* or Monty Python's *Life of Brian* and *The Meaning of Life* among countless others. Despite the sparse population of open nonbelievers and religious skeptics in politics, the entertainment industry has been overflowing with them for years, from Katharine Hepburn (1907–2003), who received the American Humanist Association's Arts Award in 1985 ("I'm an atheist and that's it," she casually told one reporter. "I believe there's nothing we can know except that we should be kind to each other and do what we can for people."), to Jodie Foster, Penn Jillette, Brad Pitt, and innumerable others in modern times.[54]

Hence, secularity has always been a major part of American culture and is undoubtedly becoming even more prominent. As this rich secular heritage has moved into the modern era, it has in many ways shaped American arts, science, literature, entertainment, and popular culture and, together with a demographic landscape that has diversified to reflect virtually all of the world's peoples and cultures, has made the notion of America as a Christian nation a delusion that is kept alive only through ignorance and religious zealotry.

Puzzlingly, America's great appreciation for secularity seems to come to a screeching halt in only one public arena: politics. This was pointed out quite effectively by Jesse Ventura, the former professional wrestler who served as governor of Minnesota from 1999 to 2003, after he ran a populist campaign as a candidate of the Reform Party. "I can't even run for office anymore," he told radio host Howard Stern in 2011. "I've come out of the closet . . . I'm an atheist." It speaks volumes that the tough, confident, and outspoken Ventura, already having once overcome tremendous odds to be elected governor of a state as a third-party candidate, conceded that his open atheism makes him incapable of further electoral victory.[55]

This is what today's secular movement seeks to change. Clearly, America has deep secular roots, a large population of talented secular individuals, and great appreciation for secularity. It would be a shame to waste this valuable resource by conceding the job of policy making to anti-intellectual religious activists. In America, personal secularity is alive and well, and today's secular movement aims to help it flex its muscle.

FOUR

SECULARITY AND MORALITY

IN 2009, TO COINCIDE WITH THE ONE HUNDRED FIFTIETH AN-
niversary of the publication of Charles Darwin's *On the Origin of Species*, religious conservatives, led by actor Kirk Cameron and minister Ray
Comfort, distributed one hundred thousand free copies of the book with
a "special introduction" written by Comfort, an introduction that gro-
tesquely distorts Darwin's ideas.[1] According to the book's website, over
seventy thousand additional copies were sold to churches and individuals
for distribution to students on college campuses. The site brags, "In one
day, 170,000 future doctors, lawyers and politicians will freely get information about Intelligent Design (and the gospel) placed directly into their
hands!"[2]

The lengthy introduction—over 50 pages—is full of wild scientific
inaccuracies and misleading information. For example, Comfort suggested
that the fossil record contains little evidence of "transitional forms" (fos-
sils exhibiting intermediate states between an ancestral organism and a
descendant), when in fact the existing record overflows with evidence of
transitional evolving species. He also claimed that certain organs, such as
the eye, are too complex to have evolved through the process of natural
selection, when in fact scientists have explained in detail that the eye has

evolved separately in nature numerous times.[3] The evolutionary explanation of the eye's origin is not so complex that a reasonably intelligent person, conducting an honest inquiry, cannot have a basic understanding of it, but Comfort seems to prefer a position of willful blindness.

Comfort also misled readers by associating Darwin's biological theory to Social Darwinism, a gross misapplication of Darwin's ideas that was popular in the late nineteenth and early twentieth centuries. Social Darwinists argued that Darwin's theory could be applied socially to justify inequality, oppression, and even racism, under the guise of "survival of the fittest" (a phrase actually coined by Herbert Spencer, not Darwin, but which is commonly used to explain natural selection). Contrary to Comfort's deceptions, Darwin's theory of evolution is purely biological and has no innate social application. Nevertheless, Comfort inaccurately portrayed Darwin as a racist and misogynist, when in fact Darwin's views on both race and gender, while outdated by today's standards, were mainstream or even liberal for his time. (He was an abolitionist, for example.) Perhaps worst of all, Comfort referred to Hitler as Darwin's "famous student," a brazen distortion that incorrectly implies that Darwin was responsible for Hitler's atrocities.

These books were handed out not to religious conservatives, but to unsuspecting students who thought they were getting a high-quality special edition of a classic writing. Few would have seen Cameron's video promoting the campaign to distribute the books, in which he warns that "an entire generation is being brainwashed by atheistic evolution" and admits that the purpose of the deception is to "get the gospel into the hands of this generation."[4] To a curious young American undergrad, who may have learned little about Darwin's theory in high school due to antievolution efforts by religious conservatives, Comfort's "special introduction" would be a heavy dose of religious propaganda.

Given the correlation between religiosity and social ills as explained in chapter 2, it is ironic that one of the worst slanders repeated about secularity is that it is the first step toward a moral breakdown that might lead to the rise of totalitarianism. This may sound outlandish to readers who are knowledgeable of history and philosophy, but the unfortunate reality is that many Americans, upon hearing the word *atheism*, immediately envision Hitler,

Stalin, and Mao. Such associations are the result of persistent misinformation campaigns, such as the aforementioned Cameron-Comfort scheme,
and this is surely part of the reason that many Americans are hesitant to
openly identify as nonbelievers.

DON'T BLAME THE HOLOCAUST ON SECULARITY

Having gone to Catholic schools as a child, I know from personal experience that the church claimed that the Holocaust was a direct result
of nonbelief. This is the kind of historical and moral claim that young
school children typically accept without question, and it was, and still is,
propagated frequently by religious leaders. Not just fringe fundamentalist preachers, but even figures as notable as the Pope have placed blame
for the Holocaust on nonbelievers. Speaking in 2010, Pope Benedict XVI
railed against "atheist extremism" and "aggressive secularism" as giving rise
to Nazi atrocities.[5] It is little wonder that so many Americans today have
such a misunderstanding of the facts.

As discussed in chapter 3, there was a long European Christian tradition (both Catholic and Protestant) that demonized Jews as the worst
element of humanity. Hitler's anti-Semitism, while obviously extreme, was
a natural outgrowth of a long-accepted climate of anti-Semitism in Christian Europe. Germany had long been a Christian society, with both Catholic and Protestant populations that were large and influential. A 1939
census, at the height of the Third Reich's power, reports that 94 percent of
Germans identified as Christian (54 percent Protestant, 40 percent Catholic), while only 1.5 percent identified as unbelievers.[6] Both Catholic and
Protestant churches remained officially subsidized by the German state
throughout the Nazi regime, meaning the government collected a church
tax and funded the churches.[7] The Holocaust occurred not because there
was a sudden tide of nonbelief in Germany, but because of a confluence of
factors that allowed long-existing Christian prejudices against Jews to rise
to the surface.

Hitler was raised Catholic (another fact that I was never told in Catholic school) and was never excommunicated by the church. The specifics of
his personal religious beliefs as an adult are impossible to determine based
on the limited evidence, but he made it clear that he was not an atheist. In

his book *Mein Kampf,* his personal memoir and manifesto, he referred to God dozens of times, at one point penning a prayer, "Almighty God, bless our arms when the hour comes." He also claimed, for example, "God does not follow the principle of granting freedom to a nation of cowards," and he spoke out frequently against atheism and in favor of religious instruction in schools.[8]

In an attempt to direct attention away from Christian anti-Semitism as the primary cause of the Holocaust, religious conservatives will often try to blame Nazi atrocities on Darwinism, because Hitler's notion of racial superiority can be seen as an outgrowth of evolutionary theory. This argument overlooks the long European tradition of anti-Semitism, which predates Darwin by well over a thousand years, and instead emphasizes that the Nazis justified their perverse theories of racial superiority on a misapplication of Darwin's sound scientific work. The illogic of this argument is stunning. Nazis misused Darwin's ideas relating to evolution as a tool in their campaign, but the root cause of their anti-Semitism was the underlying hatred that was instilled by centuries of Christian teachings, not Darwin's theories. Legitimate science is not voided because it is misunderstood or misused by sick minds.

Anyone who takes the time to read Darwin sees that he had no political or social agenda, that he exhibited no hatred toward any group of people, and that he was simply a meticulous naturalist who was fascinated by beetles, finches, and the wide variety of other animals and plants that he studied in his world travels. To the extent that he had prejudices, they were only those that were common to almost all men of his time and class. A modest man with a brilliant mind, Darwin was reluctant to reveal his scientific discoveries because he knew that they ran counter to much traditional thinking, yet he ultimately made his findings public after painstakingly documenting their validity. As a Victorian English gentleman, he had no interest in overturning the social order, but he understood that his findings would inevitably result in a radical rethinking of many long-held assumptions, particularly theological assumptions.

Ultimately, Darwin's theory of evolution by natural selection stands not on the basis of whether bad people misapplied it, or even on whether Darwin was a good person, but on its scientific soundness. In this regard, Darwin's legacy is monumental, as his theory is recognized as the foundation upon which modern biology is based. His brilliance is even more evident when we consider that he was unaware of the gene or DNA, which constitute the biological mechanism through which the process of natural selection takes place. Without knowledge of any of the molecular-level activity that results in an organism exhibiting particular traits, Darwin nevertheless developed a thorough, coherent theory on how species evolved over time. Subsequent genetic discoveries have solidified the scientific validity of Darwin's theory, and it is a sad commentary on the state of mind of religious conservatives that, despite the overwhelming evidence, they continue to insist that the world was created six thousand years ago with life in its current form.

THE CATHOLIC CHURCH AND HITLER

It is important to distinguish between the *general* role played by Christianity in creating a culture of anti-Semitism and the *specific* role played by the religion (particularly the Catholic Church) in the rise of Hitler. These are two separate issues, and confusion results when they are examined as one. Whereas there is room for some debate regarding the responsibility of the Catholic Church for allowing Hitler to consolidate his power and execute his campaign of hate, that debate should not distract from the clear historical role of Christianity in fueling anti-Semitism.

Although the degree of the Catholic Church's culpability stemming from its relationship with Hitler might be debatable, no fair assessment will have the church emerging unscathed. This subject has been covered comprehensively in other works, perhaps most notably in a book by the prominent Catholic writer John Cornwell, whose *Hitler's Pope* details both the relevant history of the church and the career of Eugenio Pacelli, who would eventually become Pope Pius XII.[9] Elected pope in 1939, Pacelli is important not only because the Second World War was waged during his papacy, but also because he was a cardinal representing the Vatican in Berlin in the decade before the war, during Hitler's rise. As will be discussed in what follows, Pacelli's role as the Vatican's chief diplomat with Berlin during the decade of Hitler's rise to power is arguably more historically significant than his subsequent role as pope during the war. Moreover, at a minimum, it is clear that the church of the early twentieth century preferred fascism to leftist alternatives (evidenced by its support of Franco in Spain, for example), had little fondness for democracy, and was not concerned about anti-Semitism until it rose to beyond crisis proportions.

Looking at the church's activities in the 1930s, the facts are somewhat unsettling. As Cornwell argued quite convincingly, Pacelli made diplomatic moves as cardinal in Berlin that almost certainly helped Hitler consolidate power. The Vatican's 1933 Concordat with Berlin, for example, depoliticized many German Catholics, thereby silencing in the early days of Hitler's regime a segment of German society that might have effectively restrained him. This diplomatic faux pas, a figurative pact with the devil exhibiting an indifference to fascism at a time when it should have been clear that Hitler represented a threat to humanity, shows a church that resembles not a divine agency, but an all-too-human institution. The level of wrongdoing that should be attributed to these actions might be debatable, but few outside the church would assess the church's actions as an example of moral perfection. And again, this blundering is wholly distinguishable from the historical role played by the church in fostering anti-Semitism.

One thing that is not debatable is that secularity played no role in the Holocaust, and it seems that Europeans as a group are most aware of this. Having been closest to the scene of the crime, Europeans have flocked to secularity since the Second World War, to the point that in many countries churches have been empty for decades. Secularity, with the lower crime rates and higher standards of living that accompany it, has thrived in Europe in the postwar years as the continent has licked its wounds and learned from its mistakes, with most of the continent seeing relative peace and prosperity in a nonreligious environment. Had atheism been perceived as the root cause of the Holocaust and war, Europeans would no doubt have rushed back to the churches in the postwar years. But they didn't.

SECULARITY AND COMMUNISM

Of course, in the first four decades after the Second World War, much of Eastern Europe didn't have the option of going back to church, because Soviet domination of that region resulted in political oppression and a loss of basic freedoms, including the free exercise of religion. Defenders of conservative religion often use this fact to encourage the public to view atheism as virtually synonymous with communism. After all, it's not hard to win a public relations battle if your audience believes that your opponents will lead society to gulags and a police state. Few intelligent and informed religious leaders truly believe such foolishness, but it's not unusual to hear preachers drawing associations between atheism and communism in an effort to instill their followers with fear.

If there were any doubt that atheism is not a slippery slope to communism, then we should take note that some of the most vehemently anticommunist public figures have been nonbelievers. For example, Ayn Rand (1905–1982), author of *The Fountainhead* and *Atlas Shrugged,* fled Russia after the Bolshevik Revolution of 1917 and was a fierce anticommunist. Though an atheist, Rand promoted a philosophy that exalted the individual, not the collective, and is popular among libertarians today. Other ardent capitalists known to be nonbelievers would include Milton Friedman and Warren Buffett, among countless others.

To ordinary Secular Americans, the suggestion that atheists are communist sympathizers, or that secularity leads to totalitarianism in any form, is insulting. The Soviet Union repressed freedom, including religious freedom and freedom of conscience, and tried to impose communist and antireligious views on its citizens. This is no more desirable than the imposition of a particular religious view, and no rational American, religious or secular, would support anything of the kind. Moreover, since pre-Soviet Russia, a monarchy that ruled with the blessing of the church, was itself a harsh, authoritarian society with few basic freedoms, we should not be surprised that the regime emerging from the Russian civil war in 1917 was something less than a Jeffersonian democracy; to blame the tyranny on atheism is either naïve or dishonest. To suggest that a Western democracy would plummet into social and political chaos if secularity were to become more prevalent is not just abstractly absurd, but demonstrably so given the evidence of the stable secular democracies of modern Europe.

MORALITY AND SECULARITY

When religious advocates proclaim that there is a relationship between secularity and fascism or communism, they are essentially challenging the moral underpinnings of a secular worldview. Religious conservatives believe that morals and values come directly from God, and without a divine ethical grounding, they argue, surely moral chaos will result. "I believe . . . that in the absence of absolute values, in the absence of a belief that your liberty comes from God, democracy becomes very fragile and weak," said Newt Gingrich, a rather hilarious statement considering his stature as a moral authority.[10] This is a common view that has been promoted by religious leaders for centuries.

This argument necessitates some consideration of where people find their morality and values. Enlightenment philosophers such as Hobbes and Locke wrote of the concept of natural law and natural rights—binding rules of morality and rights that exist in nature—later influencing Jefferson and other American founders. Though natural law could still be theoretically rooted in the divine (the Declaration of Independence states that men are "endowed by their Creator with certain unalienable Rights"), it nevertheless should be seen as a step in the direction of secularity. Natural law and natural rights, like anything in nature, can be described by sheer speculation as coming from God, but they do not by definition require God or religion, and like other things found in nature they are discovered through the use of reason.

Moreover, though "reason" may seem like an objective standard, in application it is not always so, for what seems readily apparent through reason in one society (such as women having the right to vote) may seem like a radical notion to other societies that nevertheless consider themselves reasonable. Thus, whether the source of morality is divine or natural, it seems that it is always defined by the social unit that ultimately enforces it.

Keeping this last point in mind, modern secular writers sometimes criticize even the relatively liberal concept of natural law and natural rights. Harvard law professor Alan Dershowitz, in his 2004 book, *Rights from Wrongs,* argues that rights are not divine or naturally existing but are invented by societies through experience, often by learning from mistakes. Viewed this way, free speech and free press do not reflect any inherent natural rights that were waiting to be discovered, but rather can be seen as inventions that serve the practical purpose of preventing repressive government. Such rights are wholly man-made and unnatural, Dershowitz contends. Civilization can be seen as an effort to tame the natural world, with morality and rights evolving as human societies make mistakes and learn what doesn't work and what isn't desirable. Too pragmatic to suggest a comprehensive system of morality and rights, Dershowitz instead says a better approach is a minimalist one that, while not finding unanimity on all points about what is right, at least reaches agreement on what is wrong.[11]

Applying this approach to religion and secularity, we can see why religious freedom and church-state separation are so sensible. A pluralistic society cannot reach unanimity on which religion, if any, is the right one, and it cannot reach consensus on which god, if any, should be worshiped, but all can at least agree that everyone should have freedom of conscience, that nobody should be forced to worship or to subsidize the worship of others.

As a natural phenomenon, morality is not entirely unique to humans. We are, after all, simply one of many mammals in the animal kingdom, and like many, we are social in nature. Social mammals survive via some degree of cooperative living by developing means of sharing resources and responsibilities. In this sense, the human experience is analogous to that of chimpanzees, wolves, and even dolphins. From an evolutionary viewpoint, antisocial behavior often does not promote survival in a group setting and might result in ostracism from the group, fewer mating opportunities, and fewer offspring. Thus, our species evolved to produce members that recognize, consciously and unconsciously, group rules and standards. It is these rules and standards that became the rudimentary framework of what can be called morality.

While human morality is indeed unique, it is not entirely incomparable to that of other animals. In fact, extensive evidence has been compiled of animals exhibiting selfless altruistic behavior, showing compassion, putting themselves at risk, sacrificing, and even saving the life of another. Anyone who suggests that admirable exhibitions of altruism are unique to humans hasn't taken the time to seriously consider such behavior.

Importantly, however, while ethical behavior has proven to have survival value, unethical behavior sometimes has as well. For example, violence has historically allowed certain individuals to successfully reproduce, creating offspring with similar aggressive behavioral tendencies. The same goes for stealing, cheating, and dishonesty—all of these characteristics can be found in humans and other animals, even though these behaviors may violate the rules and standards of the group. None of this should be construed as meaning that aggressive or dishonest behavior is somehow justified by the fact that our ancestors exhibited it to their reproductive advantage. On the contrary, at this stage of human development, our best hope for long-term safety and stability is to use our impressive brain capacity to learn how to live well within a desirable social and moral framework that promotes peace, creativity, justice, and prosperity.[12]

Morality can be defined by individuals and by societies, but in each case it is simply a reflection of behavioral standards that are deemed acceptable and unacceptable at that particular place and time. If individuals sometimes violate those standards, usually when it is personally advantageous to do so, such behavior is defined as immoral. This modest, naturalistic, and sensible view runs quite contrary to biblical explanations of morality, which tell of an omnipotent, omniscient, loving God who allowed a rebellious angel to influence humans as a test of faith, the theological details of which are hotly disputed even among the various Christian churches. The more fundamentalist among those churches teach that this rebellious angel took the form of a snake and successfully tempted humans about six thousand years ago, initiating the first moral flaw and paving the way for the rest of history. It doesn't speak highly of American society that those who accept literally this fabled explanation continue to garner significant political support, while those preferring the naturalistic view are perceived as marginal.

Not just morality, but religion itself can be understood naturalistically. This subject is covered brilliantly by Tufts University professor Daniel Dennett in his 2006 book, *Breaking the Spell: Religion as a Natural Phenomenon,* in which he demonstrates that the human religious impulse can be understood through evolutionary theory.[13] For example, the tendency to assume that natural events are the result of some agency can be seen not just in humans, but in other mammals as well. A dog startled by snow falling from a roof, for example, will typically respond by barking, because it assumes a possible aggressor might be approaching. Even though this "assumption of agency" is often wrong (as when snow falls off the roof due to melting, not an approaching aggressor), it is a trait that had survival value. Ancestors with that trait either fought or fled when an aggressor was in fact present, thereby living to reproduce, whereas those that didn't presume agency more often perished. (The fight-or-flight instinct, which is behind much of the stress and anxiety that we experience in modern life, is another trait that had survival value in the wild but seems to carry less utility today.) Thus, with humans exhibiting an innate tendency to assume agency, it is not surprising that early forms of religious speculation frequently attached supernatural agents (gods and spirits) to virtually all natural phenomena, nor is it difficult to see that many humans would eventually conclude that one Grand Agent (i.e., God) is responsible for creating and overseeing the universe. From this general human tendency, together with many other biological, psychological, and social factors, religious myth was probably born, and one could argue that all subsequent religious variation is just incidental detail.

Much work remains to be done in the naturalistic study of religion and morality, but the foundational argument is clear. These naturalistic analyses of morality, values, and religion almost always run contrary to the myths and explanations of traditional religion, but they reflect a growing understanding of the true place of humans within the natural world. Concepts and tendencies that once seemed inexplicable via any means other than theology—good and evil, human aggression, altruism, and so forth—are starting to be understood as phenomena that exist for wholly naturalistic reasons.

There can be no doubt that for some people, religion provides grounding for ethical behavior, but it would be a mistake to conclude that religion is necessary for morality, or that without religion there would be moral decay. The data discussed in chapter 2, showing more secular societies consistently exhibiting fewer social ills, helps prove this point. Greg Epstein, the humanist chaplain of Harvard University, discussed the issue of God-free morality in his 2009 book, *Good Without God*, in which he argued that the position that one cannot be good without God-belief is not just wrong but reflects an unfair prejudice.[14] Tendencies toward moral behavior are natural and innate, and moral standards and values are learned by individuals and societies. Experience and reason, not divine revelation, teach us what is right and wrong. We may have a sentimental attachment to the church of our upbringing, and we may even have learned some lessons about right and wrong through the religious teachings of that church, but that does not mean our underlying sense of right or wrong is of divine origins.

What is quite puzzling is the common view among some believers that they would fall into unthinkable immorality if they stopped believing in God. As my friend Herb Silverman, a founder of the Secular Coalition for America, tells audiences, if you genuinely feel that you'll start committing felonies if you stopped believing in God, then by all means keep believing! As many commentators have also pointed out, the view that one is good primarily because one wishes to win a ticket to heaven and avoid eternal damnation does not exactly paint a commendable portrait of humanity. Even when acting at our best, we would be doing so for purely selfish reasons. Other practical concerns, such as how we could possibly enjoy heaven while knowing that others are suffering eternal hellfire, or how any loving God could possibly divide his creations into categories this way, also trouble philosophers and theologians.

Morality is one area where religion has arguably maintained its relevance longer than others. Whereas centuries ago science began displacing religion as a means of acquiring knowledge and determining truth, in the sphere of morality, many people, even today, continue to see religion as providing the answers. What we are seeing, however, is that even in this area secularity is making significant advances, demonstrating that holy books and their moral codes can indeed be understood as natural phenomena, as can human morality itself. Rooted in a naturalistic understanding of the world, studied empirically and scientifically, morality is yet another realm of the human experience that is explained better by scientists than clerics.

SECULARITY AND LGBT ISSUES

The secular approach to morality can be applied to any ethical issue, but one issue that illustrates it well is the debate over LGBT rights. If morality is only derived from the dictation of ancient texts, then biblical conservatives have a solid basis for claiming that homosexuality is "bad," since the Old Testament not only says that a man lying with another man is an "abomination" but also prescribes the death penalty for such behavior.[15]

Christians urging a more accepting view of gay rights, working within the constraints of biblical interpretation, can argue only that such language should be overlooked or interpreted differently. One could contend, for example, that this particular biblical rule should not be construed as universal but instead should be seen as reflecting the value placed on procreation by one relatively small tribe, often outnumbered and in need of additional members. In this instance, the biblical prohibition against homosexuality should be treated like other Old Testament prohibitions that aren't usually emphasized nowadays, such as those forbidding tattoos or the eating of shellfish. One could also point out that in the New Testament, Jesus says nothing about homosexuality, and therefore the "new covenant" arguably does not include such a ban.

The religious debate could no doubt go back and forth endlessly, with points and counterpoints as each side asserts that its interpretation of the ancient text is correct, but it is this debate itself that baffles Secular Americans. These are modern individuals squabbling over writings that are thousands of years old, written by people who had little knowledge of natural science and couldn't have imagined the modern, technologically advanced world we know today. We have otherwise intelligent men and women accepting the translated writings of ancient people as the word of God, structuring their lives around speculative interpretations of the belief systems of a tribe that was struggling to survive and understand the world—nothing more, and certainly nothing divine.

The secular approach to gay rights gives no weight to ancient texts but simply assesses the issue from the standpoint of nature and ethics. Same-sex orientation is found throughout nature and presents no inherent threat to civilization. In a free society, the government has no business dictating the deeply personal decisions of individuals with regard to consensual sex, nor does it have the right to deny individuals with same-sex orientation the same rights as those with opposite-sex orientation. There is room for debate about particulars, and I wouldn't suggest that Secular Americans are unanimous about all issues pertaining to gay rights, but the important point is that the secular analysis disregards ancient religious doctrines, as such writings have no legitimacy in a pragmatic modern analysis that relies upon naturalism, empiricism, and facts.

At first glance, it would seem that the so-called "gay agenda" would be ir-relevant to the agenda of Secular Americans, but in practice, there is over-lap. To be on the "secular agenda," an issue will typically carry with it a question of religion, church-state separation, or discrimination against the nonreligious, and none of those factors would seem to be present in the fight for gay rights. As anyone who has actually worked on LGBT rights issues knows, however, the religion angle is never far from the sur-face—mobilizing, motivating, and often funding much of the opposition to gay and lesbian equality. While of course there are liberal churches that respect and accept gays and lesbians without judgment, conservative reli-gious groups devote enormous resources to opposing LGBT equality.

A high-profile example of this was the 2008 effort by the Mormon church to support Proposition 8, a California ballot measure to ban same-sex marriage. After a call to action by church leaders, Mormons invested heavily in the effort, with estimates stating that they donated half of the $40 million raised on behalf of the ballot initiative. In terms of volunteer time, one leader estimated that Mormons comprised 80 to 90 percent of the early door-to-door canvassers.[16] The religious activism proved success-ful, as the measure passed with 52 percent of the vote.

The religious motivation behind the opposition to gay rights is one reason—but certainly not the only one—that secular individuals and groups often take the other side. Most are already sympathetic to the ar-guments for LGBT equality, and virtually all are opposed to efforts by religious groups to impose their biblical standards of morality. Humanism, as an affirmative philosophy with progressive values rooted in humanity's knowledge and experience, naturally sees LGBT rights as an important matter of human rights. In fact, in 2010 the American Humanist Associa-tion (AHA) formed a subgroup, called the LGBT Humanist Council, for the purpose of advancing LGBT equality through education, public ser-vice, and outreach. At the AHA's 2011 national conference, Candace Gin-grich, an LGBT activist and Newt's younger sister, received the group's first annual LGBT Humanist Pride Award.

Many gays and lesbians are also Secular Americans, but of course many are religious, some even conservatively religious. LGBT individuals who want to remain within a conservative religious faith often struggle fu-tilely for acceptance and face deep-seated antagonism. What one believes about religion is a deeply personal matter, and to a large degree we cannot even consciously decide what we actually believe to be true, so gays and lesbians who remain within the structure of churches that do not accept them owe nobody an explanation. Still, from a secular perspective, the idea of a gay or lesbian individual being devoutly attached to a religion that expresses intolerance, or even hatred, toward same-sex orientation is somewhat baffling. Gays and lesbians within fundamentalist religion have sometimes been driven to self-loathing and even suicide, unable to overcome what they perceive as their sinful nature. Not surprisingly, many gays and lesbians with theistic inclinations choose instead to find an accepting environment in more liberal theistic congregations, and most of those individuals, for understandable reasons, have little interest in the secular movement.

Those gays and lesbians who are Secular Americans, however, are increasingly discovering the value of secular identity and secular groups. This has not always been the case, and in fact I still come across LGBT activists who, even though personally secular, will hesitate about identifying as such. "It was harder for me to come out to my family as an atheist than it was as gay," one AHA member told me, an experience that is not unusual. Many gays and lesbians, having struggled as outsiders for so long on the issue of sexual orientation, would prefer to fly under society's religious radar. But increasingly, many see secular activism, secular community, and secular identity as something that provides enrichment and support. A naturalistic, secular worldview sees gays and lesbians as what they are— people worthy of respect and dignity and whose sexual orientation is not the basis for any moral judgments. By approaching the issue from a naturalistic standpoint, there is simply no basis for intolerance.

Since the fight for the rights of Secular Americans is sometimes compared to the struggle of the LGBT community, a few words are in order regarding the similarities and differences between these two movements.

For starters, most would agree that discrimination against gays and lesbians in modern times, particularly before the recent successes of the LGBT movement, has been more violent and extreme than discrimination toward nonbelievers. Deadly gay bashing is still a reality even in supposedly progressive countries, as is evidenced by the brutal torture and murder of college student Matthew Shepard in 1998, a high-profile crime that spurred hate-crime legislation. Historically, the price of religious dissent could also be extreme. Giordano Bruno, who was burned alive by the Inquisition in 1600 because his scientific views were considered heresy, is a symbolic martyr of religious dissenters, and millions of lesser-known victims of religious intolerance can be found throughout the historical record. In the modern era, however, such extreme brutality for religious opinions has disappeared from most developed societies, so there is almost no danger in living as an open atheist. Though the risks of being openly gay have diminished greatly in recent years, they have not disappeared.

The threat of physical violence against nonbelievers is a rarity, but in deeply religious families the notion of openly rejecting the family religion is often seen as extremely defiant and worthy of ostracism. Most moderate American families wouldn't react so harshly to family members rejecting traditional faith, but most would hope that religious dissenters would at least keep quiet about it, and some would be uncomfortable with a family member openly identifying as atheist, let alone advocating for atheist rights. (Here again we see the stigma that especially attaches to the atheist identity, whereas a more generic secularity that doesn't identify expressly as atheist is often seen as more acceptable.) More conservative families, however, have been known to react quite harshly to the rejection of religion by a member. The blogosphere is filled with tales of young atheists who have been kicked out of their houses. One forum writer told what happened when he informed his mother that he would no longer be attending church. "At first she couldn't believe it and thought I was joking, but then reality set in and she broke down crying," he wrote. "She yelled at me for a little bit trying to understand what I was trying to accomplish, but I told her that this was something I could no longer do. Finally, my mother told me something I already was ready for, and which was that my stepdad would no longer allow me to live there. I told her I understood very well the consequences and that I had made arrangements to stay with our cousin. I left that house shortly afterwards, never again able to call it home."[17]

Another important difference between secularity and sexual orientation is the ease with which secularity can be concealed. For gays or lesbians to conceal their sexual orientation, they must often live a lie, keeping their relationships hidden from family and work colleagues. Thus, being "in the closet" translates to living a double life of sorts, a grave injustice that affects the real lives of many gays and lesbians. For an atheist to stay in the closet, the personal sacrifice is usually not so great or intimate. Being gay or lesbian also carries legal and social repercussions, such as limits on the ability to inherit a partner's estate, adoption rights, and innumerable other real-life factors. Fortunately, these legal impediments are decreasing as the LGBT movement makes progress on same-sex marriage and other avenues. Such legal and social disadvantages are not as common or serious in the lives of secular individuals, although there have been cases in which courts have viewed religious spouses more favorably than secular spouses in custody disputes. But these instances are relatively few, and for the most part Secular Americans' rejection of religion will not affect their ability to work, socialize, have the family life they desire, or otherwise function as they wish.

While there are legal disadvantages to being an LGBT citizen, official governmental hostility toward the demographic has significantly declined, thanks in large part to the successes of the LGBT movement. The same cannot be said for Secular Americans, who have only seen an increase in official hostility to their rights and equality since the rise of the Religious Right, and who now find themselves clearly relegated to a second-class status. Not content with having made In God We Trust the official national motto in 1956, many Religious Right activists are now making determined efforts to erect In God We Trust signs in as many places as possible, reminding everyone that real Americans must believe in God. Children of secular families go to school every day to be told that their nation is "under God," which can only mean that they, along with their mom and dad, are outsiders and not sufficiently patriotic. The accumulated effect of pervasive religion, from prayers at football games and assemblies to religiously influenced science and sex-education curricula, is a fact of life for many nonbelievers. To be sure, schools and other public institutions in many parts of the country exude an aura that disapproves of LGBT status as well, sometimes resulting in terrible incidents of discrimination, but at least the general trend in recent times, especially within official institutional policy and practice, has been toward acceptance. The public condemnation of nonbelievers, meanwhile, typically comes directly from federal, state, and local governments in a highly visible way, and it shows no sign of abating so long as the Religious Right is in charge.

In both the secular and LGBT movements, we have minority groups in which membership can usually be concealed from the view of the general public, although at high personal cost for gays and lesbians. We also have widespread prejudices that often result in family disapproval and various degrees of social ostracism. But with both groups, we find that a key to acceptance is identity—only by "coming out" can Secular Americans and LGBT Americans change public perceptions and gain acceptance. This, in fact, explains the difference between the success of the LGBT movement in recent decades and the lack thereof for the secular movement. Starting in the late 1970s, gay and lesbian rights activists utilized the notion of "coming out" as an important part of their campaign for acceptance. Terms like *gay pride* became common, the rainbow emblem signifying support for LGBT rights became visible, and the general notion of gay-lesbian identity became prominent. Now, decades later, we see that this identity-oriented activism paid off for the LGBT movement, as LGBT orientation has reached levels of acceptance that would have been unimaginable a few decades ago. As we will see later, today's Secular Americans are learning from this experience.

A POST-THEOLOGICAL WORLDVIEW

In all this talk about religion and morality, it is easy to lose sight of the fact that secularity is not just another alternative in the supermarket of American belief systems; instead, it can be seen as a worldview that transcends theology altogether, a worldview that is "post-theological."

While most animals can be accurately described as pre-theological, having never attained the brain capacity to contemplate deep, theological ideas, humans long ago left the pre-theological stage and became theological animals. This happened when our distant ancestors developed the brain capacity to contemplate big questions: *Where did I come from? What is this place? What caused that thunder? What happens when we die?* Having asked such questions, our ancestors lacked the real-world knowledge to accurately answer them, making speculation necessary. And thus theology was born. Struggling through life with such deep questions; seeing famine, disease, and death all around; filled with fear and anxiety, early humans needed answers. Though the explanations they made for themselves varied from one society to the next, the general notions of creation myths, supernatural agents, beliefs about death, and so forth, were common. Not surprisingly, as the human animal moved from hunter-gatherer to more settled civilizations within just the last ten thousand years or so (a sliver of time on the larger scale of human development), institutions were constructed around the primitive theological ideas that had already been circulating for many millennia. And with the development of writing in just the last few thousand years, those ancient myths and explanations could be more permanently memorialized in holy texts.

If humans entered the theological stage because they were able to ponder big questions, the post-theological stage is the result of our acquiring enough knowledge to finally answer many of them. Starting in just the last few hundred years, we have quickly filled in many gaps in knowledge, enough to give us a real sense of where humans fit within the space and time of the universe. We don't need creation myths anymore, because we have a pretty good understanding of how the earth formed and how life evolved. We also know that our planet is not the center of the universe—nor is our sun, nor is our galaxy. Though we can throw out numbers to describe the vastness and age of the universe, most of us are incapable of fully comprehending the true enormity of those numbers, and yet we at least understand that each is staggering. We know, for example, that the universe began with a big bang around 13.7 billion years ago; that our insignificant planet, more insignificant in the universal scheme than we can imagine, formed about 4.5 billion years ago; and that our species, *Homo sapiens,* came into being little more than 200,000 years ago. We don't know what, if anything, caused the Big Bang, but there is no evidence to suggest that it was caused by some kind of "superbeing with intent." Most importantly, intelligent men and women in the modern era, driven to find more answers, are likely to conduct their search through the channels of natural sciences rather than ancient theology.

The post-theological individual is not deprived of the positive benefits of theology. There is lots of room for awe, wonder, and profound thinking with a secular outlook. As Carl Sagan said, each of us is stardust, so humans can be understood as a way that the universe can observe itself.

It's little wonder that most humanists see Sagan as having more profundity and veracity than any biblical prophet or cleric. And from this naturalistic, humanistic standpoint, there is plenty of room for a life of purpose and doing good. In fact, since this one life is our only certainty, the need to live well is compelling. Old-time theological notions, whether meddling spirits or potential eternal punishment from an angry and jealous God, seem misguided and even sometimes a bit juvenile from this perspective.

Because religious institutions are so ingrained in our culture, they of course still offer personal and social benefits to many, and nobody is expecting that all of society is going to rush toward a post-theological view. To many, religious institutions offer tradition, cultural continuity, and a place to find peace of mind through ritual, meditation, and contemplation. As long as this is not infringing on anyone else's rights, this can be all good.

But with the need for theological explanations of the natural world declining, many good, ethical people simply see theology itself as unnecessary. More than ever, many now achieve these ends without institutions or beliefs grounded in the supernatural, instead utilizing humanist organizations, secular institutions, or other means. These people find peace, mindfulness, goodwill, community, ethics, perspective, and culture without the assistance of theology or religious institutions. These people are post-theological, and most of them are Secular Americans.

Having laid out all of this analysis about morality, values, and religion, it is worth pointing out that many typical Secular Americans simply do not obsess about such issues. Like most people, they try to be decent, but also like most, they know that they could probably be better and that they fall short of moral perfection more frequently than they wish they would. Of course, there are those who are deeply concerned about the complexities of these issues, but there is a tendency in discussions like this to overlook the masses, the regular people who are not so analytical. Just as many who identify as religious never think much about the underlying theology of the religion with which they identify, many Secular Americans rarely consider the question of the origins of their morality. They accept who they are, they try to be better, and they go about their daily business, perhaps never having heard of Dennett or Dershowitz, or even the popular

New Atheist authors Richard Dawkins, Sam Harris, and Christopher Hitchens. Though we may tend to think of typical Secular Americans as being college professors or research scientists, they are just as commonly the plumbers, hairdressers, and auto mechanics with whom we interact every day.

FIVE

THE DISASTER OF THE RELIGIOUS RIGHT

TO UNDERSTAND HOW THE RELIGIOUS RIGHT HAS DRAGGED down American public affairs, compare two important speeches by presidential candidates. Separated by almost half a century, the 1960 speech by John F. Kennedy, seeking to become the first Roman Catholic president, and the 2008 speech by Mitt Romney, seeking to become the first Mormon president, perfectly illustrate the descent into religious pandering that currently characterizes American politics.[1]

Speaking to a group of Protestant ministers in Houston, Texas, Kennedy exuded the intellectual confidence and statesmanlike aura that were the trademarks of his public speaking. "I believe in an America where the separation of church and state is absolute," he declared. He told the ministers that his vision of America was one "where no Catholic prelate would tell the president (should he be Catholic) how to act, and no Protestant minister would tell his parishioners for whom to vote; and where no church or church school is granted public funds or political preference."

This speech, proclaiming that neither religion nor religious leaders have any special place in politics, is even more remarkable when we bear in mind that Kennedy was addressing a group of ministers. "I believe in an America," Kennedy told the group and the watching nation, "where no public official either requests or accepts instructions on public policy from the Pope, the National Council of Churches or any other ecclesiastic source; where no religious body seeks to impose its will directly or indirectly upon the general populace or the public acts of its officials." Kennedy reminded the ministers that religious discrimination against any group should concern all Americans. "Today I may be the victim, but tomorrow it may be you," he warned, adding that he would strive to be "responsible to all groups and obligated to none," and that he felt that the "fulfillment of [the] presidential oath is not limited or conditioned by any religious oath, ritual or obligation." Kennedy reminded the clerics that he opposed the move to send an American ambassador to the Vatican (in 1984, Ronald Reagan would establish diplomatic relations with the Vatican, much to the approval of conservative Catholics who were an important part of his base), and he reiterated that he considered governmental support of parochial schools to be unconstitutional.

It is hard to imagine such a clear, unambiguous statement of support for the notion of church-state separation being made today. This becomes apparent when we consider the Romney speech, in which the presidential candidate went out of his way to pander to religious conservatives who control his party. In sharp contrast to the direct and unambiguous church-state separationist declarations of Kennedy, Romney instead devoted the great weight of his speech to assurances that he would sympathize with Religious Right views on controversial issues. God "should remain on our currency, in our pledge, in our teaching of our history, and during the holiday season, nativity scenes and menorahs should be welcome in our public places," he declared, giving religious conservatives a generous serving of red meat on so-called culture war issues.

Romney also repeatedly invoked God, making the deity the primary character in his narrative, saying, "We believe that every single human being is a child of God" and that "Americans acknowledge that liberty is a gift of God." Romney directly chided those who feel that religion should be a private affair, saying, "They are wrong," while warning against the "religion of secularism." He decried the secular character of European society, where organized religion is "withering away" and the churches are "so empty," but he failed to mention that those secular European societies have for the most part been healthy and vibrant for decades.

To make it absolutely clear that nonbelievers are outsiders in today's America, Romney declared, "Freedom requires religion just as religion requires freedom," explaining that freedom allows one to "commune with God." Romney celebrated America's "symphony of faith," a concert to which Secular Americans apparently have no ticket, because "any person who has knelt in prayer to the Almighty, has a friend and ally in me." Ironically, if we carefully consider this statement, it suggests that Osama bin Laden would have had a friend in Romney, whereas Stephen Hawking would not. How unfortunate that Romney didn't stop to realize how far astray from the realm of sanity his rhetoric had drifted in order to kowtow to the religious extremists of his party.

Romney's speech exemplifies the effect that the Religious Right has had on America—it has dragged down the discourse and distracted politicians and voters from rational consideration of issues that are truly important. It isn't Christianity that is problematic, but the righteous confluence of Christianity and politics. If politically engaged Hindus were taking over local school boards and demanding that science curricula include a lesson that promotes the validity of reincarnation, we would find Secular Americans and conservative Christians for once on the same side of a constitutional battle, suing the school system for injecting Hindu religious beliefs into science classes. This is because it is not the theological differences that are problematic but the religiously motivated political agenda. The differences in worldviews between Christians and Secular Americans would be of little significance if conservative Christians were not so insistent on shaping public policy around their particular theological outlook. Religious conservatism certainly predates the rise of the Religious Right in the late 1970s, but the new and distinctive feature of the Religious Right is not its theology but its intense political engagement.

A NEW PHENOMENON WITH VAST RESOURCES

In May 2011, Rob Boston of Americans United for Separation of Church and State, one of the country's leading church-state watchdog groups, published a list of the "worst" Religious Right organizations, the major Christian conservative groups that represent the biggest threat to Jefferson's "wall of separation" between church and state. "Collectively, these groups raise more than three-quarters of a billion dollars annually, the bulk of it tax-exempt," Boston reported, adding that "they share a deep and abiding hostility to the separation of church and state."[2] The list is reproduced in table 5.1, with an extra column added to indicate the year that each group was founded.

Group	Budget	Founded
PAT ROBERTSON EMPIRE		
Christian Broadcasting Network	$295 million	1961
Regent University	$60 million	1978
American Center for Law and Justice	$13 million	1990
Christian Advocates Serving Evangelism	$43 million	1988
THE FALWELL EMPIRE		
Liberty University	$396 million	1971
Jerry Falwell Ministries	$4 million	1956
Liberty Counsel	$1 million	1989
OTHERS		
Family Research Council / FRC Action / FRC PAC	$14 million	1981
American Family Association	$21 million	1977
Alliance Defense Fund	$30 million	1994
Focus on the Family	$130 million	1977
SBC Ethics & Religious Liberty Commission	$3 million	1845
Traditional Values Coalition	$10 million	1980
Coral Ridge Ministries	$17 million	1974
Faith & Freedom Coalition	unavailable	2009
WallBuilder Presentations / WallBuilders	Over $1 million	1989
Concerned Women for America	$11 million	1979

Table 5.1

This list is by no means comprehensive, for numerous other Religious Right groups are actively engaged in promoting the conservative Christian agenda, but it provides some sense of the size and scope of the Religious Right network. Not even included in Boston's list, for example, are Answers in Genesis, which promotes young-earth creationism; the Discovery Institute, which leads the effort to promote creationist intelligent design in public schools; and numerous other conservative Christian media outlets, ministries, and advocacy groups. All Americans concerned about the agenda of the Religious Right need to be aware that the formidable resources backing politically active fundamentalist religion far outmatch any opposing counterweight.

What is perhaps most striking about this list, however, is not the number of groups or the amount of money raised but how almost all of the groups are relatively new. Of the 17 listed, only 3 predate 1970. Organized, politically motivated religious conservatism has exploded onto the scene in America in just the last few decades. Groups that didn't even exist before the Carter administration (1977 to 1981) suddenly sprang up, attracted immense amounts of money, mobilized voters, and completely changed the social and political environment around the country. While all this was happening, those who were not enamored by the Religious Right could only watch as their country drifted toward irrational public policy and anti-intellectualism.

THEOLOGY DRIVING POLITICS

Though there are some exceptions, the vast majority of Secular Americans are not particularly evangelical about their worldview. In fact, most Secular Americans are downright secretive about their nonbelief, saying and doing nothing to call attention to their lack of religion. As such, typical nonbelievers are hesitant to criticize the religious views of others, as doing so is only going to require an uncomfortable discussion. Still, at the same time, a quick survey of the state of society forces all of us to consider the reality of America's religious landscape, where millions of Americans sincerely believe that

- the world is only a few thousand years old and evolution is a hoax[3];
- a woman's legal right to reproductive freedom, including not just abortion but also birth control, has become far too liberal[4];
- environmentalism, including concern about climate change, is primarily a liberal conspiracy, as the Bible assures us that God created the earth for man's exploitation[5];
- education should center around religion (specifically, that there should be a return of school-sponsored prayer, an injection of creationism into science curricula, the teaching of abstinence-only

sex education, a pro-Christian presentation of history, and the
posting of religious mottos and commandments in schools);

- the Rapture, or return of Jesus to escort the saved to heaven, will
likely happen in our lifetime, part of an end-times chronology that
includes a great battle between good and evil at Armageddon, the
fiery end of history and fulfillment of biblical prophecy (and that
this is a good thing, to be optimistically awaited).[6]

Such are the deeply held convictions of millions of Americans, many
of whom are politically engaged and vote for candidates along theological lines. If those adhering to such religious views were an obscure and
insignificant minority, we could dismiss them as irrelevant, but such is not
the case.

Like most citizens, Secular Americans understand and appreciate that
a pluralistic democracy will inevitably reflect a wide range of religious and
philosophical viewpoints, and most see little value in constant arguments
over whose view is "right." Differing theological views should not give rise
to animosity. After all, Secular Americans, Christians, Jews, and Muslims
disagree with Buddhists and Hindus about reincarnation, but such theological differences are rarely problematic. Each religious demographic has
beliefs and opinions that are unique—for example, Christians believe in
the divinity of Jesus, Muslims believe in Muhammad's status as a prophet,
and so forth—but each such detail is just one of innumerable cultural nu-
ances to be found within a diverse population. In a free, democratic society,
we learn to not just tolerate such differences, but to even appreciate them
as contributing to cultural richness.

The views of the Religious Right, however, are not just theological. As
a major political faction with vast resources determined to not only practice its religion but impose its views on the general society, the Religious
Right has become a genuine threat to Secular Americans and others who
value personal freedom and rational public policy. For those disinclined
toward criticizing religion (which is most of us), it is important to remember that the culture wars are ultimately about public policy, not theology.
We certainly have here a clash of worldviews—conservative theology versus reason-based secularity—but those worldviews are clashing only because critical matters of social and public policy are at stake, and religious

conservatives have chosen to use theological righteousness to justify their policy positions. We see this in the debate over LGBT rights, abstinence-only education, and countless other issues.

When conservative religion is exalted as a basis for claiming moral high ground, family values, and public policy positions, frank discussion of fundamentalist religious views is appropriate, and one's personal secularity is relevant. The Religious Right, not its secular critics, has made a political issue of its theology.

THE RELIGIOUS RIGHT'S CURIOUS CHRISTIAN ETHICS

Despite the sometimes belligerent tenor of the culture wars, most non-believers have few problems with general Christian ethical principles. As theologians and philosophers have long pointed out, most of the major ethical teachings of Jesus are common in other societies and not particularly original. For example, the Golden Rule—to do unto others as you would have them do unto you—is a restatement of a fundamental moral concept that is almost universal, a maxim that can be found in one form or another in Jewish, Egyptian, Chinese, and other teachings that predate Jesus. Other principles taught by Jesus, such as the radical pacifist notion of "turning the other cheek" in response to aggression, are less universal but can still be found in earlier teachings.

It would be absurd, therefore, to suggest that Secular Americans object to Religious Right activism because it is too assertive in promoting the teachings attributed to Jesus. Indeed, from the standpoint of many Secular Americans, the problem with the Religious Right is not that it is too Christian, but that it is insufficiently so. If all of those who call themselves Christians in America lived even remotely in accord with the teachings of the Nazarene, the culture wars as we know them would not exist. The fact is, however, that many conservative Christians find the teachings of Jesus at best quaint, and at worst repugnant.

Pacifism, for example, is an outrage to many conservative Christians who are more often eager to ramp up military budgets and utilize modern weaponry. Military spending in the United States, thanks to the ambitious efforts of conservative Christians, dwarfs that of all other countries, usually approximating or exceeding the military expenditures of all other nations combined. Though we like to tell ourselves otherwise, we are a nation that glorifies militarism and constructs much of its national economy and foreign policy around it. There is no credible argument that Christlike values could justify such a martial national character.

Now, before going further, I should mention that relatively few Secular Americans would describe themselves as absolute pacifists, and most are sufficiently pragmatic to acknowledge that, even valuing peace, in the modern world some level of military spending is necessary. Most of us recognize that ideals, such as pacifism, must sometimes be compromised, that life often necessitates a bit of a disconnect between our highest ideals and our real-world actions, and ultimately all of us must decide for ourselves the extent of such compromises. In this sense, many Secular Americans can admire teachers of pacifism—whether Jesus, Gandhi, Martin Luther King Jr., or otherwise—while also endorsing policies that would not be entirely consistent with absolute nonviolence. Such, unfortunately, is the "real world."

This acknowledgment, however, does not diminish even one iota the contradiction of conservative Christians who claim to embrace Jesus while simultaneously promoting and exalting militarism. The need for pragmatism cannot justify actions that rise to the level of direct and complete refutation of claimed principles. This is supported by statistical evidence, which shows that conservative Christians were the demographic segment that was most in favor of invading Iraq in 2003 (whereas Secular Americans were least in favor).[7] If you're asking yourself how this can be reconciled with a theology that is rooted in love and pacifism, of turning the other cheek, the answer is simple: it can't.

Yet this is precisely the position taken by conservative religious leaders who had access to the White House before the Iraq invasion. It is well known that President Bush nurtured his relationships with fundamentalist Christian leaders, making it clear to them that they had an ally in the Oval Office, and it was just such Christians who pushed hardest for war. In a famous October 2002 letter from Richard D. Land of the Southern Baptist Convention, Chuck Colson of the Prison Fellowship Ministries (President Nixon's special counsel who served time in federal prison for his role in the Watergate scandal and later became a high-profile Christian leader), Bill Bright of the Campus Crusade for Christ International, and

James Kennedy of Coral Ridge Ministries Media, Bush was told that an attack on the Iraqi people would "fall well within the time honored criteria of just war theory as developed by Christian theologians."[8]

The "Land letter," as it became known, demonstrates how rhetoric can be used to make any set of facts fit a desired argument. The Christian leaders acknowledged that a "just war" must be defensive and "may only be commenced as a last resort," but despite the fact that Iraq posed no imminent threat to the United States and that there were desperate appeals from world leaders for further discussion, Land and his colleagues said that further delay of the attack would reflect "reckless irresponsibility." In other words, a peaceful approach would be contrary to Christian principles, so get the guns blazing. Amen!

The Religious Right likes to talk about "values," but the Iraq invasion surely demonstrates an obvious failure to apply the teachings of Christianity. After all, if an enemy strikes, Jesus said, one should turn and offer the other cheek to the enemy as well. In 2003, the United States had not even been struck by Iraq, but the invasion was launched just the same, costing thousands of lives, to prevent an attack that *might* occur in the future—how Christian!

ENGAGED, BUT UNINFORMED

Let's be honest: if four in ten Americans believe the earth is only a few thousand years old, then those four in ten Americans are not thinking critically. This is not to suggest that these individuals naturally lack intelligence—many no doubt have high innate IQs—but it does mean that they are rejecting widely known facts. The antiscience mentality of many religious conservatives is well documented, and this frequently translates into a broad lack of critical thinking. If high rates of Americans "don't believe" in evolution (as if evolution is something to be "believed in"), preferring instead to be blind to established scientific facts, we should expect public policy that reflects that anti-intellectualism. Chapter 2 showed that there is a correlation between religiosity and a willingness to accept authoritarianism and dogma. This correlation points to the rejection of critical, independent thinking, a predictable end result since organized conservative religion often asserts both institutional authority and doctrinal authority

that cannot be questioned. Adherents are even referred to as "sheep," obe-
dient followers to whom facts and mandates are dictated. This necessarily
results in the downgrading of critical thinking as a core societal value, and
it has real-world consequences.

For example, when I mentioned earlier that the United States attacked Iraq without having been struck first, many Americans would disagree, pointing to the September 11 attacks as evidence that the country
had been "struck" before it retaliated against Iraq. The problem with this
argument is that there was never any credible evidence that Iraq was involved in the September 11 plot. In fact, none of the hijackers were Iraqi,
and those who plotted the attacks had disdain for Saddam Hussein and
the Iraqi government.

Nevertheless, as the Iraq invasion neared in March 2003, many Americans were in a frenzy for war, eager to attack Saddam Hussein's regime and
oblivious to the innocent bloodshed that would result, often claiming that
the invasion was some kind of payback for September 11. Surveys showed
that as many as seven in ten Americans believed, in complete contradiction to what was known at the time, that Saddam Hussein was directly
involved in the September 11 attacks.[9] Though the official justification for
war centered on a search for weapons of mass destruction (weapons that
did not exist, we later discovered), public support in the United States was
easily garnered by tapping fear, anger, and aggressive impulses stemming
from September 11. To the shock and dismay of much of the rest of the
world, Americans were eager for war while being dangerously ignorant of
important facts.

The Religious Right objects to this argument, saying that such anti-
intellectualism, even if true, cannot be attributed to conservative Christianity. This is demonstrably incorrect. For example, in the case of the
Iraq invasion, evangelical Protestants supported the invasion at almost
twice the rate of Secular Americans, according to the aforementioned
Zuckerman report. Had overall public support been as low as the support within the secular community (only 38 percent), the Bush administration would not have had the political capital to launch the war. An
uninformed population, incapable of accurately assessing information,
simply cannot utilize the democratic process wisely and effectively, because participatory democracy is reliant on informed citizens capable

of critical thinking. This is why we rarely see healthy democracy in areas where fundamentalist religion is dominant. In such societies, where there is much sympathy for holy texts mandating harsh laws and placing little value on human rights or civil liberties, a vote of the people would often result in the eventual imposition of undemocratic, authoritarian theocracy. In any society, a sizable political faction that openly espouses conservative, often fundamentalist religion should be of great concern to all who value democracy and freedom. This is precisely what America is experiencing with today's Religious Right, and those quasi-authoritarian tendencies are creating policy.

This view is supported by numerous studies that examine the dangers of fundamentalist religious belief in political affairs. An article entitled "Authoritarianism, Religious Fundamentalism, Quest, and Prejudice" by authors Bob Altemeyer and Bruce Hunsberger is particularly instructive, as it relays the findings of five studies investigating the relationships between right-wing authoritarianism, various indices of religious orientation, and prejudice.[10] The authors defined fundamentalism as believing "that there is one set of religious teachings that clearly contains the fundamental, basic, intrinsic, essential, inerrant truth about humanity and deity; that this essential truth is fundamentally opposed by forces of evil which must be vigorously fought; that this truth must be followed today according to the fundamental, unchangeable practices of the past; and that those who believe and follow these fundamental teachings have a special relationship with the deity."[11] Not surprisingly, the reported findings are not flattering toward the mind-set that seems to drive the Religious Right. Specifically, the authors reported that fundamentalist "nonquesters" (those unlikely to be searching for truth outside of their set of beliefs) are "more likely to be prejudiced, more likely to be hostile toward homosexuals, more likely to 'join a posse' to hunt down radicals, and more likely to impose stiff (punitive) sentences." Nonquesters were also found to be more submissive and "they were not more aggressive against just a few groups, but against nearly all the minorities mentioned."[12]

The authors also pointed out that fundamentalists are often certain that their religion is "a complete, unfailing guide to happiness and salvation which must be totally followed." This, they suggested, plays a role in the ethnocentrism, self-righteousness, and fear that commonly correlate to authoritarianism. The idea of "one, true religion" often drives authoritarians, leading them to believe that "there are only two kinds of people in the world: the Righteous . . . and the rest."[13]

This is one reason Secular Americans sometimes cringe at the statement, "God bless America." Besides the obvious theological nature of the statement, which presumes that good Americans must believe in a divinity, Secular Americans are also uncomfortable with the belief that God is on the side of the United States. Most nonbelievers realize that many Americans make the statement innocently and with no ill will toward other nations or individuals, but nevertheless, within the statement is the seedling of a nationalistic "God and country" belief that is worrisome. As the Altemeyer-Hunsberger report suggests, the fact that harsh authoritarianism seems to feed on such views should give all Americans, religious and secular, reason for pause.

HARDLY SIGNS OF A GREAT CULTURE

Even if fundamentalist Christianity were unlikely to lead to a more authoritarian political atmosphere, other aspects of its agenda highlight its anti-intellectual effect and necessitate attention. A $27 million Kentucky tourist attraction called the Creation Museum, for example, promotes a fundamentalist Christian view that the world is less than ten thousand years old, and has attracted millions of visitors from all over the country since its 2007 opening, far more than most museums that promote science. Fossils displayed in the museum are said to be just a few thousand years old, with the museum claiming that scientific dating methods indicating that the fossils are millions of years old are flawed. Visitors learn that floods, not millions of years of erosion, caused the Grand Canyon. Every attempt is made to explain all of natural history as a story no more than a few thousand years in duration, from the disappearance of dinosaurs (there was probably no room on Noah's ark) to the diversity of animals around the globe (the continents were probably once joined, but they separated within the last few thousand years).[14]

The fact that not only was this "museum" built, but that it is attracting large crowds, is a sad commentary on the state of American society.

The Creation Museum is relatively modest compared to the $172 million project being constructed down the road from it. Called the Ark Encounter and owned in part by the same ministry that built the Creation Museum, it is a park dedicated to providing what the *New York Times* described as a "full-size replica of Noah's ark, complete with live animals."[15] The newspaper reported that the park "aims to promote a literal interpretation of the Bible by proving that Noah had room on his vessel to fit two of every kind of animal."[16]

The Creation Museum and Ark Encounter have been the target of much mockery from comics and others looking for an easy laugh, but there is a serious side to the issue. America is considered the world's superpower, both militarily and economically the dominant nation in the world, yet much of its citizenry is fiercely loyal to a religious worldview that is in complete denial of scientific facts, to the point that enormous sums of money can be raised for the construction of such temples of ignorance. We cannot honestly say that such widespread anti-intellectualism is harmless, that it doesn't reflect a serious and deep-rooted problem that has already cost the country dearly and is only likely to result in more grave consequences. The longer we continue the denial, the more we endanger future generations.

The story gets even worse. Despite an old-fashioned concept known as separation of church and state, which would normally prohibit the government from subsidizing the construction of churches and religious institutions, the taxpayers of Kentucky are paying $40 million toward the cost of the proselytizing theme park.[17] Before the rise of the Religious Right, not only would such a public subsidy of religion have been unthinkable, but the very suggestion of the construction of such a park would have been met with laughs. But nobody's laughing today, as America enters the second decade of the twenty-first century with surveys showing that only about four in ten adults accept evolution, a figure well below most other developed societies, justifying America's reputation as a haven for anti-intellectual religious zealots.[18]

And the trend seems to be toward more and bigger religion-based theme attractions. In Orlando, for example, just a few miles from the Disney parks, is the Holy Land Experience, which features regular reenactments of the crucifixion of Jesus. The park opened in 2001 and was sold in 2007 for $37 million to Trinity Broadcasting, a Christian media conglomerate that features a wide range of televangelists willing to pray for you and take your donations via a toll-free number. Like its Kentucky counterpart, the Holy Land Experience also received special treatment from the government, when Florida officials passed a law exempting it from tax burdens based on its religious theme.

PROMOTING PRAYER AND DENYING SEPARATION

Before the rise of the Religious Right, there were certainly occasional disagreements about how to apply the concept of church-state separation. Not surprisingly, for example, some religious citizens (but not all) objected in the 1960s when school-sponsored prayer and Bible study were declared unconstitutional. But even in the midst of these disagreements, the vast majority of religious Americans agreed that the concept of church-state separation was an essential part of the Constitution; few had the audacity to suggest that church-state separation itself was a fictitious concept invented by a liberal judiciary. Yet that's exactly what we hear today as Christian preachers, politicians, and voters increasingly echo the cry that separation of church and state is a liberal conspiracy. "There is no such thing as separation of church and state," declared Ken Ham of Answers in Genesis, the group responsible for constructing the Creation Museum, adding that "Christianity in this nation is becoming outlawed more and more in various quarters." Such speeches are now commonplace at Religious Right gatherings, such as the so-called Values Voter Summit that has become a magnet for conservative politicians seeking to gain favor with conservative Christians. The 2011 summit, which included addresses from the major GOP presidential contenders, also featured content warning that secularism will result in sexual anarchy.[19]

In Congress, the most zealous opponents of church-state separation can be found in the Congressional Prayer Caucus, a group of legislators dedicated to injecting God and Christianity into public life as much as possible. The debate here is not about the scope of church-state separation, but whether church-state separation exists at all. Founded by Republican Representative J. Randy Forbes, the caucus declares via its website that its purpose is to:

1. recognize the vital role that prayer by individuals of all faiths has played in uniting us as a people and in making us a more generous, more cooperative, and more forgiving people than we might otherwise have been;

2. collect, exchange, and disseminate information about prayer as a fundamental and enduring feature of American life;

3. use the legislative process—both through sponsorship of affirmative legislation and through opposition to detrimental legislation—to assist the nation and its people in continuing to draw upon and benefit from this essential source of our strength and well-being.[20]

The levels of unintended humor and irony in this purpose statement are numerous. I'm not sure what the prayer caucus means when it says that prayer has played a "vital role" in "uniting us," because it seems that any objective analysis would conclude just the opposite. Catholic-Protestant conflict, anti-Semitism, bigotry against Muslims, and the marginalization of Secular Americans are all examples of the divisive nature of religion in America. If it makes us "more generous, more cooperative, and more forgiving," then it is not clear why so many on the prayer caucus have voted to cut spending for things like health care and education while increasing military spending. Perhaps they feel the need to "disseminate information about prayer as a fundamental and enduring feature of American life," but I'm sure many of their constituents would prefer that such proselytizing be done outside the scope of the lawmakers' professional capacity. In any case, since the caucus members wish to "use the legislative process . . . to assist the nation and its people" by promoting prayer, they obviously aren't very concerned about the Establishment Clause or the rights of nonbelievers.

Thus, while the country was facing multiple wars, financial collapse, recession, job losses, and numerous other urgent and important issues, over one hundred congressmen and congresswomen—almost one in four of the entire House of Representatives—were members of an official caucus that dedicates its time and energy to ensuring that prayer and religion are recognized as much as possible in governmental affairs. Forbes and his colleagues are constantly initiating resolutions that remind us of every detail of American history that pertains to public prayer and religiosity, lest we forget to acknowledge the pious nature of our nation. They supported a resolution to have 2010 declared the "National Year of the Bible," for example, as well as another to erect a plaque acknowledging that church services had once been held in the Capitol building.[21]

Not surprisingly, however, not one of the prayer caucus's numerous resolutions has ever mentioned the proud role that religion played as a justification for slavery, as when Southern politicians, religious leaders, and slave owners pointed to both Old Testament and New Testament passages as proof of divine approval of the South's "peculiar institution." In 1 Timothy 6:1, for example, slaves are given this advice: "All who are under the yoke of slavery should consider their masters worthy of full respect, so that God's name and our teaching may not be slandered." Similarly, 1 Peter 2:18 dictates, "Slaves, in reverent fear of God submit yourselves to your masters, not only to those who are good and considerate, but also to those who are harsh." James Henley Thornwell (1812–1862), a leading Southern theologian, spoke for many when he concluded "that the relation betwixt the slave and his master is not inconsistent with the word of God."[22] Aside from such selective omissions, however, Forbes works exhaustively to ensure that all Americans—secular and religious—recognize the importance of Christianity in government.

IN BED WITH CORPORATE INTERESTS

Even casual observers would probably notice that the rise of the Religious Right has resulted in religion becoming more prominent in American public life, but other ramifications of politically mobilized religious conservatism are not so obvious. Many of the policy positions put forward by the Religious Right are backed by big businesses with much to gain, corporations and industry groups that cleverly use religious conservatives as a tool to mask their agenda. Large oil and coal interests, for example, frequently make themselves bedmates of conservative religious leaders, funding religion-based advocacy groups that vocally challenge concerns about climate change. Though corporations are incapable of innate religious impulses, they profit immensely from fundamentalists' denial of global warming, which allows them to obstruct serious environmental regulation and legislation aimed at addressing climate change. Such alliances help the oil and coal industries stay out of the media spotlight by focusing the attention on "grassroots opposition" to environmental regulation.

One religious group with industry connections is the Cornwall Alliance, which holds itself out as a coalition "committed to bringing about a balanced Biblical view of stewardship to the critical issues of the environment and development."[23] The group maintains a dismissive stance toward many key environmental concerns, especially those that are vehemently opposed by large corporate and industry interests. In a document called "The Cornwall Declaration on Environmental Stewardship," which has been signed by over fifteen hundred religious leaders, the group says environmentalists should be concerned about some issues, such as poor sanitation in the developing world, but that other common environmental issues are based on "unfounded" fears and "undue concerns." Included on the list of concerns that are "without foundation" is "destructive manmade global warming."[24] In opposing carbon dioxide regulation by the Environmental Protection Agency (EPA), for example, Cornwall spokesperson E. Calvin Beisner sounded not like a lobbyist for big industry, but a representative of the little guy: "The potential damage from EPA regulation of carbon dioxide emissions is enormous. Energy prices would skyrocket, driving up costs of food, shelter, transportation, and everything else consumers need."[25] All of this is done from a grassroots and religious angle that would never appear to be industry-driven to an unknowing observer.

Assuring us that its views are "informed by revelation," the Cornwall Alliance emphasizes the common fundamentalist view that God wants humans to exercise "dominion over the earth." It warns that many ordinary citizens with environmental concerns are guided by "erroneous theological and anthropological positions" that result in a "tendency among some to oppose economic progress in the name of environmental stewardship." What we need is not more environmental regulation, this environmental group tells us, but more "sound theology," "economic freedom," and "market economics."[26]

The Cornwall declaration is filled with all the right buzzwords to please both the Religious Right (*dominion* is especially key, as this term is a mantra in fundamentalist circles alluding to language from the book of Genesis wherein God gives man dominion over the earth) and large corporate interests (*economic freedom* and *market economics* are particularly apt for that crowd), but on the surface, the emphasis is on religion and not big business. In this manner, Cornwall is able to hold itself out as a citizen-based grassroots organization driven by religious conviction, not an industry group aiming to maximize profits. The group boasts that it has become "one of the most prominent voices in America and internationally on issues of religion and the environment," with its spokesmen having been featured in publications such as the *New York Times*, the *Washington Post*, the *Los Angeles Times*, *USA Today*, and hundreds of other media outlets.[27]

Not surprisingly, a bit of investigating reveals that the religion-based antienvironmentalist positions of Cornwall are subsidized by oil money. In an article appropriately entitled "The Oily Operators behind the Religious Climate Change Denial Front Group, Cornwall Alliance," journalist Lee Fang reported that funding for Cornwall comes from James Partnership, a group run by individuals with business relationships tied to the oil industry and corporate-funded efforts to deny climate change. One example is the Committee for a Constructive Tomorrow (CFACT), a nonprofit that has received millions of dollars from companies and individuals tied to the oil industry that it uses to discredit the scientific basis for climate change concerns and mock environmentalists. Fang noted that Cornwall's media office denied any relationship between Cornwall and CFACT, but that in fact CFACT's founder and president, David Rothbard, who has longtime oil industry ties, has been described as a "driving force" behind the Cornwall declaration. The cross fertilization between Cornwall and CFACT, from personal relationships, business connections, and operating practices (both groups share the same fundraising firm, for example, and CFACT's publicity stunts to discredit environmentalists are regularly reported as "breaking news" for the religious audience of Cornwall's website), is widespread.[28]

"As Republican officials accelerate their efforts to weaken environmental regulations and attack climate scientists," reported People for the American Way in April 2011, "energy corporations are reaping the benefits of a decades-long effort to put a more benevolent, humanitarian, and even religious spin on their anti-environmental activism." Pointing out that Cornwall spokesperson E. Calvin Beisner, who is a CFACT board member, promotes a dominionist theology that assists industry in quashing efforts to protect the environment, the report noted that he "now boasts that approximately half of all Protestant pastors are skeptical of climate change."[29]

When Beisner describes belief in catastrophic, human-caused climate change as "antibiblical" and "blasphemous," he has friends in high places who agree. As the report pointed out, House Speaker John Boehner, to the pleasure of both his corporate and fundamentalist constituents, has described concerns about carbon dioxide as "almost comical."[30] Michele Bachmann has made a career of dismissing environmental concerns, apparently concluding that since Jesus saved the planet two thousand years ago any modern efforts would be redundant.

Corporate interests no doubt have sufficient financial capabilities to lobby effectively for antienvironmentalist positions without partnering with the Religious Right, but the utilization of religious conservatism in making climate change denial politically viable was a strategic masterstroke. Today's coalition of antienvironmentalism often overwhelms efforts at rational policy. As the People for the American Way report concludes, "Just as corporate America has infused the GOP with anti-environmental and anti-science ideology, the Religious Right is more than eager to provide cover for politicians and their corporate backers by claiming God's blessing for their dishonest assertions and destructive policies."

THE VALUE OF A SECULAR PERSPECTIVE

The environmental debate highlights an aspect of secular activism that is often overlooked by the general public and the media. Secular Americans realize that most religious individuals do not agree with the Cornwall position on the environment, that most Americans, religious and secular, support the notion of regulating polluters and protecting the environment. Even if many are not fully informed about the scientific details of global warming, even if some misinformation circulates in the public dialogue, the general inclination toward environmental protection is a strong current in America—it's something most of us teach our children and understand as an important value. Thus, when Secular Americans clash with religion-based positions such as the Cornwall arguments on environmentalism, the secular position is not bashing religion in general, but bashing public policy that rejects science and is based on a specific interpretation of religious doctrine.

It is unfortunate that many fail to see that secular activism is not about tearing down religion but building wider acceptance of secularity. Not everyone agrees with Secular American views on religion, but too many don't recognize the value that flows from recognizing and respecting the viewpoints of the secular demographic. Groups like Cornwall benefit immensely from the general prejudice that the public has for Secular Americans, because with the secular perspective removed from the debate, the conservative biblical position escapes its most serious challenge. Of course, liberal religious groups can challenge the Cornwall position, and they do, but at that point the question becomes only one of whose interpretation of scripture is correct. Frankly, we are all at risk if the question of whether to protect the environment comes down to a debate over scriptural interpretation, because the Bible is at best ambiguous on the issue and certainly not based on science. Americans who care about the environment should be eager to legitimize the Secular American demographic, not because we all agree with the secular view on theology but because we all want the rational public policy that it demands.

OVERPOPULATION DENIAL

Another issue that illustrates the need for a secular perspective—an issue that gets scant public attention because it has religious implications—is overpopulation. Like climate change, this is yet another environmental concern that the Cornwall declaration describes as "unfounded." The facts suggest otherwise.

While most Americans have a general sense that world population is increasing, the actual numbers on population growth are staggering. As the planet's population passed seven billion in 2011, most Americans were unaware that the figure passed just *one* billion only in the nineteenth century, just a few generations ago. Though modern humans have roamed the planet for over two hundred thousand years, until the invention of agriculture just a few thousand years ago our entire global population barely exceeded one million. With agriculture came slow and steady population growth, so that during the Middle Ages global population probably numbered just over three hundred million, or approximately the population of the United States today. Since that time, just in the last few hundred years, human population has been exploding, with no sign of stopping.

Rapid population growth has brought with it enormous problems—not just environmental, but also political, economic, and social—and continues to present one of the major threats to humanity. Some of the problems arising from overpopulation are obvious—widespread disease and famine that we see in much of the developing world, scarcity of resources, social and political instability—while others are more subtle. Industrialized societies are decimating the global environment as the carbon footprint of each of us dwarfs that of a typical villager in the developing world, but the strain on the planet's environment will increase exponentially as those villagers modernize. We already see what is happening in China as much of the population trades its bicycles for automobiles, with severe environmental consequences. We can only brace ourselves as this phenomenon accelerates there and elsewhere in the years ahead.

It would be bad enough if political leadership were merely oblivious to this problem, but with the Religious Right the situation is even worse—religiously conservative politicians are affirmatively opposed to rational measures that would stabilize population growth. Rick Santorum, a favorite of the Religious Right, is a harsh critic of all forms of contraception. "One of the things I will talk about, that no president has talked about before, is I think the dangers of contraception in this country," he said while on the campaign trail in 2011. "Many of the Christian faith have said, well, that's okay, contraception is okay. It's not okay. It's a license to do things in the sexual realm that is counter to how things are supposed to be."[31] Note that Santorum's opposition to birth control extends even to married couples. Empirical facts, such as widespread famine, disease, and an environment strained to the breaking point by human activity, mean less to Santorum than enforcing the sexual morality of his Catholic religion. Non-procreative sex is simply wrong, and Santorum knows this because supposedly celibate church leaders tell him so. An objective outside observer would be shocked that such an individual could have even a remote chance of winning the presidential nomination of a major party in the world's most powerful nation.

The rational approach to the overpopulation dilemma would be to make sensible population growth policies a high priority around the world, but instead the issue is often ignored. Much of the reason for this is grounded in religion, especially the influence of the Catholic Church, which aggressively opposes any effort to effectively address overpopulation. Thankfully, many developed societies (which also happen to be the more secular societies) have slowed population growth through widespread use of safe and effective contraception, but around the developing world, where population growth is most predominant, there is strong resistance to birth control measures fueled by religious motivation. This is perhaps most shameful in Africa, where millions of innocent people suffer from AIDS, but the church nevertheless maintains its opposition to condom use. In 2010, after decades of seeing innocent victims, usually women, infected with the virus due to unsafe sexual practices, the pope reluctantly approved condom use in certain instances, not including birth control, in a statement that has been seen as far too limited and ambiguous.

This is an instance where religious and secular citizens often agree, since even most Catholic Americans ignore their church and favor birth control. Yet most Americans continue to see secular activism as rabble-rousing that has little broad societal benefit. Few religious Americans consider, for example, that broad acceptance of the Secular American demographic would isolate the religious conservative position and call attention to important public policy issues that religious conservatives have successfully suppressed.

AN INCREASINGLY ASSERTIVE RELIGIOUS RIGHT

As it solidifies its position in society and grows increasingly comfortable with power, the Religious Right is growing bolder. A spokesperson for the American Family Association (AFA), for example, a leading Religious Right group with an annual budget of over $21 million (modest by Religious Right standards, but still significant), declared publicly in 2011 that America should enforce blasphemy laws.[32] To the surprise of many, such laws are still on the books in many states but, being relics from bygone days, are no longer enforced. Their mere existence, however, makes enforcement, perhaps by some right-wing culture warrior sheriff, theoretically possible. Even though such a prosecution could be opposed on First Amendment grounds (hopefully successfully so, but in today's environment there are no sure things), the fact that it is being discussed by an organization with access to high-level politicians is troubling. (AFA leadership had frequent White House access under George W. Bush and would no doubt be welcomed in the administrations of other future fundamentalist presidents.[33]) The AFA spokesperson, Bryan Fischer, justified the proposed enforcement of blasphemy laws by comparing them to a fine that was imposed on a professional basketball player for using a homosexual slur in a verbal spat with a fan. The punishment in that case, however, was imposed not by the government but by the National Basketball Association, a private entity that has rules against such behavior by its players. Nonetheless, in the mind-set of the Religious Right, any policy that punishes hostility toward gays is suspect, potentially part of the liberal plot to promote the "gay agenda," necessitating a response.

Meanwhile, because Secular Americans remain marginalized, the Religious Right marches forward with its own agenda, getting stronger with each election cycle. In 2008, Louisiana passed a law allowing fundamentalist public school science teachers to use supplemental materials in their classrooms, paving the way for Bible-based creationism to enter the curricula. High school student Zack Kopplin led a push for repeal, setting up a blog in support of the cause, lobbying legislators directly, and garnering support from scientists around the country. The Associated Press reported that although over 40 Nobel Prize-winning scientists opposed the law, Louisiana governor Bobby Jindal and conservative Christian groups insisted that it promoted critical thinking. Not all agreed. "The lawmakers of Louisiana are a laughing stock as far as the scientific community is concerned," Harold Kroto, a Florida State University scientist, is reported as saying.[34]

Such antiscience legislation is becoming more commonplace around the nation, as are measures to restrict reproductive freedom, oppose equal rights for gays and lesbians, and inject religion into public affairs. While many sensible citizens oppose such measures, sometimes successfully and sometimes not, that opposition has rarely been as well funded and organized as the Religious Right.

A prime example of the seriousness of the Religious Right is the Wedge document, a strategic plan drafted in 1998 by the Discovery Institute, a Seattle-based fundamentalist think tank. Not intended for public consumption but leaked publicly in 1999, the Wedge document exposed a detailed plan to "defeat" the modern scientific worldview and "replace it with a science that is consonant with Christian and theistic convictions." Sounding like a subversive group of revolutionaries, the Wedge strategists detailed how they will infiltrate popular culture in ways that allow them to promote intelligent design. "A lesson we have learned from the history of science is that it is unnecessary to outnumber the opposing establishment," the document declares. To do this successfully, they will "prepare the popular reception of our ideas" by skillfully utilizing popular avenues of mass communication. As such, the conspirators agreed that they "seek to cultivate and convince influential individuals in print and broadcast media, as well as think tank leaders, scientists and academics, congressional staff, talk show hosts, college and seminary presidents and faculty, future talent and potential academic allies." Those behind the document may seem like fringe characters, but given the enormous power of the Religious Right, with its widespread support in much of the country and its high-profile presidential aspirants vocally promoting fundamentalist religious positions, it would be a mistake to assume that their views are too outlandish to take seriously. They are quite open in their determination to "replace materialistic explanations with the theistic understanding that nature and human beings are created by God."[35]

With this background, it is easy to see how the Discovery Institute would promote intelligent design as a key element in its "Wedge strategy," for few actions could inject God into science more effectively than an unfounded assumption that phenomena not yet explained by science should be attributed to a supernatural deity. Such campaigns have been tried in the past, under the guise of what was once called creation science, but the effort to repackage religion as science was found unconstitutional. Of course, that's precisely what intelligent design is as well, and it wasn't long before a major trial brought the issue into the public eye.

The 2005 *Kitzmiller v. Dover Area School District* case arose from efforts by Pennsylvania school officials, with the assistance of the Discovery Institute, to inject intelligent design into the science curriculum. The dramatic trial, which lasted over two months, revealed in great detail that intelligent design, despite efforts to present it as a sophisticated approach to science, was nothing more than a religiously motivated, repackaged creationism. Federal judge John E. Jones III, a conservative Republican appointed by George W. Bush, blasted the school board in his decision: "This case came to us as the result of the activism of an ill-informed faction on a school board." The case was a humiliating defeat for the proponents of intelligent design, several of whom were shown to be outright deceitful in their efforts. In his opinion, Jones wrote, "It is ironic that several of these individuals [school board members], who so staunchly and proudly touted their religious convictions in public, would time and again lie to cover their tracks and disguise the real purpose behind the ID [intelligent design] policy."[36]

Despite this major victory for the opponents of intelligent design, efforts persist around the country to taint science curricula with unscientific, religious views. Leaders at the highest levels of government continue to support the idea of teaching intelligent design. President George W. Bush was on record as supporting teaching "both sides" of the issue, suggesting that the intelligent design argument stands on equal footing with Darwin's theory of evolution by natural selection, even though only the latter is recognized as valid by the scientific community. Giving no weight to the views of the scientific establishment, religious conservatives and the politicians they support routinely cite publications by Discovery Institute authors in their efforts to promote intelligent design.

Something has gone terribly awry when politicians at the local, state, and national levels expend enormous political capital in defense of blatant anti-intellectualism. As American student test scores in science continue to place poorly in international rankings, the Religious Right cares not for the promotion of true scientific inquiry but instead emphasizes issues such as intelligent design. All Americans, religious and secular, should be concerned.

In modern America, conservative politicians are ramping up the political religiosity in ways that would have been unthinkable just a few years ago. Texas governor Rick Perry, for one, had a much-publicized religious rally in August 2011, called "The Response: A Call to Prayer for a Nation in

Crisis," where he brazenly presented himself to the country as a vocal and fundamentalist Christian, much to the delight of the Religious Right. In front of thirty thousand emotional believers in Houston's Reliant Stadium and another thirteen hundred religious groups that were streaming the event, Perry was unrestrained in his religious enthusiasm. "Father, our heart breaks for America," he declared. "We see discord at home. We see fear in the marketplace. We see anger in the halls of government. And as a nation we have forgotten Who made us, Who protects us, Who blesses us, and for that we cry out for Your forgiveness." (The capitalized pronouns are from the event's website.)[37]

It is a sign of the times that this event, which had been planned for months, was interpreted as an unofficial kickoff event for Perry's presidential campaign. Though he later flopped as a presidential candidate, at the time Perry was perceived as being an astute politician for hosting such an event and sharing the stage with the likes of James Dobson, the rabidly antigay founder of Focus on the Family; John Benefiel, the pastor who once called the Statue of Liberty a "demonic idol"; and other controversial religious figures.[38] While today this kind of open religiosity is seen as "smart politics" for a Republican candidate seeking to enthrall the social conservatives in early primary states, such as Iowa and South Carolina, before the rise of the Religious Right such actions by a Republican candidate would have been seen as political suicide.

A week after the high-profile prayer rally, Perry officially announced his candidacy for the presidency of the United States, and he was soon leading in the polls. To the dismay of most nonbelievers, many Americans at the time apparently felt that Perry was just the kind of leader the country needed. His popularity as a candidate declined, but not because of his religiosity. (Rather, his terrible performance in debates and other missteps caused his numbers to plummet.) Indeed, with candidates such as Perry, as well as Michele Bachmann and Rick Santorum, all of whom rose to popularity at various times during the 2012 GOP contest, we are finding that a steady flow of hard-right, religiously motivated social conservatives can be expected in presidential politics for the foreseeable future.

SIX

BETTER LATE THAN NEVER

SECULAR AMERICANS EMERGE

THE LATTER DECADES OF THE TWENTIETH CENTURY SAW A SUR-
prising resurgence of politically engaged conservative religion. No comprehensive history of that time period will be accurate without a mention
of the rise of the Religious Right and its impact on American culture.
Despite this, most histories will make no mention of organized efforts by
Secular Americans to counter the Religious Right.

That's not to suggest that there was no opposition to the Religious
Right. After the Moral Majority flexed its muscle in the 1980 election,
television producer Norman Lear, well known for his liberal views on
social issues, founded the advocacy group People for the American Way
(PFAW) to combat the conservative religious agenda. Taking progressive
stances on equality, civil rights, and church-state separation while vocally opposing the Religious Right, PFAW quickly built a reputation as
a scrappy proponent of rational public policy. Other groups, such as the
American Civil Liberties Union (ACLU) and the church-state watchdog group Americans United for Separation of Church and State, also
actively opposed the Religious Right during this time period, providing

much-needed rebuttals to the likes of Jerry Falwell, Pat Robertson, and other conservative religious leaders who were on the ascent.

None of this opposition, however, seemed to slow down the juggernaut of religious conservatism that was rapidly coming to dominate the political landscape. Increasingly, mobilized conservative Christians controlled the Republican Party, and even Democrats seemed to find it necessary to bring God into their rhetoric. Though Republicans tend to be more often associated with conservative religion, it is noteworthy that Democrat Bill Clinton, in defeating George H. W. Bush in 1992 and Bob Dole in 1996, referred to faith, God, and religion more than his Republican opponents. Barack Obama, the only other Democrat to win the White House since the rise of the Religious Right, was also quick to reference his faith on the campaign trail. Clearly, the Religious Right was having an impact across the political spectrum.

THE RELIGIOUS IDENTITY FACTOR

In comparing early Religious Right groups such as the Moral Majority and Christian Coalition to opposing groups such as PFAW, the ACLU, or Americans United, one noteworthy difference between the two camps was their religious makeup. Almost all the relevant groups on the Religious Right, naturally, embraced strong Christian personal identity as a defining characteristic, giving them some level of moral authority in the eyes of many Americans. A few Religious Right groups welcomed Jewish support as well, thereby enabling the claim of "Judeo-Christian values" mentioned earlier, but diversity rarely extended any further than that.

In contrast, the high-profile groups opposing the Religious Right were rarely associated with any particular religious identity because, to their credit, they defined their values according to the accepted standards of decency of modern, democratic, pluralistic society, welcoming leadership and membership from those of all faiths and no faith at all. PFAW's mission statement, for example, states, "Our vision is a vibrantly diverse democratic society in which everyone is treated equally under the law, given the freedom and opportunity to pursue their dreams, and encouraged to participate in our nation's civic and political life. Our America respects diversity, nurtures creativity and combats hatred and bigotry."[1] It would be hard to write a statement more in direct conflict with the values of Falwell and Robertson, or further from their biblical view of America.

So while the Religious Right defined itself by religious identity, claiming values coming from God, its opposition pointed to no such moral authority, while also claiming values—such as acceptance of gays and lesbians—that many Americans saw as nontraditional. From this starting point, one can see how the debate quickly became one of "traditional family values" versus "moral relativism," a choice that leaves many social conservatives tightly grasping their Bibles. Perhaps for this reason, the opposition to the Religious Right was often quick to emphasize any religious connections, such as its liberal religious leadership and membership.

In fact, 1994 saw the formation of another group opposing the Religious Right: the Interfaith Alliance, a liberal nonprofit that included members from a wide range of faith backgrounds. Enlisting retired newscaster Walter Cronkite—at one time the most trusted man in America— as its spokesperson, the Interfaith Alliance quickly established itself as an important new voice of the "Religious Left." With 185,000 members, the group still stands as a key religion-based opponent to the Religious Right, taking positions in favor of LGBT rights, church-state separation, and general diversity and tolerance. Nevertheless, few would argue that the term Religious Left carries the same clout as Religious Right in American politics.

With the Religious Right claiming the banner of godly righteousness, its main opponents also reflexively emphasized traditional religious identity. Americans United has for 20 years been led by the Reverend Barry Lynn, a minister in the United Church of Christ, an effective reminder that not all persons of faith stand with the Religious Right. (Lynn's persistent opposition to the Religious Right once caused Falwell to quip that Lynn "is about as reverend as an oak tree.")[2] The ACLU and PFAW have also welcomed a wide range of religious Americans in board positions.

According to Roy Speckhardt, who was the Interfaith Alliance's deputy director in its early years, the result of all this was that the atmosphere in Washington had become decidedly religious by the late 1990s: "Nearly every group in D.C. formed religious outreach offices, added religious leaders to their boards, and hired religious leaders as spokespersons." This, he says, slanted the playing field away from Secular Americans. "Even progressive faith groups, as well as otherwise secular lobbying groups, unwittingly supported the Religious Right by supporting the notion that criticism of religion in any way was taboo."

With one side defining itself via conservative religion and the other defining itself as being broadly liberal but also welcoming of religion, few were speaking up for the dignity and legitimacy of Secular Americans. In fact, as even Democratic candidates drifted in the direction of visible religiosity, Secular Americans seemed to have no role in public life.

CONSERVATIVE RELIGION AND WOMEN'S RIGHTS

As we consider the origins of the culture wars, we find that many of the differences between the two camps revolve around the rights of women. In fact, perhaps no single culture-war issue has been as contentious as the question of whether a woman should have the right to terminate her pregnancy. Although the Supreme Court declared in its 1973 *Roe v. Wade* ruling that abortion was a fundamental right, that case was only the beginning of the modern abortion debate, not the end. As a result of that decision, which had nothing to do with religion or religious identity, conservative Christians mobilized into the identity-oriented movement that we now call the Religious Right, becoming the main force in the anti-choice movement.

As we see the Religious Right oppose a woman's right to abortion, it is worth remembering that conservative religion has consistently opposed almost all efforts to treat women with equality and respect, instead consistently demanding submission to male authority, denying basic rights, and condoning gross mistreatment. Biblical passages that are oppressive toward women are numerous and well known. "Christ is the head of every man, and the man is the head of woman" (1 Corinthians 11:3). "Wives, submit yourselves unto your own husbands, as unto the Lord" (Ephesians 5:22). "But I suffer not a woman to teach, nor to usurp authority over the man, but to be in silence" (1 Timothy 2:12). These are just a few rather mild examples of numerous Bible passages that relegate women to second-class status. More grisly doctrine would include that which requires a rape victim to marry her rapist (Deuteronomy 22:28) or, in the alternative, would require capital punishment for the rape victim if she was not heard screaming for help (Deuteronomy 22:24). Such passages, of course, are outdated writings from an ancient society, but these writings are the foundation for the Religious Right's attitude toward women. This view of women has manifested itself throughout history, from the position of many theologians that women should not receive anesthesia during childbirth, to the belief, still voiced by many conservative Christians, that women should not work outside the home.

These examples barely skim the surface of the misogynistic tradition within conservative religion, yet conservative Christians expect to be taken seriously when they speak out on the issue of women's reproductive rights. If conservative religion had a history of treating women with great respect, of seeing women as social and political equals of men, then at least it might claim some credibility when it takes a position of supporting the "right to life" of an embryo. Since the history of conservative religion is quite the contrary, its "pro-life" arguments seem little more than a disingenuous attempt to validate an outdated antiwoman worldview.

With the issue of women's rights, we once again see the wisdom of a naturalistic view, especially when contrasted with the misogyny of traditional religion. Viewing women's rights this way, we see not only how human social development has historically resulted in inequality between the sexes in societies, but also why equality is so necessary and morally desirable as we move forward. Rather than fixating on a role for women consistent with the standards of ancient agrarian societies of the Middle East, most Secular Americans analyze the issue from the pragmatic standpoint of modern technological society wherein women stand as equals. Few issues better contrast the forward-looking secular view with the outdated view of conservative religion.

THE IMPORTANCE OF IDENTITY

Social evolution is difficult, if not impossible, to predict, and oftentimes the progress that we expect simply doesn't happen, while unexpected progress does. The LGBT rights movement, for example, has been a stunning success that few would have predicted a few decades ago, while the surprising rise of politically influential fundamentalist Christianity, accompanied by the failure of secularity to become more predominant, has been a disappointing setback.

If we consider how the LGBT movement achieved its unexpected success, there can be no question that an important component was the notion of identity. Historically, same-sex orientation was associated with living "in the closet," as it was seen as shameful and socially unacceptable, making it virtually impossible to organize an effective social-political LGBT movement. If the members of your movement are in hiding, they cannot effectively demand recognition, respect, and social change.

It was not until the 1970s, when many gays and lesbians slowly started "coming out," that a movement began to build. Suddenly, the notion of pride, rather than shame, became a driving force, resulting in the development of major organizations such as the Human Rights Campaign (which now claims 750,000 members) as institutional advocates for LGBT rights.[3] Their success illustrates the difference between a marginalized, closeted minority and an engaged, proud minority. By showing that virtually everyone has family members, friends, work colleagues, and neighbors who are gay, the LGBT community was able to stand up for its rights, rebut attacks from opponents, and change its status within the culture.

While the Religious Right also used identity politics with its emphasis on proud Christian identity, in the early years its primary opposition lacked that strong sense of identity. Members of groups like PFAW, the ACLU, and Americans United certainly had identity, calling themselves civil libertarians, liberals, and a host of other descriptive terms, but there was nothing comparable to the strong, unifying sense of Christian identity that can be seen in the Religious Right or, for that matter, the gay/lesbian identity of the LGBT movement. Moreover, because even the Religious Right's opponents tried to associate themselves with religion, secular identity was nowhere to be found in the mix.

Indeed, as the Religious Right was gaining momentum in the 1980s and 1990s, there were no significant national groups ready to emphasize the importance of secular identity. Groups like PFAW simply didn't consider validating secular identity to be a viable strategy in discrediting religious conservatism. The few national identity-oriented secular groups that existed, such as the American Humanist Association (AHA), the Council for Secular Humanism (CSH), and American Atheists (AA), were too small to mount a serious opposition to the tidal wave of religious conservatism that was sweeping the nation. Membership numbers for these groups were low, resources were limited, and the wider culture was not looking to them to seriously challenge the Religious Right. Other secular groups, such as the Freedom from Religion Foundation (FFRF) and the Center for Inquiry (CFI), while also small, had the added disadvantage of not even being clearly identity-oriented. The end result was that in the 1980s and 1990s, those who were atheists, humanists, or otherwise secular rarely emphasized it in their social or political activism.

Unlike the secular community, the LGBT movement was seeing much progress by the 1990s as a result of its identity-oriented strategy. By the late 1980s, coming out had lost much of its shock value, at least in celebrity culture, and in the 1990s, gay and lesbian characters were becoming common in mainstream television and film. As a result, acceptance of gays and lesbians steadily increased, and public policy slowly began reflecting that tolerance.

A SECULAR MOVEMENT EMERGES

The election of George W. Bush in 2000 was a wake-up call to many Secular Americans. Whatever the good intentions of the people and organizations that had been opposing the Religious Right for two decades, there was no denying that those efforts were failing miserably. Bush had run on a platform of anti-intellectualism, scoffing at "elitist" academics, mispronouncing his words, and frequently referencing faith and conservative religious positions. He gave fundamentalist leaders access to his White House and made it clear that he sided with them on all the key issues—public expressions of faith and prayer, restrictions on women's rights to abortion, the funneling of tax dollars to Christian churches via faith-based initiatives, and even the opposition of stem cell research. Many were especially incensed that Bush's vocal religiosity didn't prevent him from pushing seemingly un-Christian public policy positions, as when he called for slashing taxes on corporations and the wealthiest individuals, cutting back on social spending, escalating military budgets, and, eventually, utilizing military force in Iraq. Bush's presidency had all the markings of a government heavily influenced by conservative, fundamentalist religion.

The nation was sharply divided after Bush's election in 2000. Not only did Bush lose the popular vote, but the election highlighted the deep cultural divide that separated social conservatives from more moderate and progressive Americans. This was an election that showed a clear map of blue states in the northeast and Pacific coast and red states in the south and interior. This division in American politics highlighted the so-called culture wars, calling attention to the vastly different worldviews of the Religious Right and Secular Americans, though at the time, the notion of an identity-oriented secular movement had not yet taken root. Given the failure to contain the Religious Right, however, it was becoming clear that new approaches were needed.

The September 11 attacks—a fine example of religious motivation at its worst—occurred in the first year of Bush's presidency, and it was in the atmosphere of post-September 11 that leaders from several secular organizations met and formed the Secular Coalition for America (SCA). They were led by secular activist Herb Silverman, a math professor who made waves in the 1990s when he ran for governor of South Carolina in order to challenge that state's prohibition against atheists holding public office. After years of battling state authorities, he eventually succeeded in challenging the state law. With that experience under his belt, he started working with national and local groups on secular activism. Silverman quickly discovered the disunity and lack of focus that prevailed in the community of organized secularism, and it was this frustration that led him to envision a coalition of the various groups and individuals that could grow into a movement. Those efforts eventually bore fruit with the formation of the SCA in December 2002.

The SCA's mission is to raise the profile of Secular Americans and to demonstrate to politicians, the media, and the public that nonbelievers are an important part of the citizenry that is finally starting to organize. But in 2003, the SCA was little more than an incubator for an idea, a shell with few assets, no employees, and no ongoing activism. It was formed as a lobbying organization, meaning that donations to it would not be tax deductible, because secular leaders knew political influence was essential to the movement's success. The SCA's role as a lobbying organization enables the coalition to do things that its member organizations, not being lobbying groups themselves, could not.

The disunity within the secular community, however, meant that only a few national organizations joined the SCA in its first year. The AHA, the oldest national secular group and one of the largest, at first refused to join because of hesitations about activism that emphasizes secularity. Historically, the AHA's public advocacy had been less identity-oriented and more inclined toward general progressive issues such as reproductive rights, peace, church-state separation, and human rights. AHA leadership at the time saw the SCA's approach as potentially too brazen.

But the AHA was itself undergoing significant changes. In 2003, the AHA elected a new president, Mel Lipman, who would steer the organization in a new activist direction, emphasizing a more identity-oriented approach to activism. In 2004, Lipman and Silverman (who was also an AHA board member) garnered enough board votes to support a motion for the AHA to join the SCA. The motion passed by one vote, including a swing vote from Tom Ferrick, at the time Harvard University's humanist chaplain, with vocal objections coming from the old guard. I had been working with Silverman since 2003, mainly corresponding by email and sharing ideas about what could be done to build a secular movement. We met in person for the first time at an SCA board meeting in Minneapolis. Herb is known for wearing T-shirts and sandals in almost all settings, and I had shown up at the event wearing ordinary clothes—nothing fancy, but a sport jacket and a collared shirt. Introducing himself to me, Herb said, "You look like you could be with the Christian Coalition!" Considering the context, I wasn't sure whether to take this as a compliment. Nevertheless, over the last decade, I've watched Herb work tirelessly to build the SCA and the entire movement, and it's been a pleasure working with him despite our wardrobe differences.

It's amazing to look at the SCA today, with an impressive Washington office steps from the Capitol, eleven national member groups, a highly professional staff of activists and lobbyists, and a distinguished advisory board of celebrities and influential activists, and think that just a few years ago, it was a newly formed entity that existed on paper only. The SCA provides a vehicle for unified political activism by which Secular Americans can, for the first time, stand together and act together.

EARLY SCA ACTIVISM

In those early days when the SCA was trying to attract reluctant groups and build itself into a national player in the culture wars, resources were scarce. The group decided that its first foray into activism would be to call attention to one of the ugliest segments of fundamentalist Christianity—televangelists. The expansion of cable television in the 1980s and satellite television in the 1990s was a boon for television preachers, who used the new media to spread their message and enrich their tax-exempt ministries, but part of this benefit was due to an unfair advantage that religious broadcasters were enjoying. In the spring of 2004, the SCA challenged, via a complaint to the Federal Communications Commission (FCC), the granting of valuable satellite television channels to televangelists. A federal regulation required satellite television providers, such as DIRECTV, to set aside a certain percentage of their channels "for noncommercial programming of an educational or informational nature"[4] to be given to nonprofits at cost—a small fraction of their value. William E. Kennard, the chairman of the FCC when the regulation was first implemented, made it clear that the public-interest channel capacity was meant for education, children, minorities, the disabled, health-care information, and innovative programming that would not be expected to be commercially viable. He said the set-aside was intended "to ensure that we have access to quality programming" and that it was expected to "raise the level of political discourse."[5] Kennard was adamant that it would benefit not just viewers but also those who produce creative and educational content. "We have a great opportunity here," he said. "There are abundant sources of quality programming. There are parents and children all across this country who are anxious for quality broadcasts."[6]

Contrary to these lofty goals, the SCA learned, DIRECTV had granted 5 of its 12 set-aside public-interest channels to religious programmers who used them to proselytize and raise money. Sometimes the programming could not even be described as noncommercial, since programs would be interrupted by commercial advertisements for religious videos and audiotapes. Just as egregious, however, was the programming itself, which fell far short of any fair interpretation of "educational or informational." For example, one programmer, the Christian company Daystar, aired a program called *Celebration* with hosts Marcus and Joni Lamb interviewing Dr. Hilton Sutton, who was presented as an expert on Bible prophecy. Sutton informed viewers that Iraq is the first place on earth that Satan is known to have appeared, a fact that he gleaned from his reading of Genesis. He also informed viewers that the Second Coming of Jesus was not imminent, though he humbly added that nobody could be completely sure about when this event will occur. "Even the angels don't know,"[7] he declared, because such knowledge is "reserved for the father." While this "educational" program aired on the public-interest channel subsidized by satellite television consumers, a toll-free telephone number and website were displayed on the television screen, asking for monetary donations.

This example is by no means unique. At about the same time, viewers of Trinity Broadcasting, another recipient of the public-interest channel capacity, could see *Believer's Voice of Victory* with host Kenneth Copeland, where tapes were offered for sale and viewers were reminded that donations could easily be made online. Almost all of the programming on these channels was some form of religious proselytizing, whether via the convulsive rants of "Pastor Jesse" or the more subdued delivery of preacher Joyce Meyer. It's hard to imagine that this was the "quality programming" that FCC chairman Kennard had in mind.

The SCA did not question the right of these preachers and programmers to broadcast their religious views, but rather the granting of public-interest channel capacity—intended for quality educational programming and subsidized by unknowing satellite television consumers—to religious organizations who were profiting from the enterprise. It is noteworthy that the religious programming in question was exclusively Christian, thereby excluding millions of Jews, Muslims, Hindus, Buddhists, Scientologists, Wiccans, and nonbelievers. Moreover, the Christian programmers on DIRECTV did not even represent a fair cross section of the Christian community, for conservative, evangelical, fundamentalist, and Protestant preachers filled the airwaves of the public-interest channels. Liberal Christianity was absent from the programming, as was tolerance for LGBT rights, abortion rights, or other liberal values.

In its complaint to the FCC, the SCA pointed out that the programming, by offering salvation while requesting money, preys upon some of the most vulnerable of the public. The rights of religious groups to proselytize cannot be questioned, but the rights of televangelists to utilize public-interest channels reserved for quality and innovative educational programming certainly can. The complaint also pointed out that DIRECTV had refused channel capacity to other truly qualified programmers, such as several universities, distance education providers, foreign language programmers, and social activist groups. Through counsel, DIRECTV denied that the granting of public-interest channels to televangelists violated the FCC's regulation. Unfortunately, in December 2004 the FCC, without a hearing, agreed with DIRECTV and denied the complaint, leaving the SCA, with its limited resources at the time, without an avenue to pursue the case further. Nevertheless, the dispute got some media attention and allowed the SCA to introduce itself as a watchdog for the interests of Secular Americans.

In 2005, the SCA started on the road of increasing Secular Americans' political influence by hiring its first full-time lobbyist, Lori Lipman Brown, a former Nevada state senator with a strong record as a civil libertarian. Instantly, the news of a full-time "atheist lobbyist" excited cable news hosts and pundits, and Brown was inundated with requests for interviews, appearing on numerous high-profile television and radio programs to discuss secular political activism.

Because atheists are so rare in politics, in 2006 the SCA sponsored a contest to locate the highest-ranking elected official in the nation who would openly identify as atheist or agnostic. As a result, Representative Pete Stark of California, a veteran Democrat from the Bay Area, "came out" publicly as an atheist, describing himself as a "Unitarian who does not believe in a Supreme Being."[8] Even before this announcement, Stark had a reputation as a supporter of church-state separation and an opponent of the Religious Right. In 2008, Stark, who has a strong progressive track record to accompany his secular credentials, accepted the AHA's Humanist of the Year Award. Subsequently, he has reaffirmed his commitment to secular government, even reading a proclamation into the Congressional Record in 2011 recognizing the National Day of Reason on May 5, a day already reserved as the National Day of Prayer (thanks to lobbying by religious conservatives). "Reason and rational thinking have made our country great," Stark's defiant proclamation stated. "The Constitution of the United States of America is based upon the philosophies developed during the historical Age of Reason and the idea that citizens engaging in rational discourse and decision-making can govern themselves. The Constitution also contains a strong separation of church and state, making it clear that government should continue to be built on reason."[9]

Concrete evidence of the secular community's progress in gaining acceptance from the establishment came in 2010 with the first-ever formal meeting between organized secular groups and White House staff. Meetings between religious leaders and the White House have been commonplace for years, of course, but never had the executive branch opened its doors in this way to listen to the concerns of atheists and humanists. Recognizing the secular community's increasing growth and organization, the Obama team invited several dozen of us for a day of discussion on various issues. We used the time to focus on just a few key areas: concerns about faith-based initiatives, legal loopholes that give religion special treatment, and discrimination against nonbelievers in the military. White House staff made it clear that they were there to listen, not to make deals or promises, and there was no suggestion that the secular community's views would necessarily shape future policy, but nevertheless there was a sense that at least our voices were being heard and taken seriously.

Having been on the outside looking in for so long, any recognition, especially coming directly from the White House, felt like progress. This perhaps explains why many Secular Americans took note of Obama's shout-out to them in his January 2009 inaugural speech. Speaking of the patchwork nature of America as a strength, not a weakness, Obama declared, "We are a nation of Christians and Muslims, Jews and Hindus— and nonbelievers."[10] A positive, inclusive reference by the president of a minority group representing such a huge portion of the population would not normally be remarkable, but such a call-out to the nonreligious was without precedent.

Secular Americans, once a disorganized and invisible segment of the population, are now coming together via the SCA. Besides lobbying, the SCA issues action alerts that convey news and information about political issues important to the secular community. These alerts, which are disseminated to over twenty thousand direct subscribers and to the memberships of each of the SCA's eleven member groups and others throughout cyberspace, spur Secular Americans to write to legislators and other government officials in response to important votes and other events. The SCA's Facebook page also keeps the secular community abreast of issues of interest. Through a "Congressional Scorecard" that can be found on the SCA's website (www.secular.org), the SCA informs secular voters of how all members of Congress vote on issues of importance. All of this creates a demographic cohesion that simply didn't exist even a few years ago.

SECULAR ADVERTISING

In 2005, the AHA launched the first major national advertising campaign by an atheist or humanist group in America. The campaign ran full-page ads in several national publications—the *Nation, Mother Jones,* the *Progressive,* and the *American Prospect*—over the course of four months, putting humanist identity and religious skepticism in front of the general public like never before. The idea of secular advertising may not sound very unusual today, but at that time it was considered controversial, even within the AHA. Many among the AHA's leadership, especially those who had been around for decades, objected to the effort, seeing the idea of promoting humanism to the general public as inappropriate. The mass of the membership, however, rejoiced at the sight of secularity in public view in this way for the first time. By subsequent standards, those 2005 AHA ads were tame, conveying positive messages that, for the most part, were not directly critical of religion. The first ad had a photo of a professional woman in a business suit with the caption, "My values? I'm a Humanist." The smaller text provided information about humanist values, such as compassion, human rights, reason, and education.

The AHA's ads created so much buzz that other secular groups quickly launched advertising campaigns of their own, first like the AHA in magazines and then in other media. A group called FreeThoughtAction, formed by two activists named Jan Meshon and Joseph Stewart, raised money to run a billboard on the New Jersey Turnpike. It simply stated, "Don't believe in God? You are not alone," with a website that provided information about secularity and secular groups. FreeThoughtAction later became an AHA adjunct, and the billboard medium proved so successful, garnering lots of attention from the media and the public, that it was soon replicated widely. The movement was now getting high-profile coverage in major newspapers and other publications, including a March 2009 cover story in the *National Journal* called "The Rise of the Godless," which reported, "Now, however, the 'Godless' are organizing, inspired in part by Bush-era abandonment of sound policy in science and other domains in favor of faith-based initiatives and evangelical influence." Reporter Paul Starobin continued: "In a growing struggle to earn recognition and respect, America's nonbelievers want 'to be viewed no longer as an offbeat and safely marginalized counterculture but as part of the diverse mainstream of American life.'"[11]

The advertising trend even crossed the pond in 2009 when the British Humanist Association began running ads on public buses. With characteristic British wit, the bus ads declared, "There's probably no God. Now stop worrying and enjoy your life." This campaign was so popular that similar bus ads soon started appearing on transit systems all over Europe and North America.

Also in 2009, the AHA launched a national effort to enable secular grassroots groups to work together to achieve higher visibility through local secular advertising. The United Coalition of Reason, an AHA project that is the brainchild of secular activist Steve Rade, finds the various secular groups in a metropolitan market and then helps them create a local Coalition of Reason (CoR) that becomes the subject of local advertising. Each billboard provides a catchy phrase calling attention to the concept of secularity, along with a website for further information. Dozens of such campaigns have been launched in cities from coast to coast, with organizations such as PhillyCoR, OrlandoCoR, and SanDiegoCoR. A list of the various local grassroots groups, often chapters of national groups, can be found at each local CoR website, allowing the groups to gain visibility and members.

Though advertising has been an effective way of raising the profile of secular groups, it has sometimes been met with hostility. In Fort Worth, Texas, for example, local clerics organized an unsuccessful boycott of the transit system after atheist ads began running on buses there in 2010. Vandals destroyed ten secular billboards in Sacramento, two bus ads in Detroit, and other billboards in Idaho and Florida, while one billboard was taken down in Cincinnati after the owner received threats.[12] In some areas, transit systems have refused to run the ads, even though the same systems routinely accept religious advertising. When this has happened, threats of legal action have usually gotten the uncooperative transit system to rethink its position, although sometimes threats alone have not sufficed. In August 2011, the AHA, through its Appignani Humanist Legal Center, had to obtain a federal court order to force the Little Rock, Arkansas, transit authority to accept advertising from the local CoR.

The legal dispute in Little Rock reflected how far the secular community has come in recent years. A decade ago, neither secular advertising campaigns nor the AHA's legal center existed, so now there is poignancy in a secular ad campaign being defended not by the ACLU or some other outside entity, but by a legal office within the movement. Together with the legal department of the FFRF, which has been the most litigious of the secular groups in recent years, the AHA's legal center is providing full-time legal advocacy specifically for the secular community.

Not surprisingly, when it comes to secular advertising, the provocative and edgier ads tend to get the most attention. When American Atheists ran a billboard during the Christmas season in 2010 depicting a nativity image with the words "You know it's a myth," the public reaction was heard far and wide, even though many Christians understand the nativity story, particularly the tale of the visits of the three wise men, to be mythological.

In fact, some interpret any secular advertising during the Christmas season as an attack on Christianity. The AHA ran bus ads in Washington DC in 2008 depicting a young African American man, wearing a Santa suit and a puzzled expression, under the caption, "Why believe in a god? Just be good for goodness' sake." The uproar, not so much from the public but from conservative commentators, was furious. "It's a stupid ad," declared Tim Wildmon of the American Family Association. "How do we define 'good' if we don't believe in God?"[13] (Perhaps the most unintentionally humorous comment on the ad was a media account that said it depicted "a fake Santa.")[14] This response to secular advertising during the Christmas season is consistent with the general annual perception, believed by many and encouraged by the media, that there is a "war on Christmas." Before the emergence of Secular Americans, however, there was little talk about any such "war," so this can be seen as another sign that the secular demographic is successfully asserting itself and making waves in the political and cultural discourse.

FINDING UNITY AND VISION

During the first Bush-Cheney term, in an effort to ensure that the broad secular community would find cohesion, the AHA organized for the first time a meeting of all the heads of major secular groups from around the country (appropriately called the "Heads" meeting). The event was so successful that it became an annual event, attracting hundreds of leaders from national, regional, and local secular groups. The annual meeting allows leaders to discuss strategies, issues and policy, and possible joint action.

In 2010, the SCA launched its Secular Decade program—one of the most ambitious long-term projects by a secular group to date—wherein it plans to launch grassroots secular groups in all 50 states. Building in part on the loose confederation of local secular groups created by the AHA's CoR program, the state secular coalitions will enable the SCA to mobilize grassroots activism even more effectively. These groups will provide a network of local activists who can contact their representatives and senators on important secular issues, proving that real constituents stand ready to advocate at the grassroots level for the SCA's position. They also can advocate on issues at the local level that might not come to the attention of the SCA Washington office. The first state group was launched in October 2010 as the Secular Coalition for Arizona, followed a few months later by another group in Alabama. By 2020, the SCA plans to have local lobbying groups covering the nation.

Another factor that fueled the emergence of Secular Americans in the last decade—a development that brought about a sense of validation and unity among nonbelievers—was the surprising success of what are now called New Atheist books. Whereas the subject of atheism had never been popular in mainstream publishing, suddenly in 2004 books on this subject began to receive widespread attention. The first was *The End of Faith* by Sam Harris, a relatively unknown author who at the time was a doctoral student. His direct attack on traditional religion, pointing to the events of September 11 as evidence of what happens when modern technology mixes with outdated religious faith, made him an instant celebrity in a secular community that, thanks to the Internet and social networking, had become much more visible than in years past. In 2006, *The God Delusion* by

Richard Dawkins and *Breaking the Spell* by Daniel Dennett followed, and in 2007, Christopher Hitchens published *God Is Not Great.*

The surprisingly wide appeal of these New Atheist books, which gained their authors the title "Four Horsemen of the Apocalypse," both energized the secular movement and reflected an already-existing energy. Though the authors of these books, with the possible exception of Dennett, are more confrontational toward religion than the typical Secular American, their assertiveness is appreciated by many who see it as necessary in light of the suffocating influence of the Religious Right. In an atmosphere of hostility toward secularity, zealous advocacy and validation are often appreciated.

Riding momentum from the popularity of the New Atheism, in 2007 the Richard Dawkins Foundation for Reason and Science launched an identity-oriented project—the brainchild of its executive director, Dr. R. Elisabeth Cornwell—that has proven widely popular. Using a scarlet "A" as its emblem, the Out Campaign encourages atheists to come out of the closet to identify openly, and millions have. Emblazoned on buttons, pins, jewelry, apparel, and other products, the Out Campaign's scarlet "A" has become a popular branding mechanism within the secular movement, and is particularly popular online, where it can be found on millions of social media profiles. Other secular symbols, such as the Darwin fish and the Flying Spaghetti Monster (a parody deity), are often nearby. Far from being a personal characteristic that must be kept politely out of view, religious skepticism is now a means of defining oneself to friends, family, and the outside world. "We are mothers, fathers, sons, daughters, sisters, brothers and grandparents," the Out Campaign declares on its website. "We are good people who have no need to cling to the supernatural."

PUSHING BACK AGAINST PRIVILEGED RELIGION

The appearance of the SCA as a legislative advocacy group came at a time when the Religious Right was becoming more assertive with its agenda. Often under the guise of "religious freedom," fundamentalists have pushed for legislation that either provides special privileges for the religious, denies rights to others, or both. Several states have passed laws, for example, permitting pharmacists to refuse to dispense prescriptions for religious reasons, thereby denying others the right to basic and necessary health care. In 2005, this resulted in a 20-year-old rape victim subsequently spending three days frantically calling dozens of pharmacies to fill a prescription for emergency contraception. When she finally found one carrying the prescription, the pharmacist on duty refused to fill the prescription on moral and religious grounds. By the time a willing pharmacist could be found, the optimal time for filling the prescription had passed.[16]

Most Americans, religious and secular, have more sympathy for a rape victim who wants access to emergency contraception than for the pharmacist who adds to her trauma by imposing his own personal morality on her. Nevertheless, because the Religious Right is so well funded and influential, such "religious refusal laws" are common around the country and difficult to overturn. The SCA, by organizing the secular demographic and working with other groups who object to the policies of the Religious Right, is lobbying for federal legislation that would prohibit pharmacists from refusing to fill prescriptions and for other measures to assure that victims of sexual assault have full access to emergency contraception.

The SCA's legislative agenda shows both how far the Religious Right has come and how far Secular Americans and others who favor rational public policy and church-state separation have to go to get the country back. Even with a Democratic administration, for example, there was no possibility of eliminating the faith-based initiatives program, which funnels tax money to religious groups for various social services programs. This is a blatant church-state violation, especially considering that there is no adequate oversight of the millions of dollars sent to churches to ensure that the money is not used to subsidize proselytizing and other nonhumanitarian activities. Candidate Obama in 2008 did not promise to eliminate the program, but he did promise that he would require churches receiving money to abide by federal laws prohibiting discrimination on the basis of religion. He did not keep even that modest promise, however, and when confronted with the issue by SCA staffer Amanda Knief in 2011, Obama lost his usual eloquence and struggled unsuccessfully to rationalize the government's privileging of religion. "This is always a tricky part of the First Amendment," he said during his rambling answer, which went on to imply that the free exercise of religion might justify discriminatory hiring even when government money is subsidizing the program. By the end, it seemed that even Obama realized the utter lack of credibility that his answer carried.[17]

While the Religious Right frequently talks about restoring religious freedom, suggesting that such freedom has been mysteriously lost, it masks the primary purpose of its legislative goals, which is to ensure that religion and religious institutions receive an elite position in society. In fact, much of the special treatment that religious groups receive in modern American society does not flow from their constitutional rights, which are somewhat limited. Instead, this special treatment comes from a federal statute passed in 1993—at the urging of the Religious Right—called the Religious Freedom Restoration Act (RFRA), and from similar laws that have since been passed by the federal government and individual states.[18] Under RFRA laws, any governmental action, even one that was not intended as being hostile to religion, that "substantially burdens" the exercise of religion is invalid. RFRA and laws like it have been used to exempt religious groups from zoning requirements, to allow special religious exemptions from drug laws, and to permit the hunting of endangered species. The SCA does not argue the wisdom, pro or con, of the underlying zoning ordinances, drug laws, or hunting laws, but instead objects to the special exemptions given to religion. This is the same kind of flawed logic that leads to pharmacists using special exemptions to refuse to do their job based on religious objections.

What all of these efforts show is that there is no end to the Religious Right's wish list, that any policy victory will be followed by another policy goal that further offends the sensibilities of Secular Americans.

Many commentators have noted that the presidency of George W. Bush was the best thing that ever happened for organized secularism in America. It was the ascendance to the White House of a proud anti-intellectual, who counted many of the Religious Right's leaders and organizations as his strongest supporters, that awakened Secular Americans to the need for organization and activism. With Bush, the secular community came to realize that activism must mean something more than fighting for church-state separation, reproductive rights, and other progressive issues, and that the idea of secular identity—building a recognized demographic category representing the millions of Americans who simply aren't religious or theistic—had been neglected for too long. It is a testament to the strength and determination of that movement that it has not lost steam as Bush's successor, who was presumed to be less hostile to the secular demographic, has taken office. In fact, as we'll see in the next chapter, steps are being taken to ensure that the secular movement becomes entrenched into the culture for years to come.

SEVEN

REASON FOR HOPE AND HOPE FOR REASON

AS SECULAR AMERICANS HAVE EMERGED OVER THE LAST FEW years, one of the most fascinating and exciting areas within the movement has been the phenomenon of student activism. Religious skepticism on college campuses is nothing new, but what's happening today is truly unprecedented. Across all lines of wealth, ethnicity, gender, and sexual orientation, students are standing up together to identify as personally secular.

The historical role of religion in higher learning is somewhat paradoxical. On one hand, by definition higher learning should be an exercise in skepticism—questioning facts, finding flaws in arguments, and developing work that can withstand intellectual scrutiny—so it should not be surprising that colleges and universities are havens for the critical analysis of religious claims and doctrines. Nevertheless, established churches have historically wielded enormous influence over social and political life in both Europe and America and, therefore, have often had close relationships with institutions of higher learning. Harvard, Yale, the College of William and Mary, and virtually all of the oldest colleges in America were mainly incubators for clergymen in their earliest years. When

Connecticut legislators founded the college that would later become Yale in 1701, they declared that they were motivated by "Zeal for upholding & Propagating of the Christian Protestant Religion" to educate "a succession of Learned & Orthodox men" who through "the blessing of Almighty God may be fitted for Publick employment both in Church & Civil State."[1] Thus, it is ironic that these bastions of intellectual pursuit, which would ultimately do more to chip away at the credibility of established religion than any other social institutions, were often established by men for whom the idea of separating God from academia would have been unthinkable.

With the Enlightenment already underway in Europe when religious men were founding the earliest American colleges, the relationship between religion and higher education was bound to eventually get tense. One obvious dilemma was that established religious institutions, which were by their nature conservative, inflexible, and reliant on ancient doctrine, needed educated, literate leadership to maintain power and legitimacy. This was not so problematic in the seventeenth and eighteenth centuries, when an advanced education did not necessarily conflict with religious authority. As the years progressed, however, Enlightenment ideas, industrialization and commercialization, the discoveries of Darwin, and other advances in knowledge made it increasingly likely that a college education would result in religious skepticism, not reinforcement. Over time, this resulted in the diminished role of religion in higher education, and as early as the nineteenth century we begin to see atheism and agnosticism as visible, sometimes even acceptable, schools of thought in establishment academia.

That trajectory continued into the twentieth century, resulting in skepticism being not the exception, but the rule in many institutions of higher education. While schools of theology can still be found in many of the great educational institutions, theology as a discipline of study is often seen as a puzzling relic from a bygone era. Much more dominant are the schools of science, technology, medicine, law, business, and liberal arts, most of which, depending on the specific institution, are likely to be populated with instructors and students who, if asked, are skeptical or ambivalent about religion. Few courses of study will expose students to ideas that are particularly sympathetic toward traditional religion. This is in part because few of those doctrines withstand a search for empirical truth, and also because many courses of study, such as history, anthropology, and gender studies, expose students to ideas that may delegitimize religion and portray it in an unfavorable light. Students learn of historical and contemporary religious justifications for the mistreatment of women, the rejection of basic matters of scientific truth on religious grounds, atrocities attributable to religion, and convincing arguments that religion is a natural phenomenon and not the product of divine revelation, to name a few examples. Thus, for anyone alive today who has attended college, it is likely that notions of atheism, agnosticism, and general religious skepticism were a part of the college experience.

A PRIMARY SECULAR IDENTITY

Despite all this, even though atheists have been a fixture on America's college campuses for decades, the situation today is unprecedented. Today's secular students, unlike their parents and grandparents, see secular identity as a primary, important part of who they are. While there were atheists and agnostics all over college campuses in the 1960s, 1970s, and 1980s, most nonreligious students in those days, if asked, would have first defined themselves as many things other than atheist or secular. They may have first seen themselves as liberal, conservative, socialist, libertarian, environmentalist, gay/lesbian, feminist, antiwar, no-nukes, or one of many other labels; in fact, their religious skepticism often would have been incidental and very low on any list of importance. Today, nonreligious students are increasingly seeing their personal secularity as a key aspect of their character and their approach to life, an identity that immediately conveys much about what they accept and reject.

Nothing better illustrates this point than the explosive growth of the Secular Student Alliance (SSA), the national umbrella organization for campus atheist and humanist groups. Founded in 2000, the SSA had less than 50 campus affiliates in early 2007, but by 2011 it had over 340. Currently, the SSA has affiliates from coast to coast and even throughout the Bible Belt. With groups such as the Penn State Atheist/Agnostic Association, Students for Freethought at Ohio State University, the Boise State Secular Student Alliance, and the University of Alabama Atheists and

Agnostics, SSA affiliates demonstrate the national significance of atheist-humanist identity on college campuses today.[2]

"We're witnessing a major shift in our society," SSA spokesperson Jesse Galef told me. "More students are proudly calling themselves atheists, which inspires others to do the same. We used to go out and find them. Now they're springing up everywhere and finding us, asking to join the movement."[3]

The reasons for this interest in secular identity are numerous. Often students point to the pervasive influence of conservative religion in their lives, which might explain why some of the strongest student groups can be found in areas known for religious conservatism. Just as reformed smokers are the strongest antismoking advocates, young people coming from fundamentalist families—having grown up with images of fire and brimstone, fear of damnation, and constant references to the Bible, God, Satan, good and evil—are often the most enthusiastic about their identity as secular individuals. With the growth of the Religious Right, the influence of conservative religion in many parts of the country is now quite overbearing, and young people who emerge from that environment as nonreligious understand the need for secular activism. Of course, even kids from moderately religious homes and nonreligious homes are well aware of the pervasive influence of the Religious Right in modern society. With mobilized religious conservatives so deeply entrenched, influential, and assertive that any young person interested in politics and social issues would have to be blind to overlook it, secular students from all kinds of family backgrounds are seeing the value of organized atheist-humanist groups as an affirmative rebuke of the Religious Right. Those interested in fighting for progress a generation ago may have targeted other political or social issues, but today's students increasingly see secular identity and activism as vehicles for change.

Another factor is September 11, which has caused many to question the role of ancient, revelation-based religion in modern society. Christian fundamentalists at home were troublesome enough for many, but Islamic fundamentalist terrorism striking major American cities took concerns to a new level. Sam Harris pointed to the September 11 attacks as his motivation in writing *The End of Faith*, the first of the popular New Atheist books, citing traditional religious faith as a most problematic phenomenon in the modern world. Many young people share his sentiments, and there can be little doubt that this at least partly explains the doubling of Americans identifying as nonreligious in recent years. "After the September 11 attacks, I began thinking that perhaps I should speak out against what I felt was a mindset that is not only wrong but dangerous," said a former student named Ian, who was attending the University of Wisconsin when deeply religious terrorists took the lives of almost three thousand innocent victims on September 11, 2001. An openly secular life stance, for many young people, is a means of affirmatively taking a position in favor of reason and against ancient superstition.

What troubled many secular students after September 11 was the religious mind-set not just of the terrorists but also of the political and military leaders fighting them. US Army lieutenant general William G. Boykin, for example, who served as deputy undersecretary of defense in the Bush administration until 2007, was vocal with his conservative Christian warrior rhetoric, casting the war on terror as a holy war with biblical implications. Repeatedly referring to America as a "Christian nation," Boykin explained how he viewed one particular interaction with a reported Muslim jihadist: "I knew my God was bigger than his," Boykin said. "I knew that my God was a real God and his was an idol."[4] America's "spiritual enemy," he is quoted as saying, "will only be defeated if we come against them in the name of Jesus." Note that these are not the words of some anonymous soldier, but of a high-ranking officer and policy maker interacting with the secretary of defense and other officials in the highest circles of power. "Satan wants to destroy this nation," Boykin warned, "and he wants to destroy us as a Christian army." Telling crowds that he goes to prayer services five times a week, Boykin praised George W. Bush as a man who, though not elected by a majority of voters, "was appointed by God."[5]

It's little wonder that nonbeliever students began to stand up as proudly secular in the face of such religious extremism emanating from the halls of their government. In generations past, the idea that elders held religious views that seemed outdated may have had little direct impact on the lives of students, but the increasing influence of the Religious Right calls attention to the error of conducting public policy from a biblical standpoint. To students who are nonbelievers, this simply highlights the importance of secular identity as a valuable, stabilizing influence.

Proud secular identity is seen as very problematic in some schools, particularly those that are connected to religious institutions. Catholic colleges such as the University of Notre Dame, for example, though usually quite liberal in trying to show acceptance of a wide variety of religious backgrounds, have made it clear that they treat secularity much differently. Whereas Muslim and Jewish groups have been welcomed by the Catholic administration of Notre Dame, efforts to form secular groups have been met with stern opposition. The tolerance on Catholic campuses for Islam and Judaism, religions that have historically been the target of open hostility and even violence from church leaders, is indeed revealing and surely a sign of the more pluralistic times, but the continued exclusion of atheist-humanist groups tells us even more. As religion diminishes in power, various religions that were once bitter enemies are more inclined to set aside differences so that they can circle their wagons together to fight the common enemy of secularism.[6]

Thus, though these major colleges hold themselves out as places that offer quality higher education for people of all faiths, the welcome mat is not really out for those of no faith at all. Secular student groups have also been rejected by other Catholic universities, including Dayton and Duquesne, as well as the world's largest Baptist university, Baylor. Clearly, the feeling is that discrimination against atheist-humanist students is acceptable. Tolerance and ecumenical attitudes will dominate, except when the parties seeking inclusion are atheists and humanists. Interestingly, in the case of Dayton, even gay and lesbian groups are allowed, in direct conflict with Catholic teaching. This is just more evidence of the need for Secular Americans to raise their profile and fight unjustified vilification.

CONNECTIONS AND COMMUNITY

Even with these motivating factors, much contemporary secular student activism would be impossible without an important modern tool—the Internet. The power of the Internet has transformed many aspects of society—social, political, and commercial—but the effect that it has had on the Secular American demographic is difficult to overstate. Being a nonbeliever before the Internet was often an experience of relative isolation, but in today's world it is almost communal, with a wide range of individuals just a few clicks away ready to share ideas and experiences, provide support and encouragement, and let secular individuals know that they are not alone. Online social networking sites give users an opportunity to openly state their religion, or lack thereof, and today there are millions of Americans publicly identifying as atheist, agnostic, or secular humanist on sites like Facebook. This simple act—revealing to one's family, friends, and coworkers that one is a nonbeliever—makes secular identity seem more ordinary and acceptable. While prior generations struggled with the issue of "coming out" to their friends and family, for the first time young people are growing up routinely seeing others openly identify as atheist, agnostic, or humanist.

Most national secular groups, such as the AHA and the SSA, have sophisticated websites with useful resources for the interested visitor: educational tools, information on grassroots organizing, podcasts, action alerts for political activism, and numerous other resources. For the Secular American more interested in local happenings than national activism, sites like meetup.com are an effective way of locating like-minded neighbors, even in parts of the country that are thought of as highly religious. Enter "humanism" and "Columbia, South Carolina," in a meetup.com search, for example, and you may be surprised to find that a local group called Freethought Society of the Midlands, with over 280 members, is having regular get-togethers in your neighborhood. Few of these local groups predate the Internet, but thanks to cyberspace, they are now fueling the movement.

Online communities can be vital in certain situations, especially for the secular student who decides to challenge authority, providing support and camaraderie that can be invaluable. In years past, any student or family challenging public expressions of religion had to face outraged Christians more or less alone.

Such was the experience of the McCollum family of Champaign, Illinois, when they objected to religious instruction in their public school in the 1940s. As a nonreligious couple, John and Vashti McCollum did not want their son participating in the religious education classes, which affirmed specific Christian teachings and were run by local religious leaders, not school staff. Though the school claimed that the religious instruction was voluntary, the McCollums' son Jim was treated as a troublemaker when he stayed out of the class. The school rewarded each classroom for full participation in the program, so Jim's class was the only one that didn't receive the reward. When the other students were in the religion class, Jim was forced to sit in the hallway outside the principal's office, in a chair reserved for children being disciplined. When the family filed suit to object to the religious education classes under the First Amendment's Establishment Clause, the hostility of the community increased to a boiling point. Jim was physically assaulted and constantly harassed, until finally he had to move out of state to live with his grandparents. The family cat was killed. As Jim's younger brother Dan said years later, "These people were supposed to be Christians, but they didn't seem to be very Christian-like to me."[7]

Not surprisingly, much of the hostility toward the McCollums came from far beyond the borders of their community. Vashti, who actually brought the suit on behalf of her son, received voluminous hate mail from all around the country. State legislators considered actions to fire John, who worked at the state university, but they were ultimately unsuccessful.

The McCollums lost their case in the lower courts, but were eventually vindicated by the United States Supreme Court in a landmark decision that established important church-state legal principles. *McCollum v. Board of Education* (1948) was one of the first cases (together with *Everson v. Board of Education* in 1947) to rule that Jefferson's "wall of separation" between church and state applies to not just federal actions, but state and local government actions as well. With the McCollum victory, religious instruction in public schools was discontinued across the country, and the legal foundation was established for subsequent efforts to challenge school-sponsored prayer and Bible readings. Another fortunate result of the McCollum family's actions was that Vashti McCollum became a high-profile spokesperson on behalf of secularity, appearing for years around the country as a respected representative of the secular community and serving two terms as president of the AHA in the early 1960s. Eventually, the McCollums' middle son, Dan, was elected to three terms as mayor of Champaign, a sign that the community may have learned something from its experience.

It takes a special kind of individual and family to challenge the established order. Even in the 1940s, millions of Americans held personal views similar to those of the McCollums, but most Secular Americans, understandably, did not wish to expose themselves to the kind of treatment that the McCollums had to endure. It was, and is, sometimes easier to simply tolerate the government's sanction of religion, even though it directly conflicts with principles held dear. Some will rationalize doing so by saying that school-sponsored prayer or Bible study is really no big deal, or that any attempt to change the status quo would surely be futile, while others will frankly admit that the price of challenging religion in schools is simply too great.

What is different about today, however, is that those who decide to challenge the system quickly discover that a large community of peers supports them. A case in point is that of Jessica Ahlquist, a 15-year-old secular high school student in Cranston, Rhode Island, who decided in the spring of 2010 to not only learn about the Constitution, but utilize it. Her public school, Cranston High School West, displayed a large banner inscribed with an official school prayer called "Our Heavenly Father," so she asked the administration to remove it. When they refused, she sued.

As would be expected, Jessica faced much hostility for standing up for her principles. Elected public officials, eager to use religion for political leverage, decried her efforts and defended the banner as part of the community's tradition. Pundits and commentators joined in, calling her a troublemaker and questioning both her motives and values. She also had to face the direct wrath of her fellow students and community, an intimidating proposition even for an adult, let alone a high school sophomore. In one instance, during morning recitation of the Pledge of Allegiance, some of her classmates turned away from the flag to face Jessica, and at the appropriate time shouted "under God!" at her, obviously relaying their disapproval of her lawsuit. What this emotional and mean-spirited response reveals, besides the students' bad manners, is that the words *under God* and similar religious rhetoric do in fact have great religious significance. Although supporters of "under God" claim that the wording serves the secular purpose of acknowledging America's religious heritage, such claims are almost always disingenuous. When a federal judge ordered the banner removed in January 2012, the public vilification of Jessica erupted again. Several florists in her area even refused to deliver congratulatory flowers to her, and the delivery wasn't made until an out-of-state florist was found.[8]

But Jessica's experience—as difficult as it no doubt was—unlike that of the McCollum family, took place in a changed technological environment. After the situation erupted in Cranston, Rhode Island, online secular communities jumped into action with an outpouring of support for Jessica. On Facebook, a new group was formed—Support the Removal of the Cranston High School West Prayer—drawing thousands of members. Secular groups like the AHA and the SCA spread word about the controversy, and bloggers quickly picked up on it. Before long, Jessica was well-known throughout the secular community, sharing her experience and finding support from other secular teens and adults. If she was going to face the wrath of angry locals intent on imposing their religious sentiments on public school students, something no young student should have to withstand, at least she did so knowing that she had the strong, visible support of thousands.

The Internet and instant electronic communication made it possible for Jessica to find solidarity with others who share her views about church-state separation and secularity, including other teens in other parts of the country who were simultaneously going through similar experiences. In Louisiana, for example, at about the same time Jessica was filing her lawsuit in Rhode Island, a student named Damon Fowler was at the center of a storm over church-state separation. Damon's school, Bastrop High, was planning on having a prayer as part of its graduation ceremony, but Damon, an atheist, told school administrators that he objected to the practice. Damon is on solid legal ground, as the United States Supreme Court had ruled graduation ceremony prayers unconstitutional in the case of *Lee v. Weisman* (1992), a decision so directly on point that one wonders why Damon would find himself in a position of having to inform school administrators that the practice of graduation prayers is unlawful. The opinion, by Justice Kennedy, makes it clear that a prayer, even an apparently nonsectarian prayer, at a public school graduation ceremony is by its nature coercive:

> As we have observed before, there are heightened concerns with protecting freedom of conscience from subtle coercive pressure in the elementary and secondary public schools. Our decisions . . . recognize, among other things, that prayer exercises in public schools carry a

particular risk of indirect coercion. The concern may not be limited
to the context of schools, but it is most pronounced there. . . . What
to most believers may seem nothing more than a reasonable request
that the nonbeliever respect their religious practices, in a school context may appear to the nonbeliever or dissenter to be an attempt to
employ the machinery of the State to enforce a religious orthodoxy.[9]

Damon was calling attention to a practice that was clearly in violation
of well-established constitutional law. A naïve observer might think that
school officials would have thanked Damon for pointing out the error, but
anyone remotely familiar with the antisecular strands of American culture,
especially in the Bible Belt, knows better. For attempting to respect the
Constitution, Damon was subjected to the kind of treatment that prior
church-state activists have experienced—threats, harassment, bullying,
and ostracism. Even his parents joined in the reaction, reportedly throwing
his belongings onto the front porch and kicking him out of the house.[10]

And after all of this, Damon's class went ahead with a prayer anyway.
In a video that was posted publicly, the Bastrop High School class is seen
loudly cheering in defiance as one of its students, who was supposed to
be leading the class in a moment of silence at Class Night, instead recited a Christian prayer. After she finished the prayer, the room erupted
in celebration, as if somehow the religious recitation was a victory for the
forces of good. Because the prayer had been conducted by a student without official permission, school administrators were able to claim that the
exercise was not part of the official agenda, thereby maintaining plausible
deniability in the face of accusations that the prayer was conducted with
their permission. There has been no indication, however, that the student
who led the prayer, supposedly against instructions of the administration,
was disciplined in any way.

Despite the mistreatment, Damon, like Jessica, quickly found himself
with a significant pool of support via the online secular community. Secular websites such as *Pharyngula*, a popular blog by P. Z. Myers, a biology
professor and outspoken atheist, and *The Friendly Atheist*, another well-
read site hosted by Hemant Mehta, a math teacher and longtime secular
activist, gave Damon's ordeal a high profile, enlisting readers to write to
school administrators and register their objections to the school's shameful

treatment of a secular student. These websites and others also helped raise over $30,000 in scholarship money for Damon.

The tactic used by the pro-prayer crowd in Louisiana to bypass church-state separation is not an isolated instance; in fact, it is a trend, evidenced by the experience of another secular student in the South in 2011. Harrison Hopkins was graduating with his class in Laurens County School District 55 in South Carolina, and he contacted school officials weeks before the graduation ceremony to remind them of the requirement that the ceremony be nonreligious. School officials responded publicly by saying that while the school would not include a prayer as part of its commencement, "the views expressed during student-led messages are solely those of the speaker and do not reflect the approval or disapproval of Laurens School District 55 or the school administration." This, of course, could be construed as a signal to student speakers that prayers were being encouraged, that the First Amendment and established church-state law were not absolute barriers to graduation ceremony prayers. One did not need prophetic powers to predict what happened. On graduation night, the class valedictorian took the stage and soon asked everyone to bow their heads and join him in prayer, much to the delight of the crowd.[11] At some point, no doubt, the question of whether such practices are constitutional will be litigated.

Like other recent secular student dissenters, however, Harrison feels motivated by the experience despite the noncooperation of his school community, and much of the empowerment stems from the supportive online community. "I don't regret filing the complaint at all," he told me. "I'm glad I did it. It has completely changed me, in a good way.... I'm reading blogs, e-books, educating myself on the secular movement. I'm talking to people about what it's like running a Secular Student Alliance affiliate, getting in touch with my college about group rules, flyering policies, and attracting members. I'm making connections with people in the movement, making new friends with people from all around."

Activists like Jessica, Damon, and Harrison are exceptional in their willingness to openly challenge the system and to put themselves on the line despite certain backlash from their communities, but they are also representative of thousands, if not millions, of other secular students who are finding pervasive public religiosity intolerable.

In fact, the Internet is even creating a global secular community, as Americans involved in secular social networking quickly connect with non-believers and nonreligious individuals from all over the world—and not just from free and open Western societies. Most Americans correctly think of Pakistan, for example, as a "Muslim country," but social networks reveal numerous Pakistanis, men and women alike, identifying as secular and expressing religious skepticism. Similarly, ordinary people, many of them students and most of them relatively young, from all over the world—Japan, India, Syria, Lebanon, the Philippines, South Africa, and many others—are expressing their secular worldview via cyberspace and social networking, shedding the weight of ancient religious beliefs and finding that there is a global community of secularity that supports them. These people would have been unknown to one another just a few years ago.

SECULAR STUDENT GROUPS AND ACTIVITIES

There is a clear need for secular communities on college campuses, as young people leaving home for the first time find themselves in uncharted territory, working out important life issues and in need of support and community. With religious conservatism so immensely powerful in America on so many levels—nationally, regionally, locally, and for many students, even within their families—many students consider the counterbalance offered by secular student groups invaluable.

This explains the rapid growth of college secular groups, which are springing up all around the country. Many of these groups are primarily social, providing a network of friends for those who choose to live without religion and who value connecting with others sharing that view. Especially in schools where religiosity is prevalent, secular students appreciate the camaraderie of fellow skeptics. Marie, a member of the Secular Student Alliance of Clemson University in South Carolina, who was raised in a conservative Presbyterian home, explained the attraction of a campus secular student group this way: "Almost everyone I meet through sports, other clubs, or anyplace on campus is almost always a religious person and actively affiliated with a group. I wanted a place where I could challenge those beliefs in an open group with other people who may have thought more about it and had different ideas from those I was raised with."

In Bible Belt schools, the idea of a secular student group is often seen as curious and puzzling, so in response some students have hosted "Ask an Atheist" events, where secular students make themselves available to answer questions from students who perhaps have never met an open atheist. At one such event at the University of South Carolina, a half dozen secular individuals told their personal stories, most of which involved a journey to a worldview of religious skepticism that conflicted with the religious beliefs of their upbringing. The student group's faculty advisor, sociology professor Barry Markovsky, is quoted in the school newspaper as saying, "I remember feeling unsupported in my beliefs. It put me at odds with every authority figure and every hero in my life, and that was terribly lonely." This is part of the reason that secular groups, including student groups, emphasize the importance of identifying openly as a nonbeliever: to demonstrate that being secular is nothing to be ashamed of. "It helped to know that love, compassion and creativity were not dulled by my lack of belief in God," Markovsky said. The question-and-answer period allows the panel an opportunity to address issues that are commonly raised about nonbelief—questions about morality, death, and inner peace—all of which, hopefully, helps to diminish the mystery and fear that the public often associates with nonbelievers.[12]

Campus secular groups are not so different from other college clubs. Some host visiting speakers for lectures about topics of interest to atheists, agnostics, humanists, or otherwise nonreligious students. Others host panel discussions, write articles for school publications, display tables at school events, participate in debates, and host social events. Perhaps most importantly, the groups create a secular community of like-minded individuals that is visible to the public, giving the students a chance to affirm their life stance and their identity while giving the public a chance to see that secular individuals are a vibrant part of the wider community.

Today, the nonreligious demographic is the only major category of religious identification that seems to be growing. While about 15 percent of Americans identified as unaffiliated with any religion in the 2008 American Religious Identification Survey, that figure was about 22 percent among those aged 18 to 29.[13] Moreover, even though the secular student movement was doing impressively without major funding, it is now attracting major financial support that is only likely to empower it more.

In giving $100,000 to the SSA in 2011, Silicon Valley entrepreneur Jeff Hawkins, inventor of the Palm Pilot, said he saw the donation as "an essential investment in our nation's future," a means of defending reason and science. "Secular student groups give our youth the confidence to promote secular causes and to counter the demonization of atheists and secular advocates," he said.[14]

SECULAR GROUPS IN HIGH SCHOOLS

Within the last couple of years, the SSA has embarked on a major initiative that could become the most important campaign of secular activism to date. Although in its first decade the SSA focused solely on building college affiliates, it has now begun building a network of secular student groups in high schools. This seemingly simply act—creating groups in public schools for students who are atheist, agnostic, humanist, or otherwise nonreligious—could do more to validate the idea of being personally secular than anything else the secular community has done.

This has religious leaders understandably concerned. "In Chicago, we now have atheist clubs in high schools," complained Cardinal Francis George in the *National Catholic Reporter*. "We didn't have those five years ago. Kids I would have confirmed in the eighth grade, by the time they're sophomores in high school say they're atheists. They don't just stop going to church, they make a statement. I think that's new."[15]

Cardinal George is right—pride in secular identity among young people is new. Ironically, we can thank the Religious Right for making high school secular student groups possible. In particular, we can thank Jay Sekulow, the head of the American Center for Law and Justice (ACLJ), an organization founded by fundamentalist televangelist Pat Robertson as the Religious Right's answer to the ACLU.

Before Sekulow rose to prominence in the late 1980s, religious conservatives had been repeatedly frustrated in their attempts to inject religion back into public schools, as landmark Supreme Court cases in the 1960s had ruled that school-sponsored prayer and Bible study were unconstitutional violations of the First Amendment's Establishment Clause. But Sekulow turned things around for the Religious Right. In the case of *Board of Education of Westside Community Schools v. Mergens* (1990),

Sekulow successfully argued, using free speech principles, that a school district could not prohibit the formation of a Christian club. If schools allow the formation of various types of extracurricular student clubs, the argument goes, then it is not right to single out religious clubs as being impermissible. Since the *Mergens* ruling, Bible clubs and other voluntary Christian-oriented extracurricular activities have become commonplace in public schools across the country.

At first glance, this would seem like a clear victory for religious conservatives who wish to use public school facilities to create a culture of Christianity within those schools. Although membership in such clubs is voluntary, public schools in communities dominated by strong Christian churches would almost certainly see strong Christian clubs, resulting in a potent pro-Christian message and bias. And even in more pluralistic communities, a high school Christian club led by a charismatic student or teacher with missionary zeal could effectively proselytize on public school grounds.

What Sekulow and others on the Christian Right probably never considered, however, is that the *Mergens* decision opened the doors not just for Christian groups in public schools, but for other groups as well. If free speech standards dictate that Christian views on religion cannot be censored, then neither can the views of Hindus, Muslims, or Jews.

Or atheists.

Twenty years ago, it was rare to find a student secular group even on a college campus, let alone in a high school. But thanks to Sekulow, secular groups are now rapidly sprouting in high schools all over the country, protected by First Amendment rights. While many secular students face opposition from administrators when they attempt to organize student groups, they are able to threaten litigation, citing the *Mergens* ruling, to get them to back down. With high school secular groups normalizing secularity, children at a young age can now learn that their classmates and others in the community are proud nonbelievers, with admirable values, who reject ancient texts and supernatural explanations of the world.

Spearheading this effort is the SSA, which now has staff dedicated specifically to providing resources to high school students interested in starting groups. Also active in this area is the Center for Inquiry (CFI), which now operates high school secular student groups through its student arm, CFI on Campus. The SSA reported over 60 requests for applications from high school groups in the first few weeks after the program was announced in 2011, and it is likely that the number of high school groups will eventually outnumber college groups.

The significance of secular groups in high schools is hard to overstate. For a minority that has long been seen as outside the mainstream, as perhaps less patriotic (to those that believe we are one nation "under God"), the legitimacy that accompanies official recognition is invaluable. It becomes much harder to vilify atheists if they are meeting in the cafeteria after school, and even harder to do so when you realize that the cute classmate that you've been admiring since eighth grade is a member. Viva secularity!

Thanks to Sekulow and his efforts, Secular Americans are finally on an even playing field with Christianity in public schools. While it will be years before we see atheist groups in the same numbers as Christian groups, which have much greater wealth and resources, secular groups have much reason for optimism. When ancient, revelation-based religious texts are compared in a fair environment to a modern, nontheistic, naturalistic worldview, the SSA and its members will have little to worry about.

From the standpoint of Secular Americans, the need for these high school secular groups is indisputable. "Coming from southeastern North Carolina," wrote Walker Bristol, a Tufts University student, "I am no alien to misconceptions regarding atheism." Bristol reported that his high school classmates responded with great concern when they suspected that he might be a skeptic, wanting to know if he still read the Bible and prayed. When he was in high school just a few years ago, the idea of high school secular groups was not even considered as a possibility, but now his younger brother and other students were taking steps to form an SSA chapter. Calling his younger brother's work "inspiring," he said, "We need secular students to be willing to stand unfettered by peer exile or parental disapproval. At the high school age, it may not always be best to suddenly and forcefully reveal your lack of belief to your friends and family. Nevertheless, if secular communities become as strong in high schools as the religious communities they might find themselves at odds with, the humanistic or atheistic student will find herself a part of a meaningful fellowship, welcomed and protected in the face of unfounded bias."[16]

HUMANIST CHAPLAINCIES

When today's high school students leave for college, strong secular student groups will be awaiting them in many universities, but in some, there will be another aspect of secular student living available—humanist chaplaincies. Many observers find the very notion of a humanist chaplaincy puzzling, because chaplaincies are inherently religious and many see humanism as inherently secular. This quandary brings us back to the explanations mentioned in chapter 1, whereby humanism can be seen as either a purely secular philosophy or, alternately, a nontheistic religious worldview, or a hybrid of the two. The decision to view humanism as one way or the other is a personal one, but the basic naturalistic and ethical worldviews of the two are virtually identical. When we refer to the notion of humanist chaplains, we lean toward the view that humanism can be seen as religious, though in the real world, even antireligious humanists may sometimes find value in utilizing a chaplaincy. For example, a humanist chaplain can perform a wedding ceremony, just as clergy from more traditional religious institutions, and this is something that even the most hard-core secularist might find useful at some point.

At the college level, a humanist chaplaincy can be a great resource of reassurance and camaraderie for secular students. While a secular student group is heavily reliant on engaged students to facilitate programming and other activities, students naturally come and go as the years pass; thus, a chaplaincy has the advantage of a fixed individual who can develop roots, institutional knowledge and memory, and who has skills to help the secular student community thrive and give it a sense of continuity.

The Humanist Chaplaincy at Harvard University was founded in 1974 by Tom Ferrick, a former Roman Catholic priest who left the church after realizing that he no longer accepted its theistic doctrines. Tom had been the Catholic chaplain at Dartmouth College and, in fact, attributes the intellectual inquiries of students there for contributing to his own religious skepticism. He was one of the first humanist activists I met when I became involved in the movement about a decade ago, and as a mentor, he was (and still is) a great example of how one can live a good, decent life with a naturalistic, humanistic worldview. As a new and energetic secular activist when I first met Tom, I was sometimes quick to voice frustration about blatant religiosity, such as when someone would offer me an unsolicited blessing. Tom, with his usual wide smile, was quick to defuse my objection. "Just remember, David," he said, "that when someone blesses you it's an act of kindness. Appreciate it for that." Of course, Tom was absolutely right, and I've learned to keep that advice in mind.

Tom steered the Humanist Chaplaincy at Harvard through its first three decades, developing a reputation as an ecumenical and respected leader in the religious community of the nation's oldest university. When he retired a few years back, he was succeeded by Greg Epstein, who quickly became an important leader in the secular movement, often emphasizing the value of humanists coming together in community and contributing to society. Greg's first book was entitled *Good Without God,* and in discussing the book he tells crowds that to him, the "good" is more important than the "without God."

Secular students at Harvard derive much benefit from the chaplaincy, which recently opened a humanist center in Harvard Square that has quickly become a hangout and a valuable resource in bonding the secular community together. The chaplaincy organizes community service projects, hosts social events and lectures, and even facilitates group meditation sessions. Epstein has also attracted high-profile names to the chaplaincy, such as Salman Rushdie, Joss Whedon, Seth MacFarlane, Stephen Fry, the MythBusters, and others, as speakers and award recipients, raising the profile of both humanism and the chaplaincy.[17]

Many humanist leaders envision a day when humanist chaplaincies are as commonplace on college campuses as Catholic, Baptist, Methodist and Mormon chaplaincies. Other college humanist chaplaincies have been established in recent years at Stanford University, American University, Rutgers University, Columbia University, and Barnard College, but with hundreds of major colleges and universities around the country, it will probably be years before humanist chaplaincies are as commonplace as their Christian counterparts.

SECULARITY AS A COURSE OF STUDY

Yet another developing area on campuses is the field of secular studies. Starting in the fall of 2011, Pitzer College in Claremont, California, inaugurated a department of secular studies—the first in the nation—focusing on understanding "political/constitutional secularism, philosophical skepticism, and personal and public secularity," according to Phil Zuckerman, a Pitzer professor instrumental in initiating the program. "We are interested in studying the development of naturalistic worldviews and ethical positions devoid of supernatural assumptions." He pointed to the growth in America's secular demographic as an important reason for launching the program.[18]

The secular studies program at Pitzer follows the 2005 launch of the Institute for the Study of Secularism in Society and Culture at Trinity College in Hartford, Connecticut, the first such institute linked to a university focusing on studying the role of secularity in the world, and the 2008 founding of the Non-Religion and Secularity Research Network (NSRN). With dozens of researchers from academic institutions all around the world, the NSRN describes itself as "an international and interdisciplinary network of researchers" aiming to organize research and facilitate discussion about secularism.[19] Outside of academia, an organization known as the Humanist Institute has, since 1982, been providing intensive courses in the study of humanism, a program that has produced many leaders within the wider humanist and secular communities. The Humanist Institute became an adjunct of the AHA in 2011, and plans are in the works to broaden its programs and others like them.

The study of secularity is seen by some, particularly the organized atheist-humanist communities, as long overdue and a natural complement to religious studies. Though some critics claim that virtually all of academia is secular, arguing that therefore a program in secular studies is redundant, Zuckerman emphasizes that no traditional academic programs concentrate specifically on understanding secularity. The idea is not to bash religion but to carefully consider how secularity intersects with other social phenomena. Students in the Pitzer program will be studying historical secularity, psychological and neurological aspects of secularity, and a wide range of issues relevant to the secular individual and society. Since the Pitzer program is something new, Zuckerman is cautiously optimistic. Will it succeed, and will other institutions replicate it? "God only knows," he wrote. "Just kidding."[20]

All of this secular student activity—the popularity of secularity among young people, the college and high school groups, the chaplaincies, and now the field of secular studies—bodes well for the future, as it normalizes secularity, removes the mystery, and establishes it as familiar. Whereas secular students in prior generations may have apathetically drifted back to the family church or synagogue to get married, the solidification of secular identity among students makes other options, like ceremonies performed by humanist celebrants and chaplains, or even secular ceremonies conducted by civil officials, more likely to become the norm in the future. Secularity is now a real alternative, not just a default status for someone who has "lost" his or her faith; it offers a respectable identity and forward-looking life stance, not a stigma that is best hidden from public view. If successful, these students are the individuals who will escort the Religious Right off the stage of public influence and into the chapters of history books.

EIGHT

WHEN "HAPPY HOLIDAYS" IS AN ACT OF HOSTILITY

THE SO-CALLED CULTURE WARS ARE A YEAR-ROUND PHENOM-
enon, but they reach a fever pitch each year during the holiday season (or
perhaps I should say the *Christmas* season).

Because of my role as a secular activist, many people are surprised to
learn that I celebrate Christmas. As I explain to those who ask, I have no
problem denying the existence of God, but Santa Claus is another matter
entirely. Like most Americans who were raised in Christian families, each
December I put up a tree in my living room, give and receive presents, and
enjoy the festive atmosphere of the holiday season with family and friends,
even though I don't go to any religious service or believe any of the theological claims associated with the holiday.

Although conservative commentators would have you believe that
Secular Americans abhor the holidays and do everything possible to ruin
Christmas for true believers, in the real world most nonbelievers celebrate
the major holidays of their cultural upbringing. December in America
means Christmas or Hanukkah for most. Each holiday season, as millions
of Americans mingle at parties with friends and coworkers, they circulate

among nonbelievers and religiously apathetic individuals who think little of the theological undertones of the seasonal celebrations. To most Americans, the season itself is known as "the holidays," and it is a time to wind down the year, share cheer, and remind ourselves of the importance of peace on earth and goodwill toward our fellow humans.

For the Religious Right, that's a problem.

One would expect that, in a pluralistic society with a variety of important holidays occurring at the same time of year, a generalized greeting of "happy holidays" would be seen unanimously as the best way to please all and insult none. The Religious Right, however, construes references to "happy holidays" as a sign that secular progressives are overtaking American society and forcing their anti-Christian agenda on unsuspecting citizens. The Catholic League, for example, initiated a "Christmas Watch List," a sort of blacklist of municipalities, high-profile individuals, and private companies that fail to expressly promote Christmas. Communities that use the words "holiday tree" rather than "Christmas tree" for a tree on a public square will make the list, as will any entertainer who satirizes a Christmas song in a manner considered disrespectful by the Catholic League's leadership. Their arbitrary logic can lead to puzzling conclusions, such as when the group objected to a film called *Black Christmas,* a violent movie released on Christmas day, by saying, "It's not so much the plot of 'Black Christmas' that bothers us—a wacko who terrorizes college girls at Christmas—it's the fact that the [producers] are back again, choosing a title and an opening date to make their latest statement."[1] Thus, violence against women is not problematic to these devout Catholics, but perceived disrespect to the Christmas holiday is cause for uproar.

Similarly, the American Family Association (AFA) has called for boycotts of major retailers that are, in its judgment, too timid in promoting the Christmas holiday.[2] Though such complaining by conservative Christians may seem unimportant to an outsider, because of their numbers they get the attention of retailers. The AFA proudly declared victory in 2010 after it called for a boycott of Dick's Sporting Goods because the chain used "holidays" instead of "Christmas" in its ads. The AFA boasted that Dick's backed down less than 24 hours after the group sent an action alert to 2.3 million Christian activists. "This is a huge win for the pro-faith community," declared an AFA spokesperson, suggesting that any acknowledgment of non-Christian holiday festivities amounts to oppression toward Christians.[3]

Fanning the flames of this victimization mentality is the pro-Christian media. Bill O'Reilly has been known to attack public schools for sponsoring nonreligious holiday activities, riling up his viewers with tales of governmental officials who seem to care little for nativity scenes and other religious symbolism.[4] In a great irony, it was discovered a few years ago that O'Reilly's network, Fox, was selling on its website *O'Reilly Factor* "holiday ornaments" designed for "holiday trees." Once the hypocrisy was revealed, the web page was soon taken down.[5]

But the real irony is that while Christmas has, in fact, been stolen from real Christians, the theft has nothing to do with a secular plot. As O'Reilly and his loyal fans whine about not being wished a "Merry Christmas" by overworked sales clerks making close to minimum wage, they do so in the midst of an orgy of consumption known as the Christmas shopping season. If ever there were an activity that completely contradicts the theological foundation that it purports to promote, it is the gluttonous materialism that surrounds and permeates the holiday that celebrates the birth of Jesus of Nazareth, the simple carpenter who preached humility.

This would be laughable, except that millions of Americans, correctly sensing that something is not quite right with the Christmas season, are quick to accept the absurd argument that Christmas has been hijacked by secular progressives who, damn them, have the nerve to wish us "happy holidays." This senseless logic is more evidence of how America's lack of critical thinking manifests itself.

The contrived "War on Christmas" is just one of numerous so-called culture-war issues, areas where conservative religion clashes with secularity in modern American life. Ever since Darwin published his theory of evolution by natural selection in 1859, thereby requiring the scientific community to fend off the wrath of religious leaders who insist that biblical explanations cannot be challenged, the culture wars have raged in one form or another in popular culture. The Scopes Monkey Trial of 1925, where a Tennessee teacher was prosecuted for teaching Darwin's theories, highlighted the weakness of the creationist position and helped build support for the teaching of evolution, but the strong antievolution current in

America never really disappeared and, in fact, has seen stunning resurgence in recent decades. Whether the issue is evolution, school prayer, abstinence-only education, or one of a host of others, we find a persistent clash of two seemingly irreconcilable views of reality.

Though the real rise of the Religious Right occurred in the late 1970s and early 1980s with the formation of the Moral Majority, strong tensions could be felt before then, with both sides claiming occasional victories. In the 1940s, for example, the first Supreme Court cases applying the Establishment Clause to the states were decided, including the *McCollum* case, discussed in chapter 7, which banned religious instruction in public schools. In the 1950s, exploiting the public's anticommunist sentiments during the Cold War, religious lobbyists succeeded in inserting "under God" in the Pledge of Allegiance to the Flag and in making In God We Trust the national motto. And in the 1960s, the Supreme Court again applied the Establishment Clause to ban school-sponsored prayer and Bible instruction in public schools.[6] All of these controversies were a mere prelude to the much more constant and intense culture wars that occurred after the emergence of the Religious Right in the latter decades of the twentieth century. Not surprisingly, these disputes and many others remain far from settled today, and a closer look at a few of them provides a better understanding of the ongoing differences between the worldviews of the Religious Right and Secular Americans.

PRAYING IN SCHOOL

One of the biggest myths circulating in American culture is that prayer has been banned from public schools. Students are, in fact, free to pray in school, even together in groups if they wish. Only school-sponsored prayer is forbidden, as the government is supposed to be neutral on matters of religion. "Once government finances a religious exercise, it inserts a divisive influence into our communities," said Justice William O. Douglas in his concurring opinion in *Engel v. Vitale,* the 1962 case that struck down school-sponsored prayer. "The First Amendment leaves the Government in a position not of hostility to religion, but of neutrality. The philosophy is that the atheist or agnostic—the nonbeliever—is entitled to go his own way. The philosophy is that, if government interferes in matters spiritual, it will be a divisive force. The First Amendment teaches that a government neutral in the field of religion better serves all religious interests."[7]

Neutrality is very simple, yet the Religious Right insists that neutrality toward religion is, in fact, hostility. Not content with the right to pray without government sponsorship, activist religious conservatives aggressively push for school-sponsored prayer, even claiming that the return of school-sponsored prayer will solve many of the social and educational problems that plague public schools.

Even mainstream pundits sometimes accept the "prayer is banned" rhetoric and express a longing for the "return" of prayer. Writing in the *Washington Examiner*, Gregory Kane, who described himself as "a Roman Catholic, but not a very good one," said in a 2010 column that he sympathizes with those who feel "that America went to hell in a handbasket once God or any mention of God was kicked out of public schools."[8] Kane ignored the fact that children have a fully protected constitutional right to pray in their schools and can even form prayer clubs and Bible clubs if they wish; instead, he equated a court ruling against state-sponsored prayer as having "kicked out" God from schools. In sympathizing with those who feel that the country has gone "to hell in a handbasket," Kane suggested that we "ask ourselves what harm has come from the 1962 Supreme Court decision that banned prayer and Scripture reading from the nation's public schools."[9] Without providing any supporting evidence, he concluded that the moral decline of America (assuming there has been one) is somehow attributable to the court ruling. (In response to this argument, I contend that any moral decline of America might just as easily be attributed to the injection of "under God" into the Pledge of Allegiance to the Flag just a few years earlier.)

A better refutation of this unsubstantiated argument, however, is the fact that most countries with better educational rankings than the United States have no state-sponsored school prayer. In one study, only 11 of 72 countries surveyed (15.7 percent) had state-sanctioned school prayer. The report pointed out that the vast majority of the major countries of the world—including nations from Western Europe, Central America, and Asia—have rejected state-sanctioned prayer in public schools, noting that 8 of the 11 countries with state-sanctioned school prayer are nations with religious demographics that are much more homogeneous than the United

States.[10] If we cross-reference this report to a 2009 study ranking educational systems around the world, we find that nine of the ten top-ranked systems had no government-sponsored school prayer.[11] (Finland was the only top-ten country with school prayer, while one other, Canada, had school-sponsored prayer in a minority of its provinces.)

The area of education provides a useful contrast between the goals of Secular Americans and those of the Religious Right. Whereas social conservatives see a return to state-sponsored prayer in schools as a central issue in the education debate, Secular Americans instead emphasize real issues of education—improving math and science curricula, encouraging critical thinking, and funding public schools. Social conservatives, when they aren't complaining about school prayer, focus their energy on other matters that, in one way or another, relate to supporting religion and have little to do with real education, such as working to water down the teaching of evolution or lobbying to divert tax dollars to religious schools.

THE ATTACK ON TEXTBOOKS

Exceptional academic performance often requires that religious dogma be ignored, and this is an undesirable option for the Religious Right. Religious conservative leaders are well aware that over 90 percent of the members of the National Academy of Sciences—the most distinguished scientists in the country—reject belief in a personal God.[12] This doesn't mean that most religious conservatives won't gladly utilize scientific technology when it becomes available, whether in the form of the newest mobile phone, the latest lifesaving medical advancement, or an erectile dysfunction drug, but it does mean that, when necessary, scientific truth will be ignored and discredited. This is why we find even nationally known politicians expressing skepticism about evolution. Michele Bachmann is quoted as calling those who accept evolution "a cult following" and falsely claims that "there is a controversy among scientists about whether evolution is a fact or not."[13] Only in a society that is hostile to science could a leader of national stature make such statements.

It is in this atmosphere that we find religious conservatives, dubiously claiming to be interested in education, leading efforts to place stickers disclaiming the validity of evolution onto science textbooks. In 2002 in Cobb

County, Georgia, for example, after about two thousand parents reportedly complained about the teaching of evolution, science books were modified with stickers that read, "This textbook contains material on evolution. Evolution is a theory, not a fact, regarding the origin of living things. This material should be approached with an open mind, studied carefully and critically considered." Three years later, a federal judge ordered the stickers removed.[14] Still, other school districts utilize similar tactics. To an outside observer, it is fascinating that religious activists take so much interest in discrediting evolution, while they simultaneously pay no attention whatsoever to other scientific ideas like, say, atomic theory. They obsess about evolution only because they fear it. In a plainly visible way, understandable to even a child, the concept of evolution shatters literal biblical doctrine about human origins, and with it the notion of biblical inerrancy. Their concern is not with scientific accuracy; instead, their actions reflect only a rabid determination to obstruct science when it conflicts with their religious doctrine.

It is noteworthy that the sticker effort was not fueled by just a few assertive activists but by a groundswell of mass complaints about the teaching of sound science. This is most troubling, for it suggests that the problem is not just a few fringe characters but a deeply rooted cultural disdain for scientific analysis, a preference for religious dogma over rationality. It also points to the need for Secular Americans to come together and fight back with reason against such anti-intellectualism. This is not to suggest that only Secular Americans are capable of reason and intellectual endeavor; certainly many rational and highly intelligent voices can be heard from individuals of religious faith. But the marginalization of Secular Americans deprives the public dialogue of an important viewpoint that is aligned with scientific integrity and honest critical analysis. The mistaken perception that all acceptable opinions, liberal and conservative, originate from the camp of theism necessarily gives the advantage to anti-intellectual viewpoints by excluding an important demographic that strongly advocates for critical thinking, sound science, and reason-based policy. This calls out for a visible Secular American emergence.

The attack on science is the most obvious example of the Religious Right's negative influence on education, but it's not the only one. With increasing influence, religious conservatives have now begun a campaign to rewrite history textbooks to reflect views that are more supportive of its positions. The most visible recent instance of this was the 2010 textbook controversy in Texas, where religious conservatives proposed radical alterations to textbook standards in order to downplay the Founding Fathers' commitment to secular government as well as other accepted secular traditions in America. Because Texas is a huge market for primary school textbooks, the effect of its standards goes far beyond its borders, since publishers conforming to Texas standards will inevitably market those same books in other areas as well. Under the new standards, students will now be taught to question whether the notion of separation of church and state is a fundamental principle of American democracy, since those express words are not found in the Constitution. Thomas Jefferson, who used the "wall of separation" metaphor to explain his understanding of the First Amendment, was removed from the list of figures whose writings inspired the revolutions of his era, whereas St. Thomas Aquinas and John Calvin were added.[15]

Such historical revisionism is of course made possible only by the growing influence of the Religious Right, and it again demonstrates how the marginalization of the Secular American demographic hinders rational policy. Secular Americans and others who are appalled by this assault on education cannot simply rely on religious liberals who appreciate the value of reason and educational integrity to fight back. The successful emergence of Secular Americans, as a respected and valued element within the public discussion, would redefine the terms of the debate.

SYMBOLIC ISSUES GOING BEYOND SYMBOLISM

One way the Religious Right marginalizes Secular Americans is by equating patriotism with religion. This phenomenon is not unique to the United States; savvy political leaders have blended the notions of God and country since ancient times. The practical political and military value of convincing a citizenry that an all-powerful deity favors them, as opposed to those scoundrels in the enemy camp, is a well-known and often-used tool of leadership. This tactic, however, is not only useful in motivating infantry and football teams, for it can also be used to keep secular viewpoints outside the acceptable mainstream range of opinions. If "everyone" agrees that God blesses America, then those who don't believe in God must be on the fringes of society. Nonbelievers might be allowed to stay and enjoy our liberties, but their viewpoints certainly don't reflect mainstream opinions or values. And there's no chance we'll elect them to public office.

Religious conservatives pulled off this strategy through three masterstrokes in the 1950s, at the height of the Cold War. This was a time when the communist Soviet Union had emerged from the Second World War as America's main rival, and fears of war, even all-out atomic warfare, were prevalent. Senator Joseph McCarthy had gained notoriety through his anticommunist witch hunts, careers were ruined by blacklists that labeled good Americans as enemy sympathizers, and even the youngest of schoolchildren understood that anything "communist" was bad. Karl Marx (1818–1883), who wrote the *Communist Manifesto* and whose *Das Kapital* was the major work of political economy upon which communism was based, was an atheist who called religion the "opium of the people."[16] Soviet communism was especially uncompromising in its suppression of religious freedom, and to patriotic Americans in the postwar era, the godless enemy made America's religiosity all the more important.

In this fierce anticommunist atmosphere, religious conservatives became influential because religion was a useful political tool in distinguishing true American values from those of the enemy. Religious groups lobbied for the inclusion of religious rhetoric in public life, and they won. The first big victory was in 1952, when they succeeded in passing, with little vocal opposition, legislation requiring an annual National Day of Prayer. In the years between its passage and the rise of the Religious Right, the yearly event was typically kept fairly low-key, but since the 1980s it has become an important symbol for both sides in the culture wars. In 1988, legislation passed setting the first Thursday of May as the date for the National Day of Prayer (whereas previously, each president was free to choose any day each year for the declaration), a formalization that pleased evangelicals who wanted to see the day gain a higher profile. In fact, since the 1980s, a conservative evangelical organization called the National Day of Prayer Task Force, a group operated exclusively by Religious Right leaders (its chairwoman is Shirley Dobson, wife of Focus on the Family founder James Dobson), has been advocating and organizing events around the National

Day of Prayer, sometimes with presidential approval. During George W. Bush's administration, for example, the task force worked closely with the White House to make the National Day of Prayer an event that furthered the task force's mission of "promoting prayer observances conforming to a Judeo-Christian system of values."[17] Despite working directly with government, the group boldly proclaims its religious mission, saying it "exists to communicate with every individual the need for personal repentance and prayer . . . and to mobilize the Christian community to intercede for America's leaders and its families."[18]

To his credit, President Obama has kept the day relatively low-key, with little or no high-profile proselytizing or promotion of Christianity. In return, as noted in chapter 3, he has been sharply criticized by the Religious Right for this approach. Since Obama has taught constitutional law, it's possible that his lack of enthusiasm for the National Day of Prayer simply reflects his understanding of the Constitution.

Most who oppose the National Day of Prayer have no problem with those who wish to observe it, but only with the governmental endorsement of it. If churches choose to join together to declare a National Day of Prayer, that would be an exercise of religious freedom, but by utilizing the government to do so, religious conservatives only prove that their real agenda is to propagate the idea that their religious views deserve special public stature.

One indication of how Secular Americans have mobilized to oppose the agenda of the Religious Right can be found in the secular community's answer to the National Day of Prayer: the National Day of Reason. Since 2003, the AHA and the Washington Area Secular Humanists have promoted the National Day of Reason, which is usually held on the same day as the National Day of Prayer, as a means of both objecting to the unconstitutional governmental day of prayer and showcasing the value of reason. Many national and local secular groups use the National Day of Reason to hold blood drives or do community service, thereby showing that people can take action to solve problems rather than rely on supernatural intervention.

The National Day of Prayer, like many culture-war conflicts, centers on an issue that at first glance appears symbolic, or perhaps to some, even trivial. Many Secular Americans might shrug their shoulders at a government-sponsored National Day of Prayer, thinking it is not worth raising a fuss about, even though they know it is a church-state violation. What we have learned, however, is that the appeasement of the Religious Right only encourages it to more aggressively promote religion through government. We see this in how the rather benign National Day of Prayer approved by President Truman in 1952 evolved into triumphant annual evangelical grandstanding during the George W. Bush administration.

The next major setback for Secular Americans was in 1954, when religious lobbyists succeeded in adding the words "under God" to the Pledge of Allegiance to the Flag. Before then, the wording of the pledge was simply "I pledge allegiance to the flag of the United States of America, and to the Republic for which it stands, one nation indivisible, with liberty and justice for all." To distinguish the United States from its godless adversary, religious conservatives, led by the Knights of Columbus, lobbied hard for the insertion of the words *under God* into the pledge (making it "one nation under God, indivisible . . ."), and a bill making this change was passed and signed into law by President Eisenhower on Flag Day in 1954.

Just two years later, religious activists won another victory when they successfully lobbied for legislation making In God We Trust the official national motto, again primarily as a direct rebuke to the atheist Soviet Union. Although the United States never had a legislatively declared national motto before In God We Trust, the de facto national motto had always been E Pluribus Unum, a Latin phrase meaning "out of many, one," which was emblazoned by the Founding Fathers on the Great Seal of the United States in 1782. Indeed, so many people thought of E Pluribus Unum as the national motto that no one thought to pass legislation declaring it so. The phrase beautifully reflects the nature of American federalism (out of many states, one nation), and as we became a nation of diverse immigrants, it also came to reflect the nature of the population—out of many peoples, one American people. The selection of E Pluribus Unum as the nation's motto is a fine example of the wisdom of the Founding Fathers.

Compare the poignancy of E Pluribus Unum to In God We Trust, a motto promoted by religious interests and adopted during an era of fear. The contrast between these two mottos perfectly illustrates America's descent from the sophisticated Enlightenment thinking of the framers to the simplistic anti-intellectualism of modern times. The religious motto inevitably excludes millions of Americans, and not just atheists and agnostics but also Hindus, Buddhists, pagans, and others who practice polytheistic, nontheistic, or pantheistic religions that do not recognize a single, monotheistic God. Clearly, In God We Trust is an agenda-driven motto that does not represent the sentiments of all Americans.

Having succeeded in passing legislation declaring In God We Trust to be the national motto, religious conservatives now push aggressively for visible placement of the motto as widely as possible, to ensure that all Americans, religious or secular, will be exposed to the theistic declaration as often as possible. A bill in 2010, for example, encouraged the placement of plaques reading "In God We Trust" in all public schools, a move that would cost millions of dollars in the midst of a budget crisis.

When a legal challenge to the In God We Trust motto was heard at the Ninth Circuit in 2007, six groups filed amicus ("friend of the court") briefs in its defense. Despite claims by the motto's supporters that it does not promote religion but rather should be seen as having some kind of secular purpose relating to history or heritage, a look at those six amicus organizations reveals that the defenders of the motto all share a religious agenda. In addition to Pat Robertson's ACLJ, which has been mentioned previously, the others are as follows:

1.   National Legal Foundation (NLF).[19] The mission of the NLF is "to prayerfully create and implement innovative strategies that, through decisive action, will cause America's public policy and legal system to support and facilitate God's purpose for her. We do not merely wish to carve out a 'safe haven' for religion. Nor do we want to go back to some better day. Rather, we want to go on to something greater than we have ever known before." The NLF even discusses how it will achieve its mission by "vigilantly protecting America's legal system from being usurped to ends which run counter to God's purposes." Note that the zealous advocates at the NLF repeatedly claim to not just believe in God but to know God's purpose, a clear danger signal that Secular Americans should take seriously. As if this weren't enough, the group also says it will be "creatively using the legal system to undo the damage

of those who have called good 'evil' and evil 'good'" and "pursuing legal and policy means of ensuring that all levels of government reward good and punish evil."[20]

2.   Foundation for Moral Law (FML).[21] Headed by Roy Moore, the former Alabama Supreme Court judge who was removed from office because he refused to obey a federal court order requiring the removal of a Ten Commandments display, the FML exists "to restore the knowledge of God in law and government and to acknowledge and defend the truth that man is endowed with rights, not by our fellow man, but by God!"[22] (The exclamation mark is theirs.)

3.   United States Justice Foundation (USJF).[23] Probably the least overtly religious of the six amicus groups defending the motto, the USJF was cofounded and is currently headed by conservative activist Gary Kreep. Kreep, who also cofounded the Religious Right advocacy group the Family Values Coalition, bragged in 2011 that the USJF "has been hammering" Obama on the question of his American birth. The USJF did, in fact, file or support six lawsuits against Obama on the issue of his birth.[24]

4.   Liberty Counsel.[25] With ties to Jerry Falwell's Liberty University, this is a public-interest law firm with a serious religious mission. The group operates under a lengthy "Christian doctrinal statement" that asserts, among other things, that "there is one God, infinite Spirit, creator, and sustainer of all things, who exists eternally in three persons, God the Father, God the Son, and God the Holy Spirit." Getting into great theological detail, the document includes statements such as, "All things were created by God. Angels were created as ministering agents, though some, under the leadership of Satan, fell from their sinless state to become agents of evil." It calls the Bible "inerrant" and "authoritative in all matters." Adam was a real person who, by disobeying God, brought sin and death into the world. After relaying much more detail, the statement concludes that "the return of Christ for all believers is imminent. Those who are not saved will be forever separated from God in hell. Those who are saved will live forever in heaven in fellowship with God."[26] Despite being a law firm, the organization couldn't be more overt in its religious mission and purpose.

5.   Thomas More Law Center.[27] This is another nonprofit law center with an explicitly Christian mission. It describes itself as "dedicated to the defense and promotion of the religious freedom of Christians," adding that its "purpose is to be the sword and shield for people of faith" and "to defend and protect Christians and their religious beliefs in the public square."[28]

Together with the ACLJ, these groups represent the "friends of the court" who take great interest in the motto In God We Trust. True pluralism, in a form that sees different groups as equals and deserving of respect, is anathema to these defenders of faith, who are quite uninhibited about expressing their intentions. Their obvious religious interests, together with their admitted goal of promoting religion in public life, call into question the arguments for allowing the religious motto.

In *Aronow v. United States*, the 1970 Ninth Circuit case that first ruled that the motto did not violate the Establishment Clause, the court stated that the motto's "use is of patriotic or ceremonial character and bears no true resemblance to a governmental sponsorship of a religious exercise."[29] It might be true that the motto has a "patriotic" and "ceremonial" purpose, but because it defines patriotism with religious terminology, the motto is also an endorsement of religion that discriminates against nonbelievers. Surely, the fierce religious advocacy behind the motto's defense proves this point.

VALIDATING A VISION OF AMERICA

These issues of government-sponsored religious expression are an important part of the Religious Right's effort to define America, marginalize Secular Americans, and shape public policy. This is why many Secular Americans are starting to see these issues as being far from benign. On the surface, a day of prayer may seem like no big deal, as may a religiously inspired national motto or the insertion of two words, "under God," into the Pledge of Allegiance. But beneath the surface is a consistent effort to assert a specific conservative religious vision of America, a vision that sees Secular Americans as second-class citizens at best. This conservative Christian vision sees itself as the rightful heir to the Founding Fathers, with all other views, even liberal religious viewpoints, as subservient to a particular understanding of God's plan.

To ordinary middle-class citizens who do not circulate in conservative religious circles, talk of America playing a special role in fulfilling biblical prophecy may sound like the kind of beliefs that would emanate from some obscure outpost of religious extremism, but in fact, such views are quite prevalent in fundamentalist Christian circles. The Religious Right even has ways of communicating that would go unnoticed by ordinary voters who are not aware of the relevant rhetoric. In an early GOP presidential debate in 2011, for example, Michele Bachmann described America's foreign policy role by saying, "We are the head and not the tail." To ordinary voters, this would not have appeared to be a religious statement, but Christian Right voters understood clearly that Bachmann, a true believer and not just an opportunistic politician utilizing religion for her own personal gain, was referring to Deuteronomy 28:13: "The Lord will make you the head and not the tail."[30] This passage is interpreted as meaning that Christians should be leaders in society, particularly in politics—not passive followers or disengaged. These are critically important signals to conservative Christians, who interpret virtually all events biblically. This would be less troubling if biblical prophecy called for cooperation, peace, justice, and other desirable ends, but fundamentalist Christianity is apocalyptic, seeing mass destruction and all-out warfare between good and evil as inevitable. In fact, 41 percent of Americans (and 58 percent of white evangelical Protestants) in a 2011 survey believe Jesus Christ will return by 2050, ushering in end times.[31]

Whereas most of us hope to build a world of peace and prosperity, to the believing fundamentalist, the prophecy of Armageddon is an event to be optimistically anticipated. With nuclear weapons now at our disposal, it is unsettling to realize that some of these true believers see their use as probably inevitable, part of God's plan.

The predominance of this view highlights the need for rational viewpoints to have more visibility. If Secular Americans do not believe in the inevitability of Armageddon, if they instead argue that human problems can be best addressed by intelligent inquiry and rational analysis, they must assert themselves as part of mainstream dialogue, and all nonfundamentalists should welcome their viewpoints as providing a valuable contribution to policy making.

SCOUTS' DISHONOR

One culture-war issue that highlights efforts by religious conservatives to define patriotism as synonymous with conservative religion is the controversy over discrimination against Secular Americans and gays by the Boy Scouts of America (BSA). Unlike the Girl Scouts of America, which welcomes both nonbelievers and lesbians, the BSA has strict policies forbidding nonbelievers and open gays from membership or volunteer positions. Founded in 1910, the BSA benefitted greatly during the intensely patriotic times of the first and second World Wars, and the subsequent postwar baby boom provided a perfect environment for the expansion of the group that had become synonymous with core American values. Today, however, scouting is struggling to cling to its patriotic and wholesome image, as more Americans associate the BSA with intolerance and controversy.

When objections to the discriminatory policies are raised, BSA defenders are quick to point out that the issues have been litigated and the complaints have been unsuccessful. The Supreme Court, in its 2000 ruling in *Boy Scouts of America v. Dale,* found that the BSA, despite being federally chartered, is a private organization and, therefore, based on the constitutional principle of freedom of association, can set its own membership criteria.[32] While some still debate the legal argument despite the court ruling, that debate detracts from the more important issue of whether the discrimination is right.

Many people are surprised to learn that the BSA is considered a private organization, because its image is so closely tied to patriotism. Few caricatures are more quintessentially American than that of the Boy Scout, the wholesome young lad who helps old ladies cross the street and contributes to the good of his community. This image has been built in part because the government has nurtured the BSA since its inception, with numerous special advantages that no other "private" groups have seen: free use and special privileges in public lands, free rent in public buildings, government subsidies for jamborees and other events, and other governmental benefits that ordinary nonprofits can only dream about.

Few politicians dare to challenge the BSA's patriotic credentials, but nevertheless in recent years, the group has struggled with image problems and parents have been less eager to sign up their children. According to one source, traditional BSA enrollment steadily declined over 30 percent from 1989 to 2009, going from 4.2 million members to 2.8 million, with consistently declining numbers almost every year during that period despite a growing youth population.[33] The BSA has lost much of its corporate and charitable support due to its discrimination controversies, including the funding of about 50 local United Ways and corporations such as Hewlett-Packard, IBM, Levi Strauss, and CVS Pharmacies.[34] Despite this, national BSA leadership, which is greatly influenced by conservative religious groups, stubbornly resists change. For example, the Church of Jesus Christ of Latter-Day Saints, or Mormons, currently one of the largest sponsors of BSA units, has stated that it will withdraw from the BSA if it is forced to accept gays.

Not surprisingly, many Secular Americans participate in scouting while ignoring the religious requirements, including the theistic language of the Boy Scout oath, which includes a promise "to do my duty to God and my country and to obey the Scout Law." Many nonreligious and nontheistic Americans have learned to swallow their pride and recite such language despite their true beliefs, perhaps interpreting "God" as "Nature" or otherwise rationalizing the exercise.

For those who cannot keep their true beliefs hidden, however, the consequences are harsh. Darrell Lambert, a 19-year-old Eagle Scout from Seattle, found this out in 2002 when he revealed his nonbelief to his scoutmaster, only to be quickly expelled. BSA leaders were unapologetic, with one saying, "It's not discrimination, it's policy." Despite Lambert's years of scouting, numerous awards, and exemplary record, the scout leader concluded, "Anybody who doesn't believe in God isn't a good citizen. . . . If an atheist found a wallet on the ground they would pick it up, plunder the money, and throw the wallet back on the ground."[35] If such stories are rare, it's because most nonbelievers choose to either stay away from scouting in the first place or conceal their religious skepticism. Still, Lambert's experience was not unique, for the BSA continues to enforce antisecular policies. In 2009, Neil Polzin, who had previously served on the board of directors of the Secular Student Alliance, received a letter from his local scouting council that read, "We have received information that has compelled us to revoke your registration. You must immediately sever any relationship you may have with the Boy Scouts of America." Having discovered Polzin's secularity, the local council concluded that he was unfit for scouting, including his job as an aquatics director at a BSA camp.[36]

Many nonbelievers understandably resent that the BSA's official stance discriminates against their worldview, especially since many Americans see the BSA as exemplifying ideal patriotic values. As politicians, the media, and much of the public exalt the BSA for these values, openly atheistic kids are banned from participation. And even while perpetuating the myth that there is some kind of moral deficiency in a naturalistic, secular worldview, the BSA continues to enjoy special treatment from the government and the media. This is why agitation, public information campaigns, and vocal opposition to the BSA's official policies of discrimination are likely to continue until changes are made.

In some places, that change is already happening. Although official national BSA policy excludes gays and atheists, at least some local scouting councils quietly ignore the discriminatory policies. When I was invited to a fundraiser near my community for a local scouting group, I informed the organizer that I couldn't attend because I couldn't support an organization that discriminates against nonbelievers and gays. But the organizer told me not to worry, that the locals didn't pay attention to those discriminatory policies of the national BSA office, and assured me that the local council welcomed gay and secular members and volunteers. Interestingly, however, when a local humanist group asked that same scouting council if it would publicly reject the discriminatory policies, it wouldn't do so. The local council was ignoring national rules by welcoming nonbelievers and atheists, but doing so only covertly so that the BSA national headquarters wouldn't know. Some would say that this compromise is sufficient, that atheists and gays should be content with this effort to include them, but this view overlooks the fact that the local scouting council is failing to stand up to the official, discriminatory views of the national BSA. It's nice that the local groups will quietly accept gays and atheists, but it isn't right that they must sneak behind the backs of bigoted national leadership to do so. Obviously, the BSA still has a long way to go.

MILITARY DISCRIMINATION

Just as the BSA is sometimes seen as a training ground for future soldiers (certified Eagle Scouts are entitled to a pay upgrade upon enlistment), the BSA's discrimination against Secular Americans is a prelude to what can be found in the military. Unlike the BSA, there is no ban on nonbelievers in the military, but frequently the basic principles of religious freedom and equality are forgotten. Secular Americans routinely face overt discrimination in the military, where God and religiosity are important aspects of the warrior culture. Fortunately, in recent years secular soldiers have been pushing back with some success.

In the last chapter, we saw how Lieutenant General William G. Boykin unabashedly portrayed the country's military mission as being righteous and holy. As a "Christian nation," America must use its "Christian army" to defeat its "spiritual enemy" and can do so only "if we come against them in the name of Jesus," according to Boykin.[37] Expressly stating that he sees America's mission as a fight against Satan, Boykin exemplifies the conservative Christian mindset placed in a most dangerous role—that of a military leader. While it would be inaccurate to suggest that Boykin's statements reflect the views of all, or even a majority, of America's military leadership, it would be just as mistaken to suggest that he is some kind of bizarre anomaly. On the contrary, as we will see, the proliferation of extremely conservative Christianity in America's military is widespread. Given the nature of conservative Christianity and its sharp emphasis on good versus evil, both historically and in its future prophecies, it shouldn't be surprising that some men and women with righteous, biblical worldviews are attracted to the military. This presents a problem not just for the nonbelieving soldier who wishes to serve his or her country with dignity, but if left unchecked, it endangers the entire country and even those outside America's borders.

For instance, in today's military, soldiers are frequently given "voluntary" opportunities to attend religious services. There's no absolute requirement that soldiers attend the conservative Christian service, but if they don't, they may find themselves scrubbing latrines for several hours or doing other undesirable tasks. It's not surprising that, given such options, the interest in finding Jesus is almost unanimous. Such anecdotes are common among current soldiers and veterans.

Fighting back against this treatment are two groups: the Military Association of Atheists and Freethinkers (MAAF)[38] and the Military Religious Freedom Foundation (MRFF).[39] As the names suggest, MAAF concentrates primarily on protecting the rights of atheists and other nonbelievers, whereas MRFF defends all aspects of religious freedom, including the rights of Muslims, Jews, and other minority religious groups, as well as Secular Americans. Both groups have been vital in calling attention to the pervasive conservative Christian bias within the military.

MAAF, led by former army officer and West Point graduate Jason Torpy, is quick to rebut the often-repeated falsehood that "there are no atheists in foxholes." At the group's website, there is a list of hundreds of current or former military personnel who describe themselves as "foxhole atheists." One well-known example of a foxhole atheist was Pat Tillman, the professional football player who left his lucrative contract with the Arizona Cardinals after September 11 to fight in Afghanistan. This selfless sacrifice made Tillman one of America's highest-profile soldiers, a great poster child for the Bush administration as it rallied support for its wars. When Tillman was killed in 2004 (by what was later revealed as friendly fire, but at the time was reported as an enemy ambush), much of the nation was stunned. Ceremonies took place around the country, memorials were constructed, and the Cardinals retired his number posthumously.

What was not so widely reported, however, was that Tillman was a Secular American. Tillman was reported to have been very well read, with a nuanced understanding of religion and philosophy, and even his own family described him as a nonbeliever. When Senator John McCain and California first lady Maria Shriver made remarks at Tillman's funeral with religious overtones, Tillman's brother Richard responded by saying, "He's not with God, he's fucking dead. He's not religious."[40]

Not surprisingly, the media, the government, and the public paid little attention to Tillman's atheism, since it was at odds with the patriotic notion of "God and country" that accompanied discussion of the war. In fact, the only references to Tillman's atheism by the military were statements expressly criticizing it. When his family began suspecting a cover-up surrounding the details of the friendly fire incident and demanding answers, a high-ranking officer suggested that they were not at peace with his death because they were atheists who believed that their son was now just "worm dirt."[41] If the military had made such shockingly insensitive statements about any other minority group, particularly in the context of the death of a high-profile hero, a significant scandal would have undoubtedly erupted and disciplinary measures would have been taken. Since the derogatory comments were directed at atheists, however, they were barely reported in the media.

This disrespect toward Secular Americans is what MAAF and MRFF try to combat, though the task is difficult because conservative Christianity is deeply enmeshed in American military culture. A disproportionate percentage of military personnel come from Bible Belt states with conservative Christian views, and the nonconformity and freethinking of nonbelievers are not seen as desirable traits in a disciplined military environment. If the public has a general tendency to believe that religiosity and patriotism are intertwined, that view becomes magnified dramatically in the hyperpatriotic atmosphere of the military.

The problem of military religiosity received some media attention in 2005 due to a number of complaints at the United States Air Force Academy in Colorado Springs, Colorado. An investigation by Americans United for Separation of Church and State resulted in a scathing assessment of the school, finding that "specific [constitutional] violations and the promotion of a culture of official religious intolerance are pervasive, systematic, and evident at the very highest levels of the Academy's command structure." Americans United found that the school demonstrated "hostility toward those who do not subscribe to and practice evangelical Christianity." Upper-class cadets frequently pressured underclass cadets to attend chapel and undertake religious instruction. Visitors from Yale Divinity School reportedly observed one chaplain, Major Warren Watties, encourage cadets at a worship service to proselytize those who had not attended and to inform them that they would "burn in the fires of hell" if they were not receptive. Far from being seen as an unfortunate anomaly, Major Watties was named chaplain of the year by the air force in 2005.[42]

Air force cadets were routinely encouraged by chaplains to "witness" to other cadets, according to the report, in order to convert them to evangelical Christianity. Cadets who resisted conversion were placed in a "heathen flight," a humiliating, segregated forced march back to their dormitories. Even the school's football coach contributed to the atmosphere, hanging a banner in the locker room declaring Team Jesus and telling all players that he expected to see them in church. Mandatory prayers were common at academy meetings, and faculty members routinely introduced themselves to the classes as born-again Christians and encouraged their students to convert. ("I didn't want to be born again," one veteran explained to me. "I chose to grow up the first time.") Christian cadets were given special passes to attend religious study sessions, whereas Jews and others who wished to attend religious meetings had to use their own free time.

Complaints by students were ignored, according to the report, and many cadets reached the conclusion that "mimicking their superiors' religious beliefs and practices was necessary to succeed at the Academy" and to avoid harassment and disapproval from those with the power to punish. The report also found the violative conduct reaching the highest levels, with even Brigadier General Johnny Weida, in his official capacity as commandant of cadets, promoting his evangelical Christian faith. Weida developed secret code words used with evangelical cadets as part of a sophisticated strategy for proselytizing other cadets. The report states, "General Weida has cultivated and reinforced an attitude . . . that the Academy, and the Air Force in general, would be better off if populated solely with Christians."[43]

The air force responded to complaints about the situation at the academy by forming an investigative panel, which concluded that indeed there had been "insensitivity" but no "overt religious discrimination." Air force lieutenant general Roger A. Brady, who led the 16-member panel, said the academy leadership "had the best intentions toward the cadets" and were perhaps a bit too overzealous at times in expressing their religious faith. This, he said, was because it is sometimes difficult to define the boundary between acceptable and unacceptable religious expression. The panel pointed out that 92 percent of Christian cadets indicated that they believed the religious climate on the campus was acceptable, but only 50 percent of non-Christians agreed, a number that reveals a serious problem considering the reluctance of cadets to criticize superiors.[44]

The resignation of one academy chaplain, Captain Melinda Morton, who was a member of a team asked to draft a religious tolerance program, is notable for what it reveals about military attitudes. According to several sources, Morton resigned from the air force after being removed from her administrative post at the academy. Her superiors were upset not at the overzealous evangelism she reported, but at the complaints about it, whereas she saw the complaints as valid. "They fired me," she said. "The problem is, I agreed with those reports."[45]

The military's religious favoritism was apparent in 2010 when the Billy Graham Evangelistic Association cosponsored an event called "Rock the Fort," a Christian festival at the Fort Bragg base in North Carolina. With a stated purpose of converting as many soldiers and families as possible, the event received much support from the base and its leadership despite vocal protests from secular groups and others. In response to the outcry, military leadership eventually promised to allow a secular festival, but when proposals were put forward, the official response was not supportive. Eventually, however, secular organizers were able to get approval for an event in the spring of 2012 called "Rock Beyond Belief," featuring musicians and high-profile secular speakers such as Richard Dawkins. Such an overtly pro-atheist event at a major military installation is a sure sign of progress for secularism.

Another reflection of religious bias can be found in new "spiritual fitness" requirements that have become popular throughout the military. The army's new Global Assessment Test, for example, ranks soldiers for fitness in five areas, one of them being their "spiritual" fitness. "Spirituality" does not necessarily translate to a belief in supernatural concepts but instead could be understood as psychological soundness or strong character. The army defines spiritual fitness as "strengthening a set of beliefs, principles or values that sustain a person beyond family, institutional and societal sources of support" and providing "a sense of purpose, meaning, and the strength to persevere and prevail when faced with significant challenges and responsibilities."[46] This definition leaves some room for a secular interpretation, but for many, "spirituality" is virtually synonymous with religiosity, and even the military itself seems confused on this issue. For example, a Navy web page on the subject pointed out that belief in God is not a necessary element in spirituality, but the image linking to the page was a pair of praying hands on a Bible. Because of Secular American concerns, amplified by organizations such as MAAF, the army in February 2011 published a new order stating that all spiritual portions of training must be considered optional, not mandatory.

If secular military personnel are to avoid being swept up in religious practices and biases, intentional or unintentional, a vigilant defense of secularity will be necessary. With even top commanders showing strong favoritism toward a specific conservative religious viewpoint, and with official criteria for "fitness" utilizing quasi-religious rhetoric, secular soldiers and sailors will need advocates defending the secular worldview in the military environment.

For this reason, one of the highest priorities of MAAF in recent years has been a campaign to allow humanist chaplains in the military.[47] According to MAAF figures, the vast majority (about 97 percent) of the over three thousand chaplains in the military are Christian, even though only about 69 percent of the general military population identifies as Christian.[48] Atheists and agnostics in the military, according to Defense Department statistics, reportedly outnumber Jews, Muslims, and Buddhists, each of which already has chaplain representation.[49] In fact, the actual secular population in the military is quite substantial, with about 23 percent of the general military population stating that they have no religious preference. Only the outdated assumption that "there are no atheists in foxholes" would explain the refusal to provide a humanist alternative.

Unfortunately, military brass has difficulty accepting the idea that nonreligious recruits often have little interest in traditional religion. Torpy, the MAAF president, pointing out that posttraumatic stress and suicide are major problems in today's military, argues that humanist chaplains could help successfully counsel some soldiers in need, particularly those who are not being helped by chaplains from traditional religious backgrounds.[50] Nevertheless, Torpy told me that the Pentagon seems to be unresponsive to the idea. "After nearly a year of outreach by me at all levels, there is little conclusion to be made other than that they choose not to help," he reported. It is unclear whether this lack of enthusiasm for humanist chaplains is merely the result of common bureaucratic inertia or affirmative opposition to the recognition of humanism as a respected worldview. Military chaplaincy status would obviously convey a valuable legitimacy upon the secular worldview, and for this reason, it would not be surprising if conservative religious elements in the military obstructed progress.

With conservative religion so evident in the military, it is understandable that conspiracy theorists have little difficulty concluding that elements in the military are scheming to promote a religious agenda and suppress secularity. Whether there is an organized, conscious conspiracy— or instead, perhaps, just a long-standing systemic tendency to favor religion—is open to debate. Either way, however, Secular Americans again find themselves as marginalized outsiders whose patriotism might be seen as suspect.

In ancient times, references to God were a reliable way of assuring loyalty and motivating a population for war, but one would expect that as humanity moves forward, the primitive practice of equating patriotism with religion would dissipate. A civilized society in the modern world, especially one with by far the most massive military machine the planet has ever seen, surely doesn't want or need a military led by evangelicals who truly believe that the apocalypse might happen in their lifetime. Yet this is precisely what we've got—a military that proudly embraces fervent religiosity as a desirable element. This is yet another example of why the emergence of Secular Americans, as a moderating influence, is so important.

NINE

A NEW PLAN
OF ACTION

THE SECULAR COMMUNITY HAS STEPPED UP EFFORTS IN RECENT
years to raise public awareness of church-state issues, oftentimes through
the courts. The last decade has seen litigation involving each of the three
McCarthy-era religious statutes—the National Day of Prayer, the addition of "under God" to the Pledge of Allegiance, and the In God We Trust
motto.

At the forefront of much of this litigation has been Michael Newdow,
a California emergency-room physician and lawyer, who has filed several
cases challenging governmental endorsement of religion. The best-known
case is *Elk Grove Unified School District v. Newdow,* which, until it was
overturned on a technicality, resulted in a ruling declaring that the "under
God" wording in the Pledge of Allegiance was unconstitutional.[1] Newdow, representing himself, claimed that the wording violated the Establishment Clause, unlawfully intermingling religion and government. To
the surprise of many, the Ninth Circuit Court of Appeals agreed, ruling in
Newdow's favor in a 2002 decision.

Even though the Ninth Circuit stayed its own ruling pending review by the Supreme Court, many reacted with outrage that God might
be removed from the Pledge of Allegiance. Public officials, instead of

responding maturely—perhaps by reminding their constituents that the religious wording was added only in 1954 (many Americans were unaware of this fact) and that surely it marginalizes Secular Americans (especially atheist children who must deal with pledge recitations regularly in public schools)—reacted with a pathetic display of political and religious pandering, with many members of Congress expressing indignation at the court's decision. Representatives and senators gathered on the steps of the Capitol to recite the pledge together, with the "under God" language, sending a message back to their districts that they supported governmental endorsement of religion and God. Even supposedly liberal lawmakers, such as California senator Dianne Feinstein, threw Secular Americans under the bus. "I find the Ninth Circuit Court's opinion embarrassing at best," said Feinstein. "This nation from its foundation has had a belief in God, and has a long tradition of expressing that belief."[2] Of course, the outcry from right-wing commentators was predictably virulent, as were the numerous angry messages and death threats that Newdow received, ironically, from devout followers of the pacifist Jesus.

Unfortunately for Newdow, Secular Americans, and the Constitution, when the case went up to the Supreme Court, the Ninth Circuit's ruling was reversed on a technicality—specifically, on grounds that Newdow, as a noncustodial parent of his school-aged daughter at the time, lacked standing to bring the case. Ever persistent, Newdow brought the case again with new plaintiffs so that the standing issue was no longer a factor, but when it got to the Ninth Circuit the second time, the court—no doubt recalling the public outcry in response to its earlier decision—ruled differently. In a two-to-one decision in March 2010, the court reversed itself and said that the "under God" wording did not violate the Establishment Clause.[3] Newdow appealed to the Supreme Court, but this time he was denied a hearing.

Newdow has filed other Establishment Clause cases over the last decade as well, challenging "under God" in other judicial circuits, challenging the In God We Trust motto, and raising other objections to religiosity in government. His efforts, as well as those of a secular group from Wisconsin known as the Freedom from Religion Foundation (FFRF), have led to some of the highest-profile Establishment Clause litigation in recent years. Most of this litigation hasn't borne fruit, however, as the modern federal judiciary has tended to reaffirm governmental religiosity and view the rights of Secular Americans dismissively.

FFRF's most significant Establishment Clause case, *Hein v. FFRF,* resulted in a 2007 ruling by the Supreme Court that struck a significant blow against church-state separation.[4] In the case, FFRF challenged the Bush administration's executive order establishing so-called faith-based initiatives, a policy that directed millions of dollars annually to religious organizations to enable them to deliver social services. Many Americans were concerned that this financial arrangement crossed the line of church-state separation, enabling religious institutions to use the government as a cash cow. Not surprisingly, conservative Christian religious organizations were by far the largest beneficiaries, and there were numerous concerns that money from the program was being used not just for delivering social services but also for proselytizing and other religious purposes.

To bring a lawsuit, however, a plaintiff must establish that he or she has standing, which usually means that he or she alleges harm caused by the defendant's actions. As a general rule, status as an ordinary taxpayer does not confer the right to sue the government, because such "taxpayer standing" would open the door for lawsuits challenging virtually every action taken by the government. An exception to the taxpayer standing rule exists for Establishment Clause cases, however, because the courts recognize that there is often no way of challenging Establishment Clause violations otherwise. If a town erects a religious symbol on its green, for example, it would often be difficult for a citizen to challenge it without taxpayer standing.

In bringing their case challenging the faith-based initiatives program, FFRF and other plaintiffs claimed taxpayer standing. But when the case got to the Supreme Court, in a five-to-four plurality vote, the court dismissed the plaintiffs' claim on grounds that the exception for taxpayer standing applied only to cases that challenged legislative governmental action, not actions taken by the executive branch. In his dissent, Justice David Souter said that there is no basis for drawing a distinction between executive and legislative action for standing purposes and that "every taxpayer can claim a personal constitutional right not to be taxed for the support of a religious institution."[5] The clear signal from the plurality, however, was that Establishment Clause challenges will be viewed skeptically by the conservative court. The flow of federal tax dollars to churches continues in the Obama administration under the name Faith-Based and Neighborhood Partnerships.

In 2011, FFRF was struck another serious blow in its efforts to enforce the Establishment Clause. A year earlier, in the case of *FFRF v. Obama*, FFRF had won a great victory when it obtained a ruling from a federal district judge that the National Day of Prayer was an unconstitutional violation of the Establishment Clause. In its ruling, the court said, "Its sole purpose is to encourage all citizens to engage in prayer, an inherently religious exercise that serves no secular function in this context. In this instance, the government has taken sides on a matter that must be left to individual conscience. When the government associates one set of religious beliefs with the state and identifies nonadherents as outsiders, it encroaches upon the individual's decision about whether and how to worship." Secular Americans and others who value church-state separation celebrated this victory, but the celebration was short-lived. When the case was appealed to the Seventh Circuit, the court ruled against FFRF in April 2011, again on standing grounds.[6]

The unmistakable message from federal courts in recent years is that Establishment Clause plaintiffs are navigating unfriendly waters. The general trend is toward a narrower, less separationist view of the Establishment Clause, with federal courts increasingly upholding the mix of government and religion, frequently interpreting standing rules to bar plaintiffs from even arguing their claims.

ANTI-SECULAR JUDGES

Since Ronald Reagan took office with the help of the Religious Right in 1981, the federal courts at all levels have seen an influx of conservative judges with great tolerance for governmental religiosity. During that time period, a legal movement known as "originalism" has grown from obscurity to become an influential jurisprudential philosophy, including in the Supreme Court. Originalism became popular largely through the work of a conservative legal group known as the Federalist Society, which was formed in 1982 in response to what was seen as a liberal bias in American law schools and the judiciary. The group's earliest supporters included notorious conservatives such as Robert Bork, Edwin Meese, and perhaps most notably, Antonin Scalia, who joined the Supreme Court in 1986.

An originalist, in theory, seeks to interpret the Constitution by looking almost exclusively to the original intent of the drafters, usually by considering only the literal text of the document. For this reason, originalists object to the notion that the Constitution holds a fundamental right to privacy, for example, because no such right is literally expressed in the Constitution. Since a woman's right to an abortion under the landmark 1973 case of *Roe v. Wade* is based on the fundamental right to privacy, most originalists see *Roe* as bad law and would like to overturn it. But this hardly conveys the true radical nature of originalism. The right to privacy was also key to the 1965 case of *Griswold v. Connecticut*,[7] which ruled that states cannot outlaw the use of birth control. And it goes further. While it may not be surprising to learn that originalists see no basis for constitutional protections for gay rights, it gives one pause to consider that even desegregation rulings, such as the 1954 *Brown v. Board of Education*[8] decision that declared "separate but equal" to be unconstitutional, as well as rulings protecting women's equality, are also suspect from an originalist view.

When conservatives pitch originalism, nostalgic sentiments may sometimes give some appeal to the idea of turning the clock back to the time of the framers. Still, one must consider whether eighteenth-century standards are a sensible approach in modern society. The practice of flogging, for example, was legal and acceptable well into the nineteenth century, and under an originalist interpretation of the Constitution would not be deemed to be unconstitutionally cruel and unusual. Maybe, as musician Billy Joel once remarked, the good old days weren't always so good.

One important point to bear in mind when considering originalism is that even the Constitution itself is not today what it was over two centuries ago when the framers drafted it. Most importantly, the Fourteenth Amendment, adopted in 1868 shortly after the Civil War, now makes the fundamental protections of the Bill of Rights applicable to the states. So while a literal reading of the section of the First Amendment declaring that "Congress shall make no law respecting an establishment of religion, or prohibiting the free exercise thereof" would seem to apply only to federal legislation (because it specifies that *Congress* shall make no law), the

Fourteenth Amendment applies these protections to the states as well. This notion would have been foreign to the founding generation, and in fact, in the early years of the Republic, many states had established religions. Those established religions were discontinued by the states voluntarily, not by the federal Constitution. Thus, an originalist approach to the Constitution does not resolve questions of governmental religiosity at the state level, because one still must consider how the Fourteenth Amendment, adopted long after the framers were dead, affects the issue.

Most conservative legal scholars simply argue for an extremely limited view of the Establishment Clause, but an outside observer can only speculate as to whether such views are rooted in sincere application of originalist judicial philosophy or a more outcome-oriented personal sympathy for governmental religiosity. Some judges, however, such as Supreme Court Justice Clarence Thomas, take a more radical stance, arguing that the Fourteenth Amendment doesn't even apply the Establishment Clause to state and local governments.[9] Under this sentimental view, governmental religiosity at the state and municipal level would know almost no limits. Not only would the state of Connecticut be free to once again use citizens' tax dollars to support the Congregational Church, but with successful lobbying, the Church of Scientology could become the established church of California or any other state. Given the influence and resources of many religious institutions, such developments wouldn't be as outrageous as they may seem at first glance, as only a few more votes on the Supreme Court prevent them from becoming realistic possibilities.

When Justice Scalia joined the Supreme Court in 1986, he was often a lone wolf. In his early days on the bench, Scalia developed a reputation as a vocal dissenter and uncompromising contrarian, often in philosophical isolation and known for venomous rhetoric. A devout Catholic who criticizes his church only when it exhibits hints of liberalism or modernism, Scalia is a social conservative whose antisecular opinions have, not surprisingly, endeared him to fundamentalist Protestants. He has defended their right to teach creationism in schools, for example, and has forcefully argued that government should subsidize the education of divinity students. While Scalia's aggressive style hasn't changed, his status as lone wolf certainly has, for the last three decades have seen the Federalist Society and the conservative movement in general produce a population of judges who make Scalia's views appear almost mainstream. Such judges can be found not only throughout the lower levels of the federal judiciary, but also on the Supreme Court, where Scalia is now often in the majority, joined by Clarence Thomas, Samuel Alito, and the court's chief justice, John Roberts, all of whom have originalist sympathies and Federalist Society connections.[10]

The legal setbacks of the last decade—with high-profile court decisions against secular positions in cases such as *FFRF v. Obama, Hein v. FFRF,* and *Elk Grove Unified School District v. Newdow*—are a clear indication that federal courts are not rolling out a welcome mat for the emerging secular demographic. With the federal courts so hostile to church-state separation and the rights of nonbelievers, a new approach is needed. Secular Americans have come to realize that they can no longer rely on the Establishment Clause alone to protect their rights.

A NEW LEGAL STRATEGY

In light of the string of federal court decisions that have thwarted attempts by Secular Americans to enforce the Establishment Clause, it is clear that new legal strategies must be considered, that the old way of thinking will no longer work. At the AHA's Appignani Humanist Legal Center, we developed an approach that is inspired, strangely enough, by the successes of both the Religious Right and the LGBT community.

As discussed in chapter 7, through careful strategizing the Religious Right found a way to overcome the Establishment Clause obstacle in public schools, and because of this, religious clubs are commonplace in public schools today, especially in communities with large, engaged conservative Christian populations. Like the Religious Right a generation ago, today's secular community is in need of a new approach to its legal challenges. With the Establishment Clause becoming less effective and federal courts less welcoming, it has become imperative to find a better strategy.

One possible answer is to look to the success of the LGBT community. In a 2003 Massachusetts case, *Goodridge v. Department of Public Health,*[11] same-sex couples successfully argued, not under federal law but instead under the Massachusetts state constitution, that their state constitutional rights were violated by the government's refusal to grant them marriage licenses. Due process and equal protection guarantees of the state constitution, the *Goodridge* plaintiffs argued, prohibited the state from denying same-sex couples the right to marry. The court agreed, and the *Goodridge* decision became a landmark precedent, legalizing same-sex marriage for the first time in America. Even though the decision applied only in Massachusetts, it immediately opened a nationwide debate on same-sex marriage and began a trend that has seen same-sex marriage become legal in several more jurisdictions. Some polls now indicate that popular opinion on gay marriage has finally reached a majority level, clearly showing that society is moving toward acceptance of gays and lesbians.[12] This trend is seen in the 2011 repeal of the military's long-standing "don't ask, don't tell" policy, finally allowing gay and lesbian service members to step out of the closet. All of this is the result of a movement for LGBT acceptance that has been ongoing for decades, a struggle that has made massive strides despite opposition that frequently is extremely bitter. The *Goodridge* decision was a key milestone in that struggle, a catalyst for much of the progress over the last decade.

It would be an overstatement to claim that the *Goodridge* case is responsible for all of the recent successes that the LGBT movement has seen, as clearly the movement had been making steady progress for decades, but it would be just as mistaken to downplay the breakthrough importance of the case. It was indeed a pivotal moment. Whereas before *Goodridge* most public debates about gay and lesbian couples centered around the question of whether civil unions should be permitted, suddenly after *Goodridge* the notion of civil unions was more frequently the "conservative" position taken by those who argued against gay marriage.

The AHA's new legal strategy is modeled after the *Goodridge* case. To understand the implications of this, it is important to first consider the rather strange nature of Establishment Clause jurisprudence. Most minorities claiming discrimination—racial minorities, ethnic minorities, and women, for example—pursue their rights through the courts by claiming equal protection. They allege that they are members of a class of people who historically have been discriminated against, that in fact they are now being discriminated against, and that the court should provide a remedy for that discrimination. Religious minorities, however, have rarely pursued their rights via this equal protection avenue, even though such protection is generally considered to be available. Instead, religious minorities have usually ignored or downplayed those arguments and enforced their legal rights via the First Amendment—specifically for atheist-humanist plaintiffs, the Establishment Clause. There are several reasons for this, but the most obvious one is that the First Amendment's religion language attracts attorneys and judges toward those arguments. From a constitutional standpoint, plaintiffs claiming discrimination based on race or gender have no place to turn other than equal protection and due process, so those cases naturally gravitate to those arguments. Plaintiffs claiming religious discrimination, however, have a deep pool of religion-oriented jurisprudence within the First Amendment, with express constitutional religion language and extensive case law directly addressing religion and religious freedom. As such, plaintiffs and courts in cases involving religious minorities have rarely pursued equal protection arguments, strongly preferring instead the familiar territory of the First Amendment's religion language.

Though the Establishment Clause has historically proved to be an effective legal tool, modern plaintiffs should be aware of its limitations. Not only are federal courts interpreting it narrowly, but it lacks the identity-oriented focus that accompanies traditional equal protection cases. Consider, for example, that even a devout Christian can bring an Establishment Clause case to remove a Christian symbol from a public park. In fact, this is exactly what happened in the case of *Salazar v. Buono,* a 2010 Supreme Court case in which a Christian plaintiff, who happened to believe in church-state separation, sued for removal of a Christian cross from a national park. Interviewed on *Religion & Ethics Newsweekly* on PBS in 2009, the plaintiff Buono is quoted as saying, "I want the cross on every Catholic church. I want the cross in my home. But I don't want the cross to be permanently placed on federal government public lands or any other public lands for that matter."[13] Thus, issues of identity and discrimination are not necessarily relevant elements in Establishment Clause cases; instead, the central issue is more impersonal, considering only whether the state has committed a technical violation through government-religion commingling.

By contrast, an equal protection argument makes the plaintiff's identity a central issue, because to prove the case the plaintiff must establish membership in a "suspect class" (that is, a class of people, such as a racial group, who are understood to be frequent targets of discrimination). Unlike with many Establishment Clause scenarios, equal protection plaintiffs almost always come before the court declaring their class identity and demanding that the government stop discriminating against them. For these reasons, one can see how notions of pride—black pride, gay pride, and so forth—are often associated with struggles for equality, because a key motivating factor behind the activism, whether a lawsuit or a march down Main Street, is personal identity.

It is precisely this identity-oriented element that the secular movement lacked for so long. Whereas the LGBT movement was fueling itself with pride, encouraging its members to "come out" to family, friends, and coworkers, most Secular Americans were still largely invisible. The majority was more ambivalent about religion than affirmatively nonreligious, and many identified by default with the religion of their upbringing. Moreover, by utilizing Establishment Clause jurisprudence, even the few who chose to litigate found themselves in lawsuits that downplayed the importance of their identity and rarely made an issue of the institutional discrimination against them.

That is what the AHA's new legal strategy seeks to change. Taking a lesson from both the Religious Right (by setting aside traditional arguments in favor of a different legal theory) and the LGBT movement (by utilizing the equal rights clause of the Massachusetts Constitution), a Massachusetts lawsuit was filed in 2010 seeking a declaration that the rights of humanist and atheist families are violated by the enforcement of a state law requiring daily recitation in public schools of the Pledge of Allegiance to the Flag's "under God" wording. The suit asks the court to order that either the original version of the pledge without the "under God" language be used, or that no pledge be said at all. As of this writing, the case is still pending, but an early ruling in the case gives reason for optimism, as the court denied the defendant's motion to dismiss by stating that the "plaintiffs' factual allegations support a reasonable inference that [daily recitation of the 'under God' version of the pledge] violates their equal protection rights."[14] Additional cases in other jurisdictions, emphasizing secular identity and discrimination, are certain to follow.

Though religious conservatives are quick to suggest that Secular Americans who object to the "under God" wording of the pledge are unpatriotic, the details of this lawsuit demonstrate otherwise. The plaintiffs are not trying to scrap the pledge but to utilize pledge wording that does not marginalize them or suggest that nonbelievers are less American than their religious neighbors. In schools where the pledge is recited each morning, Secular American children are being told in a formal school ceremony that the religious views of their family are simply wrong, that the nation is, in fact, under God. Never mind what Mom or Dad say about the issue, because belief in God is patriotic; if you believe otherwise, your credentials as a good American might be suspect.

This is a real-life dilemma for many secular families—one that no family should be forced to confront. Decent, hardworking, taxpaying families are seeing their children indoctrinated into a particular theological view. One Secular American father described to me the confusion raised by his six-year-old daughter, who came home from school with questions. "She's a confident little girl and she knows that we are good citizens," he explained. "But she takes words seriously, and she was obviously troubled by the fact that the school was saying one thing and her parents were saying another." In this situation, he and his wife gave their daughter the assurances she needed, explaining a bit of the history of the pledge and the reasons for the wording, but they nevertheless resent that, on a daily basis in school, she must confront a religious truth claim that contradicts their family's beliefs. "Why should my child go to school every day to be told by the school, in an official flag-salute ceremony with teachers and classmates, that the religious views we've been teaching her are wrong?" the father asked. "We teach her good values, right from wrong. She's a good girl, and her family's religion shouldn't be disparaged by her school." The mother expressed concern that the "under God" wording strongly implies that nonbelievers are less patriotic than those who believe. "This is a patriotic exercise, let's be clear about that," she said. "So if this official patriotic ceremony, conducted every day with hand over heart, declares that our country is under God, then obviously the inference is that true patriots must believe in God. That's always made me uneasy, but now that my kids are getting to school age it really worries me."

Secular Americans such as these have every right to demand equal protection under the law. And they are finally doing it.

THE NEED FOR POPULAR SUPPORT

Legal battles will inevitably be part of any movement for rights and equality, but it's important to keep in mind that sometimes they bring unintended consequences.

Prior to 1973, the general trend in America was toward the liberalization of abortion laws. With the Supreme Court's ruling in *Roe v. Wade*, however, the social and political dynamic changed dramatically, and there is little doubt that the court decision helped to enable the formation of the Moral Majority later in the decade. In those formative years of the Religious Right, it was the abortion issue, and the *Roe* ruling in particular, that energized many, and in fact the issue continues to be the main obsession of many conservative activists. In hindsight, it is uncertain whether the Religious Right would have mushroomed into the force it became if the liberalization of abortion laws had been allowed to continue gradually, and democratically, through legislative measures. Raising this question necessarily raises numerous other issues, perhaps most importantly the question of whether it is ever wise to refrain from pursuing a successful judicial outcome if it seems within reach. Though a comprehensive analysis of the abortion issue is outside our parameters, the question is raised here because it is an example of an unintended consequence—one, in fact, that has direct relevance to the secular community, since that unintended consequence was the formation of the Religious Right.

It is a well-known fact that major court decisions tend to rally those who object to them to social and political action, but that doesn't mean Secular Americans would prefer to be on the losing side of important lawsuits. Most Secular Americans will gladly welcome decisions such as *Engel v. Vitale,* the 1962 Supreme Court ruling banning school-sponsored prayer; *Abington School District v. Schempp,* the 1963 ruling banning mandatory Bible reading in public schools; and even cases such as *Griswold* and *Roe,* which are not inherently religious cases but which challenge the standards of conservative religion. Nevertheless, Secular Americans should be mindful of the sometimes negative impact of judicial victories and the obvious advantages that come with straightforward, legislative victories driven by popular support.

This is another reason why the organization of the Secular American demographic into a coherent, recognizable segment of the population, and the electorate, is so important. Progressive policy victories, whether judicial or legislative, are not safe so long as there is a massively powerful, organized segment of the population working to overturn them. As such, with Secular Americans being a potent answer to politically active religious conservatism, popular recognition of the legitimacy of the secular demographic should be seen as a necessary prerequisite to long-term progress.

David Habecker, a town trustee from Estes Park, Colorado, found out the hard way that the general public has very little respect for secularity. Having served in office for 12 years, Habecker was surprised in 2004 when the town trustees decided to begin their meetings with a recitation of the Pledge of Allegiance. He participated in the ceremony for a few months but finally decided that he would no longer do so. A self-described agnostic, he objected to the "under God" wording of the pledge and to the notion of publicly pledging loyalty in general. His nonparticipation quickly became a local controversy, and his opponents were soon at work to demonize him for exercising his conscience. He was removed by a recall election in 2005. "This country was founded on religious tolerance," the dismayed public servant said. "This wasn't religious tolerance."[15]

Habecker's experience illustrates the need to educate the public about the legitimacy of the secular worldview and the value that is lost by discriminating against nonbelievers. The popular misperception that secularity is unpatriotic, that Secular Americans aren't contributing to the greater good, needs to be corrected, and the effort to do so is one of the central aspects of today's secular activism. "They said I turned my back on the flag, that I'm not patriotic," said Habecker, who spent countless hours working for the citizens of his community for over a decade before he was removed in a campaign of antisecular prejudice. "They said I didn't support the troops in Iraq, which is completely false."[16]

Because of the public's views about Secular Americans in politics, there is much talk nowadays within the movement of forming a political action committee to give Secular Americans a means of financing candidates who recognize the importance of nonbeliever rights. Some are skeptical that many candidates would accept "atheist money" in a publicly visible way, but others argue that this is precisely what is needed to earn legitimacy and raise awareness of discrimination. Though openly atheist candidates will most likely remain a rarity on the public scene for the foreseeable future, atheists-humanists should at least be able to publicly support a nonatheist candidate who supports equality without ruining that candidate's chances of election.

In fact, there is some evidence that fear-based attacks on candidates for circulating with Secular Americans are likely to backfire. In 2008, incumbent North Carolina senator Elizabeth Dole ran a negative ad against her opponent, Kay Hagan, alarmingly calling attention to the fact that a well-known atheist activist had hosted a fundraiser for Hagan. Even in this Bible Belt state, however, voters disapproved of the scare tactic (although, interestingly, in response to the ad, Hagan felt that it was necessary to publicly affirm her religiosity). The ad fell flat, and Hagan subsequently unseated Dole in the election, thus providing a glimmer of hope that secularity will not always be seen as political poison.

The acceptability of secularity in politics can be viewed not just from the standpoint of whether atheism is seen as poison, but from whether religion is given undue exaltation. Before Americans open their arms to embrace openly atheistic candidates, a more modest sign of progress would be the showing of some disapproval when candidates spout religious rhetoric. When GOP candidate Herman Cain declared in the fall of 2011, for example, that God had told him to run for president, a more rational electorate would have reacted with either shock or laughter—or perhaps both—seeing such a ridiculous statement as a sure sign that he is unfit for the Oval Office. Instead, the statement seemed to have no effect on Cain's perceived stature as a candidate. To anyone interested in rational public policy, this must be seen as troubling.

TEN

A SECULAR FUTURE

WHEN MOST OF US WERE YOUNG, AT SOME POINT WE THOUGHT about what the world of the future would look like. We imagined advanced technology that revolutionizes communication, transportation, and medicine. Dreamers among us envisioned a more enlightened society, a world in which long-standing barriers to harmonious and prosperous human interaction would be finally overcome. Few of us, when thinking about humanity boldly advancing into the future, would simultaneously call to mind images of Jerry Falwell and Pat Robertson, fundamentalist preachers seemingly offended by modernity and obsessed with biblical explanations of the world. Instead, when thinking about humanity breaking through present-day constraints, we would look to visionaries such as Carl Sagan or, for science fiction fans, writers like Isaac Asimov and *Star Trek* creator Gene Roddenberry. Though all three are dead now, it is not coincidental that Sagan, Asimov, and Roddenberry each worked closely with the secular movement, Asimov even having served as the AHA's president from 1985 until his death in 1992.[1] Similarly, there's a reason why you won't find many great science fiction stories with plot lines portraying their protagonists journeying to a distant galaxy to attend Christian prayer services.

Despite our tendency to link morality to religion, in our hearts and minds we know that traditional religion is rooted in an ancient world and that its foundational texts were written by people who had little comprehension of the universe. While traditional religion can be an important link to our past, for many of us it does not represent a bridge to the future. For this reason, today's secular movement looks for the answers to life's big questions through natural, not supernatural, avenues. Though relatively few of us are scientists by profession, we recognize that science—and the technology that flows from it—represents the best hope for the future of humanity. Contrary to what many on the Religious Right will claim, this does not mean that Secular Americans "worship" science, but only that they see it as the most practical approach to reality available. Moreover, to the extent that our vision of the future includes a united human family, perceived barriers such as nationalism, ethnicity, and of course religion must necessarily diminish in significance. All of this points to a future that appreciates secularity as a valid worldview and sees the divisive, revelation-based religions of the world for what they are: the efforts of uninformed ancient men to understand a frightening world.

If we are wondering which worldview—that of conservative religion or that of secularity—offers us the best hope for a grand future, we should picture ourselves sitting in front of a television set with a choice of watching two types of programming. On one program, we have Christian televangelists assuring us that hellfire awaits those who don't accept their ancient myths, but on the other we have today's great scientific communicators, Neil deGrasse Tyson and Bill Nye ("the science guy"), both of whom are recent AHA awardees. Tyson and Nye offer hope in the form of a humanity that harnesses scientific knowledge to build a better world, whereas the best hope that televangelists can offer is a future in which a loving Jesus returns to save believers and condemn all others to eternal suffering. Increasingly, more Americans are recognizing that the naturalistic, scientific approach to reality offers more real hope than that of conservative religion.

THE NEED FOR COMMUNITY

Within the secular movement, especially among humanists, there is often talk of the need to create alternatives to religious communities in order to promote secularity. Organized religion may have it all wrong when it comes to explanations of the natural world, but there can be no denying that it still offers one valuable benefit to many: community. Religious congregations offer membership in a group of like-minded individuals with shared values, providing a sense of belonging that can be both reassuring and empowering. Religious ceremonies provide a means of acknowledging life milestones like weddings, coming of age, and funerals, and congregations also give members a vehicle for doing charitable work in their communities. Socially, they are a forum through which individuals and families can interact on a regular basis, providing a sense of stability and security not always available elsewhere.

For all of these reasons and more, a frequent drumbeat among secular activists is that we must work hard to build communities, akin to religious congregations, across the country as a means of encouraging nonbelievers to come together and establish a visible presence in the wider society. This is not a particularly new idea, as humanist leaders such as Felix Adler were working toward this concept even back in the nineteenth century. Today, some still talk of the need to build a humanist center—a place for nonbelievers to congregate as believers do—in every city and town in the land, with all of the benefits but none of the dogma and creed.

Still, the idea of quasi-religious (or even outright religious) humanist or atheist congregations has never really taken off in American culture, and it is questionable whether it ever will. As a leader within organized humanism, I would be pleased to see humanist centers springing up across the country, but the reality is that many no longer find the traditional benefits of religious communities relevant in modern society. After all, even among believers, only half of the population attends religious services regularly, meaning that even many believers see religious congregations as unnecessary much of the time.

Today, innumerable social and technological developments have provided alternative means for fulfilling needs that were once under the exclusive domain of faith communities. Communication and interaction with others is so easy now, via computers, mobile phones, and other sophisticated technologies, that we need no longer rely on a weekly religious service as our primary means of finding community. The modern lifestyle, for all of its shortcomings, allows people to connect and feel some sense of community without the need for the common bond of a local religious congregation. For this reason, even though the notion of humanist congregations has natural appeal, many secular activists see the idea as a potentially distracting development in the midst of a larger general trend toward secularity that is occurring anyway.

As modern developed countries learn to educate, provide health care, and ensure the general welfare of a diverse population, there is less reliance on religious community and charity. This partly explains why conservative religion so often abhors the modern social welfare state, where the public sector fills many roles once served by religion. It's little wonder that secularity is most prominent in the social democracies of Europe, where the notion of the public sector serving many essential community needs is widely accepted. Even in the United States, which can hardly be described as a social democracy, people often find a link to others through employment, education, clubs, and many other nonreligious means. Understanding this, we can see why most Secular Americans and others, while not always liberal social democrats, often see community as something that can be defined outside the parameters of religious belief or identity. This concept of community bears little resemblance to the tight local religious communities, often determined by ethnicity as much as faith, that were once central to the social order. In many ways this new concept of community is replacing them. As society moves to the future, with or without formal secular congregations sprouting up across the land, Secular Americans and many others will see the modern notion of community as important. This may not mean meeting as religious congregations do on a weekly basis to hear sermons about morality and charity, but it does mean connecting with like-minded individuals and groups to share ideas and interests, whether through online social networks, clubs, jobs, or informal networks of friends.

A TIME OF DIVISION

Since the Civil War a century and a half ago, America has never been as divided as it is in these early years of the twenty-first century. There has always been some conflict in America—racial, class, and otherwise—but nothing as widespread and visible as today's persistent and passionate clash of worldviews. With a nonstop news cycle and a blogosphere that produces boundless information, opinion, and ranting, the warring parties within American politics and society are in a seemingly permanent state of contention.

Even during the social upheaval of the 1960s and 1970s, that strife was at least focused on a few specific issues: Vietnam, civil rights, feminism, Watergate. Among the older generation and conservative elements there was stubborn resistance to change, but the sense of disunity was insignificant compared to the deep, fundamental differences that divide much of America today. With the rise of the Religious Right, enormous pockets of the population have found validation (one could even say philosophical grounding) for reactionary views that see modernity itself as evil, science as a threat, most of humanity as ultimately damned, and ordinary progressive values of pluralism and tolerance as dangerous. Unlike the division over the Vietnam War or the struggles for racial and gender equality of years past, today's culture wars are not focused on one major issue of foreign or domestic policy, but reflect a much more broad, deeply philosophical and theological disagreement over the very nature and future of humanity.

Sadly, even many who are not fundamentalists disparage secularity and associate conservative religion with wholesome, traditional values. As we've seen, the enormous influence of the Religious Right has affected foreign policy, the economy, education, church-state separation, environmental protection, and corporate power; it even spills over into the bedrooms and personal lives of ordinary citizens. That such a phenomenon is happening at this point in history, that a man or woman could conceivably sit in the White House believing the world to be only a few thousand years old and Armageddon to be near, should be of utmost concern to all rational citizens, not just of America but of the world. If this description seems exaggerated, consider that Sarah Palin, whose religious views can only be described as fundamentalist, was on the GOP ticket in 2008, and that candidates like Michele Bachmann, Rick Santorum, and Rick Perry have been serious contenders, at times even front-runners, for the presidential nomination of their party. Many point to George W. Bush as a true believer from the Religious Right, and few rational citizens have fond memories of that administration. It is almost certain that fundamentalists, many of whom will make Bush seem mild by comparison, will be running for the nomination for years to come.

Understanding this, we see that the emergence of Secular Americans is the Religious Right's worst nightmare, because religious extremists have only been able to exert so much influence in American politics by successfully marginalizing secularity. Having thrived in an environment in which virtually all politicians—liberal, moderate, or conservative—pay no attention to the interests of nonreligious citizens, in which the prevailing paradigm dictates that religion is seen universally as synonymous with morality and virtue, the Religious Right trembles at the thought of atheists, agnostics, and otherwise nonreligious Americans being respected and appreciated as a valuable segment of society. For this reason, all of those nonbelievers who are disheartened by the rise of the Religious Right should join the emergence of the secular demographic and openly declare themselves Secular Americans, and believers who affirm progressive, inclusive values should welcome the emergence.

The twentieth century may have been the "American Century," but now the nation looks ahead into the twenty-first century with justified trepidation. America remains by far the world's greatest military power, but economically, it is extremely vulnerable and its dominance is almost certain to diminish as other world economies develop. Popular culture is perhaps America's most significant export, but despite this the rest of the world often sees America as a dysfunctional society that is hardly worthy of emulation. We are perceived as violent and dangerous, anti-intellectual, and dominated by big business, with a quality of life that is materially good but culturally barren. Our rates of incarceration leave the international community "mystified and appalled," according to the *New York Times,* as we have only 5 percent of the world's population but almost a quarter of its prisoners.[2] Americans live in a state of insecurity that is largely unknown in other developed countries, with no guaranteed health insurance, relatively weak social safety nets, and growing wealth disparity that is resulting in the disappearance of the middle class. Whereas European workers enjoy lengthy vacations (with a statutory minimum of 20 to 25 vacation days in most countries), Americans on average must work at the same job for a quarter of a century before receiving similar benefits.[3] The gap between CEO pay and that of average workers continues to widen to perverse proportions, a trend that ignited with the rise of the Religious

Right and its eagerness to work for public policy that favors large business interests and dismantles the governmental regulatory and welfare apparatus.[4] Meanwhile, the public education system is in shambles, the corporate sector has grown into an institutional behemoth that controls government at the expense of ordinary citizens, and there is no sign that real change is on the horizon.

One major step that America can take toward addressing these issues is the simple act of acknowledging the validity of the Secular American viewpoint, particularly its advocacy of reason and critical thinking. The impact of secularity goes far beyond the obvious realm of religion, reaching into political and social areas having no relation to questions of divinities. This may seem puzzling to a casual observer, especially since Secular Americans are a diverse group that does not share one common political viewpoint. It may seem strange to suggest that the rise of Secular Americans would have any discernible effect on America's broad social and political landscape. The presence of Secular Americans, however, can influence numerous aspects of society by delegitimizing anti-intellectual efforts. Just as the presence of racial minorities as respected citizens invalidates racist views that were once predominant, and just as the presence of women in leadership positions makes claims of male superiority seem outdated, the righteous claims of moral authority from the religious fundamentalist camp are quickly impeached when Secular Americans are given a place at the table.

No amount of sugarcoating can hide the stark reality that American democracy is in serious danger in the early years of the twenty-first century. Voter turnout and citizen participation in government are shamefully low, reflecting an apathy and powerlessness that permeate society. Three in ten Americans cannot even name the vice president,[5] let alone other high-ranking government officials, yet a pop singer like Lady Gaga is almost universally recognized. We hear about facts like these quite frequently, but it's time we face them.

Complaints about Americans being uninformed, disengaged, and not thinking critically, while hardly flattering, should not be construed as allegations of stupidity. As author Noam Chomsky has pointed out, Americans in many ways demonstrate impressive intelligence[6]—they can memorize sports statistics, relay details of the personal lives of celebrities, and recall television episodes from a generation ago. However, ask them to intelligently assess the actions of their government, the influence of corporate interests, or the details of any legislative proposal, and you will often be met with either blank stares or cynical dismissals. What this tells us is that Americans have been lulled into powerlessness, a process that Chomsky calls "the manufacture of consent."[7] This dangerous process has many causal factors—the consumer culture, corporate-controlled media, an economy that makes it difficult for ordinary citizens to be informed and engaged, a subpar educational system, the easy availability of distractions, and even natural human aversions to the sausage-making of real participatory democracy—but all of them point to a population that has become inept at critical thinking and protecting its own interests.

Religion is not solely responsible for the intellectual shortcomings of America, but it is increasingly clear that the proliferation of fundamentalist religion is a factor, and the marginalization of Secular Americans further contributes to the problem. Many fundamentalist Christians no doubt have great intelligence, but intelligence alone does not immunize its holder from anti-intellectual tendencies, dogmatism, and a willingness to give more weight to unsupported personal beliefs than to objective evidence. Whenever the role of religion in government is discussed, the correlation between the rise of politically active religious fundamentalism in the late 1970s and the subsequent decline of American democracy should become the elephant in the room. As we see Governor Rick Perry responding to a catastrophic drought in Texas by calling for prayer—a faith-based approach to both meteorology and governance—the damage inflicted upon America by over three decades of the Religious Right becomes clear.

We must ask ourselves if critical thinking is a true American value or just a subject that receives quick lip service. In the twenty-first century, society cannot simultaneously marginalize its secular citizens and claim to value education and critical thinking. When over 90 percent of the scientists in the National Academy of Sciences are nonbelievers but society nevertheless demonizes the secular demographic and favors leadership by religious fundamentalists, the need for change becomes apparent.[8]

MAKING EDUCATION AN AMERICAN VALUE

Of course, not all Secular Americans are college professors and scientists, and certainly even the most rational among us are prone to occasional emotional decision making and impulsive behavior, but there can be no question that as acceptance of secularity grows, the center of gravity moves in the direction of reason and critical thinking. Evidence begins to mean something, debates are more likely to be won on merits rather than sound bites, and groundless conspiracy theories are less likely to gain traction. Mistakes and poor judgments are still possible, but the quality of the overall discourse surely rises as appreciation of rational thinking becomes more prevalent.

Manipulation of the public is as old as politics, and the rise of Secular Americans cannot be expected to eliminate ploys by cynical and opportunistic leaders. Still, such ploys are more likely to be met with strong resistance as the secular demographic emerges. Surely there will be less of an inclination to view patriotism and conformity as synonymous, and there will be less patience for superficiality and anti-intellectualism in politics in general. With all the critical issues facing the country, it's almost surreal that major news outlets devote substantial time to considering which candidate voters would most enjoy having a beer with. Real issues, meanwhile, are covered in a cursory manner, usually with little more than sound bites. Candidate debates are typically not debates at all, but carefully crafted press conferences in which substance is irrelevant and image is all-important, in which the superficiality of the candidates is challenged only by that of the media pundits who offer "expert" opinions that are more akin to celebrity buzz than serious policy discussion. Debate participants are unlikely to be judged by their record or their policy positions, but a silly, insignificant verbal slip might doom a candidacy. Similarly, pundits will conclude that a candidate "won" a debate if he or she quips a clever sound bite.

The emergence of a recognized Secular American demographic will improve the country's intellectual atmosphere, not because all Secular Americans are intellectuals (in fact, some in the AHA like to remind me that they made me president after they decided they wanted the organization to be less intellectual), but because they value reason and critical thinking. To the extent that today's schools prepare most students for anything, it is a life of conformity, material acquisition, and service to corporate interests. As we have seen, science education in America, thanks in large part to the Religious Right, is an embarrassment, with many communities aggressively opposing the teaching of rudimentary science material. Relatively few American students pursue higher education in medicine or natural sciences, because our society instead directs a much larger number, including many of the brightest students who wish to get rich young, toward business and finance. There is no reason to go through the hassle of medical school when you can get an MBA much more easily and make even more money, especially if you land a job on Wall Street or in a lucrative corporate position.

An educational phenomenon known as Channel One News perfectly illustrates how an anti-intellectual society is vulnerable to predatory corporate interests. Channel One provides schools with free use of television equipment, but in return the schools must agree to submit their students on a daily basis to the company's 12-minute commercial programming. So accepting have Americans become of commercial bombardment that few even question this daily in-school television advertising of beauty products, junk food, military recruitment, soda, videos, and computer games. The entire package is an insult to the intellectual endeavor that schools are supposed to promote, a superficial procorporate marketing pitch that reinforces short attention spans and a consumption mentality. The company boasts that it reaches six million teens in approximately eight thousand schools each day across the country. A wealthy society like America, if it had sensible priorities, would have little trouble funding schools and would ensure that basic media equipment could be provided without sacrificing the student body before an altar of commercialism for 12 minutes each day. Such sensibility seems elusive in modern America, however, where commercial dominance is accepted without question and parental activism in education is more likely to focus on ensuring that Darwin's theory of evolution is kept out of the science curriculum.

With the emergence of Secular Americans, education will again become a real American value. Despite being founded by men who appreciated science and saw reason as the best guide into the future, America has drifted away from its Enlightenment principles in the decades since the rise of the Religious Right. Only an affirmative decision to break the restrictive chains of the Religious Right can usher in a renewed sense of priorities. Secular Americans can bring about this change by demanding respect, because a successful secular emergence can serve as a catalyst for building consensus around common, real-world values.

NONBELIEVERS IN POLITICS

One important yardstick in measuring the success of the secular emergence will be the participation of openly secular candidates in politics. Open nonbelievers in politics are common in much of the rest of the world, but for some reason in America, the notion of a nonbeliever making public policy seems unthinkable. Atheist or agnostic politicians have been democratically elected not only in the developed world (including former Australian prime minister Bob Hawke, for example, and British politicians such as Clement Attlee and Neil Kinnock, among numerous others), but are now being seen even in less-developed nations with strong religious roots. In Chile, for example, Michelle Bachelet, an agnostic, served as president from 2006 to 2010.

In America, however, secularity is still too often seen as political poison. Representative Pete Stark of California challenged that paradigm in 2005 when he disclosed his nonbelief, but few high-ranking elected officials have joined him. Strangely, at the same time, Americans are generally comfortable with, and even appreciative of, cultural criticism of religion when it comes from nonpolitical sources—think of the huge popularity of comics such as George Carlin, for example, or the epic status of the irreverent Monty Python films. But Americans nevertheless refuse to carry that cultural appreciation with them into the voting booth. Contempt of organized religion and declarations of secularity are commonplace in mainstream art, music, television, and film, but we seem aghast at the idea that our elected officials would openly sympathize with such popular sentiments. One of the great challenges of the secular movement is to transfer the esteem for secularity that is so prevalent elsewhere in the culture into the political realm. As we saw in the last chapter with the experience of

David Habecker, the Colorado agnostic who was removed from office in a recall election when he objected to "under God" in the Pledge of Allegiance, the public seems to forget its appreciation for nonbelievers when it enters the voting booth.

None of this is to suggest that there aren't atheists in high places—only that they are coy about admitting it. Several dozen members of Congress have privately admitted personal secularity to inquiries by the Secular Coalition for America, but they were unwilling to "come out" publicly for fear of electoral repercussions. This must change if Secular Americans are to become equal partners. Not only do we need more Secular Americans in government, but we need an environment where those who are already there can openly identify as such.

In fact, although we can't prove that there has ever been an atheist sitting in the White House, we can certainly demonstrate that a former Secular American has been elected. Though it is rarely discussed in the media, Barack Obama's memoir, *Dreams from My Father*, reveals that he was raised by a secular humanist mother and, by all indications, was himself a secular humanist well into adulthood. He described his mother as "the kindest, most generous spirit I have ever known, and that which is best in me I owe to her."[9] This remarkable woman, whom Obama clearly not only loved and respected but also truly admired as an exceptional personality, was a religious skeptic, a rationalist, and a secular humanist. At no point in the book did Obama suggest that his mother exhibited any theistic tendencies or beliefs in supernatural religion; in fact, quite the opposite was true. Hers was not a faith in divine intervention in any form, but "a faith that rational, thoughtful people could shape their own destiny."[10] Obama's childhood was rich with experiences that made him worldly, but he gave no indication that he was persuaded by any theology as he was growing up. He opened his eyes during prayer at a Catholic school to discover that no angels were floating about, and he was scolded for making faces during Koran reading at a Muslim school in Indonesia.[11] "I was not raised in a religious household," he declared in his second book, *The Audacity of Hope*. "Without the help of religious texts or outside authorities she [Obama's mother] worked mightily to instill in me the values that many Americans learn in Sunday school: honesty, empathy, discipline, delayed gratification, and hard work. She raged at poverty and injustice. . . . Most of all, she possessed an abiding sense of wonder, a reverence for life and its precious, transitory nature."[12]

Obama's naturalistic life stance was one that he carried into adulthood. He preferred to put aside tribalism and instead view all of humanity as one tribe.[13] When he moved to Chicago to work as a community organizer, he was not a believer or a churchgoer, but when he attempted to engage in community activism, he found that his rejection of religion was an obstacle. With unions so weak, one mentor told him, churches provided the best available institutional base for activism.[14] Still, even seeing this practical use for religion, Obama continued to describe himself as a "heretic" and a "skeptic" who was "wary of expedient conversion."[15]

So we can see that up until Obama accepted Christianity as an adult, not long before entering politics, he was a Secular American.

Despite this somewhat encouraging story, most Secular Americans long for a day when an open religious skeptic can successfully run for office. While many would prefer that candidates not even be asked about their faith, in today's political climate candidates cannot reasonably expect questions of religion to be ignored. As such, Secular Americans would be wise to confront the issue head-on, with the expectation that candidates expressly declaring personal secularity should be accepted by the public. As today's generation of secular students goes out into the world, it may not be long before we see openly atheist, agnostic, humanist, or other nonreligious Americans running for public office.

BEYOND TRIBALISM

Another aspect of secularity that greatly benefits society is its ability to break down tribalism. Humans, like many social animals, have evolved to think and act with loyalty to their social group and hostility to outsiders, and this general tendency still manifests itself today despite the complex human social organization that has evolved through the millennia. Human history can be understood as a progression from clans and small tribes to larger tribes, city-states, and eventually nations. Regardless of the type of organization, humans are naturally inclined toward in-group and out-group thinking and seeing a wide variety of situations through the paradigm of "us against them." Author Carl Coon, a career diplomat and former ambassador to Nepal, in his book *One Planet, One People,* described this phenomenon. "Those falling into the 'them' category are seen as less equal, less deserving of humane treatment, than people in the in-group," Coon wrote. "Ethnocentrism and even a touch of xenophobia still lurk in the inner recesses of most of our minds."[16]

This phenomenon is deeply ingrained in the human psyche and is frequently used by political and military leaders, who rely heavily on tribal sentiments to validate aggression, but it can also be seen in a wide variety of other settings. Sports rivalries, for example, are a forum for tribal expression, where we sometimes see otherwise sane individuals reacting passionately to the outcome of games that, objectively speaking, are meaningless in their lives. Usually tribal emotions are kept under control when the subject is a simple sporting event, but we sometimes see fans develop true hatred for opposing teams that cannot be rationally justified. Soccer riots, for example, have sometimes gotten deadly, and in America we have come to expect violence and vandalism in the home cities of professional teams that participate in championship games. Tribal passions run deep.

It would be naïve to think that we could purge all tribal tendencies from our genetic code, nor would we want to do so even if we could. Still, in an age of weapons of mass destruction, the necessity of keeping us-against-them thinking in check is obvious. Family and community loyalties, both of which are aspects of tribalism, have their place, and appreciation of one's particular cultural background can be an enriching experience, but overzealous nationalism that demonizes outsiders can be extremely dangerous in the modern world.

The us-versus-them mentality fueled by religion is responsible for conflicts between Muslims and Christians, Catholics and Protestants, Shiites and Sunnis, Hindus and Muslims, and innumerable other instances of hateful sectarian violence. To be sure, economic and political factors are often at work in these conflicts as well, but the role of religion in persuading one group that another is "different" and "foreign" is undeniable.

As Coon, who also served two terms as AHA vice president, pointed out, there is reason for optimism: "People are disposed to be kind to people they know. With the information age upon us, we are all getting to 'know' each other. Despite all the conflict and commotion all around us, the prospects for broad-based attitudinal shift, in the direction of internalized respect and even affection for everyone everywhere, have never been better."[17] If human history can be understood as a series of ever-larger in-groups, we can only hope that eventually we will see the world as one big in-group. Compare this practical worldview to that of fundamentalist religion, which often sees internationalist efforts such as the United Nations as evil and a sign of end times. This is not to suggest that religion must disappear or that our unique cultural differences must be discarded in the name of some monolithic ideal of worldwide brotherhood and sisterhood, but it does suggest that a forward-looking, big-picture attitude is valuable in the modern era.

And nothing encapsulates forward, big-picture thinking like a secular, humanistic view that sees the world not through the eyes of ancient men, but through reason and accumulated knowledge. Secular Americans do not claim to have found that elusive concept called Absolute Truth, which the major religions claim was delivered to them thousands of years ago via divine revelation, but the secular worldview provides an avenue toward a truth that, while perhaps less than absolute, allows humans to move into the future with reliable knowledge and hope. Within such parameters, we humans can see ourselves as all of African descent, and we can construct systems of ethics and values that allow for peace, creativity, and prosperity.

THE ISSUE OF THE CENTURY?

A century ago, W. E. B. Dubois made a prophetic statement. "The problem of the Twentieth Century is the problem of the color-line," he wrote, accurately predicting that America's struggle to come to grips with racism would be the key social issue in the decades that followed. A century later, even with an African American man sitting in the White House, it would be erroneous to suggest that America's racial issues are resolved. But certainly progress has been made, and we can reasonably expect that the problem of racism will not be the defining issue of the next century. The country has moved from a culture of Jim Crow, lynchings, and socially acceptable racial prejudice to one in which our laws and social customs reflect, even if imperfectly, an understanding that we are one human family and that racism is an evil. Bigotry is not extinct, and economic and social barriers too often mean an unequal playing field, but thanks to the hard-won victories of the civil rights movement, American society has made huge leaps forward.

Today, as we consider what will be the key issues of the coming century, religion jumps to the forefront—specifically, how to deal with fundamentalism at home and abroad, the tensions between religion and science, the appropriate place for religion in a pluralistic society, public attitudes toward secularity, and all of the numerous issues surrounding the intermingling of religion and politics. As we see with the deep divisions of the culture wars, America's struggle to come to grips with religion, especially the baffling phenomenon of religiously motivated political extremism, is likely to define the country in the decades ahead. All other issues—economic policy, foreign policy, social policy—will be greatly affected by how America addresses the religion issue. Breakthrough progress is possible on the one hand, and unthinkable disaster on the other.

As we look to the future with hope and optimism, few of us think of Pat Robertson and James Dobson as the leaders who will show us the way. Modern Christian fundamentalism is rooted in the past, and it represents a reactionary and fearful response to the challenges of modernity. A bright American future is not possible with fundamentalist thinkers in charge, with men and women who look for biblical explanations for all worldly phenomena, who feel that all human events are a mere prelude to the Second Coming of Jesus, who don't just love their country but feel that it plays a mysterious role in biblical prophecy, who reject categorically the notion that humans can solve human problems, and who believe with every fiber of their being that men, women, and children are inherently wretched and can be saved only by their omnipotent and omniscient creator.

Contrary to popular belief, Secular Americans do, in fact, believe in prophecy—just not the kind that the Religious Right promotes. If America allows itself to be controlled by religious fundamentalists who honestly believe that life can be explained as a struggle between good and evil and that the world is inevitably heading to all-out calamity, this can be seen as paving the way for self-fulfilling prophecy. If the country's political leaders stand with the men and women who look forward to welcoming Jesus as he rides through the sky as the Bible promises, humans will soon be in a position to make end-times prophecies come true, though such worldwide destruction certainly won't be accompanied by a returning divinity.

If we wish to avoid the fulfillment of such prophecy, we should make a place at the table for values that are not biblical, but secular and humanistic. The religious extremists have had unwarranted influence for far too long, and they need to take their theology back to their homes and churches where it belongs—away from the halls of government. Religious freedom is a cherished American value, but religious predominance is not. As such, the outcome of the Secular American movement will undoubtedly be a pivotal event in the American chronology.

AFTERWORD

ANOTHER WEDDING

RICH, LIKE MY FRIEND MARIA FROM THE FIRST CHAPTER, WAS born into a Catholic family. His parents, and every generation before them as long as anyone can remember, had been married in a Catholic church. And like Maria, Rich is a nonbeliever, a secular humanist who approaches the world from a naturalistic standpoint and who has no use for the myth or creed of ancient religion. I've known Rich since he was a baby, and I could see from the time that he was young that he loved science. We had a few conversations about religion over the years, and his perspective was always one of religious skepticism. His worldview was shaped not by dogma, but by reason and critical thinking. As he grew up, he was one of those lucky individuals who always knew what he wanted to do, so it was no surprise when he went off to college to pursue degrees in science and environmental studies.

I was happy for Rich when he told me a few years back that he had found that special someone, and when I met his girlfriend, Darryl, I could see that he had found a great partner; they were a happy couple, and I was happy for them. It wasn't too long before there was talk of an engagement and plans for a wedding.

Rich and Darryl, however, are a generation younger than Maria, and there would be no Catholic wedding for them. When I received the wedding invitation, I had to smile. They would be married by a humanist celebrant in a secular ceremony in a private hall near the campus of the University of North Carolina in Chapel Hill. The chain of Catholic weddings, no doubt going back many generations through Rich's ancestors to Ireland and Italy, was over, and in its place, Rich and Darryl were tying the knot with a secular wedding that expressed their true beliefs and values. Both are young professionals with great careers, and they have since settled down in North Carolina, where they now have two beautiful children whom they are raising in secularity.

Secular Americans have made great strides in the last decade, but the hole in which the secular community found itself after decades of Religious Right predominance was a very deep one. We are not out of that hole, and at this point, we have no way of knowing whether the emergence will be a complete success. If open nonbelievers are being routinely elected to office even in the Deep South in our lifetime, we can declare victory. If the movement fizzles as conservative religion uses its influence to further suffocate the corpus of American public life, we can shake our heads and explain to future generations that at least we tried.

In the meantime, we can only hope. And act.

Unlike with some movements, however, the "act" needed does not necessarily involve marching in the streets or "sticking it to the man" in any way. To promote secularity and fight back against the Religious Right, the simple act of identifying openly, and frequently, as a Secular American can be an extremely effective tactic. We need not convert believers (though, as leader of a national secular organization, I must confess that I'm always open to the idea of debating religion), as we can make significant headway merely by convincing those within our demographic to be more vocal and visible. Like the enormously successful LGBT movement, we can win just by showing up and demanding respect. If the motto of the LGBT movement was "We're here. We're queer. Get used to it!" the motto of the secular movement can be "We don't believe. We won't leave. Get used to it!"

The more we remind our relatives, neighbors, and coworkers that nonbelievers are everywhere, and the more we chip away at the mistaken notion that "real Americans" are believers, the closer we get to victory. The *Goodridge* case that legalized same-sex marriage in Massachusetts contained powerful language that talked about the nature of prejudice against gays and lesbians, but that language is just as relevant to nonbelievers. In his concurring opinion, Justice John Greaney wrote,

> The plaintiffs are members of our community, our neighbors, our coworkers, our friends. . . . [T]heir professions include investment advisor, computer engineer, teacher, therapist, and lawyer. The plaintiffs volunteer in our schools . . . and have children who play with our children. . . . We share a common humanity and participate together in the social contract that is the foundation of our Commonwealth. Simple principles of decency dictate that we extend to the plaintiffs . . . full acceptance, tolerance, and respect. We should do so because it is the right thing to do.[1]

Indeed, most Americans, whether they realize it or not, interact on a daily basis with nonbelievers—ordinary people who work in America's hospitals and schools and malls. As these Secular Americans stand up to identify openly, demanding nothing more than respect, civility, and equality, profound effects on public dialogue and policy are inevitable.

It is important to realize that there are very significant factions that vehemently oppose the changes that would result from a successful Secular American emergence. Social conservatives, obviously, see secularity as inherently evil, and as such will continue to advocate for the marginalization of nonbelievers. Beyond that, however, as we have seen, there are other powerful interests that profit immensely from irrational and fear-driven public policy, and those interests will no doubt see any movement toward critical thinking and rational public policy as a threat. For this reason, all those who comprehend the dire need for change should support and encourage the Secular American movement. If the emergence is successful, the country and the world will never be the same.

APPENDIX

SECULAR COALITION FOR AMERICA'S 2011 CONGRESSIONAL REPORT CARD

For the full text of the scorecard, visit the Secular Coalition for America's website: http://secular.org/content/scorecards.

LEGISLATION

RC 93
Would have eliminated all federal funds to Planned Parenthood Federation of America.

RC 204
Would have expanded federal funding for religious schools in D.C.

RC 236
Would have acknowledged Congress accepts climate change is occurring.

RC 601
Would have amended the Securities Act of 1933 to allow certain church plans to be exempt from registration and disclosure requirements.

RC 673
Would have established a special envoy to promote freedom of religious minorities in the Near East and South Central Asia.

RC 816
Would have reaffirmed "In God We Trust" as national motto and encouraged all public buildings to display such motto.

HR 473
Would have required the conveyance of specified land to the Boy Scouts of America. This was a voice vote.

GRADES

- ≥70% = A
- ≥60% = B
- ≥40% = C
- ≥30% = D
- ≤29% = F

Note: No member of the House received a perfect score because of the voice vote for HR 473, the vote to approve a land conveyance to a Boy Scout council. Due to the fact that the House approved the conveyance by a voice vote, meaning no one asked for a record of the vote, the Secular Coalition chose to give every member of the House a negative score rather than not count this vote at all.

An asterisk (*) denotes that the score is incomplete because Representative did not vote at least once in the scored votes. Two asterisks (**) denote that Representative was not in office for the full term.

State	District	Party	Grade
ALABAMA			
Aderholt, R.	4th	R	F
Bachus, S.	6th	R	F
Bonner, J.	1st	R	F
Brooks, M.	5th	R	F*
Roby, M.	2nd	R	F
Rogers, Mike	3rd	R	F
Sewell, T.	7th	D	C
ALASKA			
Young, D.	At Large	R	F*
ARIZONA			
Flake, J.	6th	R	F*
Franks, T.	2nd	R	F
Giffords, G.**	8th	D	0
Gosar, P.	1st	R	F
Grijalva, R.	7th	D	B*
Pastor, E.	4th	D	C
Quayle, B.	3rd	R	F*

(continues)

State	District	Party	Grade
Schweikert, D.	5th	R	F
ARKANSAS			
Crawford, E.	1st	R	F
Griffin, T.	2nd	R	F
Ross, M.	4th	D	C
Womack, S.	3rd	R	F
CALIFORNIA			
Baca, J.	43rd	D	C*
Bass, K.	33rd	D	C
Becerra, X.	31st	D	C
Berman, H.	28th	D	B*
Bilbray, B.	50th	R	F
Bono Mack, M.	45th	R	D*
Calvert, K.	44th	R	F*
Campbell, J.	48th	R	F*
Capps, L.	23rd	D	B*
Cardoza, D.	18th	D	B*
Chu, J.	32nd	D	A
Costa, J.	20th	D	B*
Davis, S.	53rd	D	B*
Denham, J.	19th	R	F
Dreier, D.	26th	R	F
Eshoo, A.	14th	D	B*
Farr, S.	17th	D	B*
Filner, B.	51st	D	A*
Gallegly, E.	24th	R	F
Garamendi, J.	10th	D	C
Hahn, J.**	36th	D	D*
Herger, W.	2nd	R	F*
Honda, M.	15th	D	A
Hunter, D.	52nd	R	F*
Issa, D.	49th	R	F*
Lee, B.	9th	D	B*
Lewis, Je.	41st	R	F
Lofgren, Z.	16th	D	B*
Lungren, D.	3rd	R	F
Matsui, D.	5th	D	C
McCarthy, K.	22nd	R	F
McClintock, T.	4th	R	F
McKeon, H.	25th	R	F*
McNerney, J.	11th	D	B*
Miller, Ga.	42nd	R	F*
Miller, Ge.	7th	D	B*
Napolitano, G.	38th	D	C
Nunes, D.	21st	R	F

(continues)

State	District	Party	Grade
Pelosi, N.	8th	D	C
Richardson, L.	37th	D	C
Rohrabacher, D.	46th	R	F*
Roybal-Allard, L.	34th	D	C
Royce, E.	40th	R	F
Sanchez, Li.	39th	D	C
Sanchez, Lo.	47th	D	B*
Sciff, A.	29th	D	C
Sherman, B.	27th	D	C
Speier, J.	12th	D	A*
Stark, P.	13th	D	A
Thompson, M.	1st	D	C
Waters, M.	35th	D	B*
Waxman, H.	30th	D	C
Woolsey, L.	6th	D	C
COLORADO			
Coffman, M.	6th	R	F
DeGette, D.	1st	D	B*
Gardner, C.	4th	R	F
Lamborn, D.	5th	R	F
Perlmutter, E.	7th	D	B*
Polis, J.	2nd	D	C
Tipton, S.	3rd	R	F
CONNECTICUT			
Courtney, J.	2nd	D	B*
DeLauro, R.	3rd	D	B*
Himes, J.	4th	D	C
Larson, J.	1st	D	C
Murphy, C.	5th	D	B*
DELAWARE			
Carney, J.	At Large	D	C
FLORIDA			
Adams, S.	24th	R	F
Bilirakis, G.	9th	R	F*
Brown, C.	3rd	D	C
Buchanan, V.	13th	R	F*
Castor, K.	11th	D	B*
Crenshaw, A.	4th	R	F
Deutch, T.	19th	D	C
Diaz-Balart, M.	21st	R	F*
Hastings, A.	23rd	D	C
Mack, C.	14th	R	F*
Mica, J.	7th	R	F*

(continues)

State	District	Party	Grade
Miller, J.	1st	R	F
Nugent, R.	5th	R	F
Posey, B.	15th	R	F
Rivera, D.	25th	R	F
Rooney, T.	16th	R	F
Ros-Lehtinen, I.	18th	R	F
Ross, D.	12th	R	F
Southerland, S.	2nd	R	F
Stearns, C.	6th	R	F
Wasserman Schultz, D.	20th	D	C
Webster, D.	8th	R	F
West, A.	22nd	R	F
Wilson, F.	17th	R	B*
Young, C.	10th	R	F*
GEORGIA			
Barrow, J.	12th	D	B*
Bishop, S.	2nd	D	A*
Broun, P.	10th	R	F
Gingrey, P.	11th	R	F*
Graves, T.	9th	R	F
Johnson, H.	4th	D	A
Kingston, J.	1st	R	F
Lewis, Jo.	5th	D	B*
Price, T.	6th	R	F
Scott, A.	8th	R	F
Scott, D.	13th	D	C
Westmoreland, L.	3rd	R	F
Woodall, R.	7th	R	F
HAWAII			
Hanabusa, C.	1st	D	C
Hirono, M.	2nd	D	C*
IDAHO			
Labrador, R.	1st	R	F*
Simpson, M.	2nd	R	D*
ILLINOIS			
Biggert, J.	13th	R	C
Costello, J.	12th	D	B*
Davis, D.	7th	D	C
Dold, R.	10th	R	C
Gutierrez, L.	4th	D	A*
Hultgren, R.	14th	R	F*
Jackson, J.	2nd	D	C
Johnson, T.	15th	R	D*

(continues)

State	District	Party	Grade
Kinzinger, A.	11th	R	F*
Lipinski, D.	3rd	D	D*
Manzullo, D.	16th	R	F*
Quigley, M.	5th	D	C
Roskam, P.	6th	R	F
Rush, B.	1st	D	A*
Schakowsky, J.	9th	D	B*
Schilling, R.	17th	R	F
Schock, A.	18th	R	F
Shimkus, J.	19th	R	F*
Walsh, J.	8th	R	F
INDIANA			
Buchson, L.	8th	R	F*
Burton, D.	5th	R	F*
Carson, A.	7th	D	B*
Donnelly, J.	2nd	D	C
Pence, M.	6th	R	F*
Rokita, T.	4th	R	F*
Stutzman, M.	3rd	R	F*
Visclosky, P.	1st	D	C
Young, T.	9th	R	F
IOWA			
Boswell, L.	3rd	D	B*
Braley, B.	1st	D	C
King, S.	5th	R	F
Latham, T.	4th	R	F*
Loebsack, D.	2nd	D	B*
KANSAS			
Huelskamp, T.	1st	R	F
Jenkins, L.	2nd	R	F
Pompeo, M.	4th	R	F*
Yoder, K.	3rd	R	F
KENTUCKY			
Chandler, B.	6th	D	C
Davis, G.	4th	R	F
Guthrie, B.	2nd	R	F
Rogers, H.	5th	R	F
Whitfield, E.	1st	R	F
Yarmuth, J.	3rd	D	C
LOUISIANA			
Alexander, R.	5th	R	F
Boustany, C.	7th	R	F

(continues)

State	District	Party	Grade
Cassidy, B.	6th	R	F
Fleming, J.	4th	R	F
Landry, J.	3rd	R	F
Richmond, C.	2nd	D	B*
Scalise, S.	1st	R	F
MAINE			
Michaud, M.	2nd	D	B*
Pingree, C.	1st	D	C*
MARYLAND			
Bartlett, R.	6th	R	F
Cummings, E.	7th	D	B*
Edwards, D.	4th	D	C
Harris, A.	1st	R	F*
Hoyer, S.	5th	D	C
Ruppersberger, C.	2nd	D	C
Sarbanes, J.	3rd	D	C
Van Hollen, C.	8th	D	C
MASSACHUSETTS			
Capuano, M.	8th	D	B*
Frank, B.	4th	D	C
Keating, W.	10th	D	C*
Lynch, S.	9th	D	A*
Markey, E.	7th	D	C
McGovern, J.	3rd	D	C
Neal, R.	2nd	D	C
Olver, J.	1st	D	B*
Tierney, J.	6th	D	C
Tsongas, N.	5th	D	A*
MICHIGAN			
Amash, J.	3rd	R	F
Benishek, D.	1st	R	F
Camp, D.	4th	R	F*
Clarke, H.	13th	D	C
Conyers, J.	14th	D	C
Dingell, J.	15th	D	B*
Huizenga, B.	2nd	R	F
Kildee, D.	5th	D	C
Levin, S.	12th	D	C
McCotter, T.	11th	R	F*
Miller, C.	10th	R	F
Peters, G.	9th	D	C
Rogers, Mike	8th	R	F
Upton, F.	6th	R	F

(continues)

State	District	Party	Grade
Walberg, T.	7th	R	F*
MINNESOTA			
Bachmann, M.	6th	R	F*
Cravaack, C.	8th	R	F*
Ellison, K.	5th	D	C
Kline, J.	2nd	R	F
McCollum, B.	4th	D	B*
Paulsen, E.	3rd	R	F*
Peterson, C.	7th	D	D*
Walz, T.	1st	D	C
MISSISSIPPI			
Harper, G.	3rd	R	F*
Nunnelee, A.	1st	R	F*
Palazzo, S.	4th	R	F*
Thompson, B.	2nd	D	B*
MISSOURI			
Akin, W.	2nd	R	F*
Carnahan, R.	3rd	D	C
Clay, W.	1st	D	B*
Cleaver, E.	5th	D	A
Emerson, J.	8th	R	F*
Graves, S.	6th	R	D*
Hartzler, V.	4th	R	F
Long, B.	7th	R	F
Luetkemeyer, B.	9th	R	F
MONTANA			
Rehberg, D.	At Large	R	F
NEBRASKA			
Fortenberry, J.	1st	R	F*
Smith, A.	3rd	R	F
Terry, L.	2nd	R	F
NEVADA			
Amodei, M.**	2nd	R	F*
Berkley, S.	1st	D	C
Heck, J.	3rd	R	F
NEW HAMPSHIRE			
Bass, C.	2nd	R	F
Guinta, F.	1st	R	F
NEW JERSEY			
Andrews, R.	1st	D	B*

(continues)

State	District	Party	Grade
Frelinghuysen, R.	11th	R	C*
Garrett, S.	5th	R	F
Holt, R.	12th	D	C
Lance, L.	7th	R	F
LoBiondo, F.	2nd	R	F
Pallone, F.	6th	D	C
Pascrell, B.	8th	D	B*
Payne, D.	10th	D	C
Rothman, S.	9th	D	B*
Runyan, J.	3rd	R	F
Sires, A.	13th	D	C
Smith, C.	4th	R	F
NEW MEXICO			
Heinrich, M.	1st	D	B*
Lujan, B.	3rd	D	C
Pearce, S.	2nd	R	F
NEW YORK			
Ackerman, G.	5th	D	A
Bishop, T.	1st	D	B*
Buerkle, A.	25th	R	F
Clarke, Y.	11th	D	C
Crowley, J.	7th	D	B*
Engel, E.	17th	D	C
Gibson, C.	20th	R	F
Grimm, M.	13th	R	F
Hanna, R.	24th	R	F
Hayworth, N.	19th	R	F
Higgins, B.	27th	D	C
Hinchey, M.	22nd	D	B*
Hochul, K.**	26th	D	F*
Israel, S.	2nd	D	C
King, P.	3rd	R	F
Lowey, N.	18th	D	C
Maloney, C.	14th	D	C
McCarthy, C.	4th	D	C
Meeks, G.	6th	D	B*
Nadler, J.	8th	D	A
Owens, W.	23rd	D	B*
Rangel, C.	15th	D	C*
Reed, T.	29th	R	F
Serrano, J.	16th	D	C
Slaughter, L.	28th	D	B*
Tonko, P.	21st	D	C
Towns, E.	10th	D	C
Turner, R.**	9th	R	F*
Velazquez, N.	12th	D	C*

(continues)

State	District	Party	Grade
NORTH CAROLINA			
Butterfield, G.K.	1st	D	C
Coble, H.	6th	R	F*
Ellmers, R.	2nd	R	F
Foxx, V.	5th	R	F
Jones, W.	3rd	R	F
Kissell, L.	8th	D	C
McHenry, P.	10th	R	F*
McIntyre, M.	7th	D	C
Miller, B.	13th	D	C
Myrick, S.	9th	R	F
Price, D.	4th	D	C
Shuler, H.	11th	D	D*
Watt, M.	12th	D	B*
NORTH DAKOTA			
Berg, R.	At Large	R	F
OHIO			
Austria, S.	7th	R	F
Boehner, J.	8th	R	0

(* Traditionally, the Speaker of the House rarely votes on
floor bills. As such, Rep. Boehner did not receive a grade.)

State	District	Party	Grade
Chabot, S.	1st	R	F
Fudge, M.	11th	D	C
Gibbs, B.	18th	R	F
Johnson, B.	6th	R	F
Jordan, J.	4th	R	F
Kaptur, M.	9th	D	B*
Kucinich, D.	10th	D	C
LaTourette, S.	14th	R	F
Latta, R.	5th	R	F*
Renacci, J.	16th	R	F*
Ryan, T.	17th	D	C
Schmidt, J.	2nd	R	F
Stivers, S.	15th	R	F
Sutton, B.	13th	D	C
Tiberi, P.	12th	R	F*
Turner, M.	3rd	R	F
OKLAHOMA			
Boren, D.	2nd	D	D*
Cole, T.	4th	R	F
Lankford, J.	5th	R	F
Lucas, F.	3rd	R	F
Sullivan, J.	1st	R	F

(continues)

State	District	Party	Grade
OREGON			
Blumenauer, E.	3rd	D	A*
DeFazio, P.	4th	D	B*
Schrader, K.	5th	D	B*
Walden, G.	2nd	R	F
PENNSYLVANIA			
Altmire, J.	4th	D	C
Barletta, L.	11th	R	F
Brady, R.	1st	D	B*
Critz, M.	12th	D	C
Dent, C.	15th	R	C*
Doyle, M.	14th	D	C
Fattah, C.	2nd	D	A*
Fitzpatrick, M.	8th	R	F
Gerlach, J.	6th	R	F*
Holden, T.	17th	D	C
Kelly, M.	3rd	R	F
Marino, T.	10th	R	F
Meehan, P.	7th	R	F
Murphy, T.	18th	R	F
Pitts, J.	16th	R	F
Platts, T.	19th	R	F*
Schwartz, A.	13th	D	C
Shuster, B.	9th	R	F*
Thompson, G.	5th	R	F
RHODE ISLAND			
Cicilline, D.	1st	D	C
Langevin, J.	2nd	D	C
SOUTH CAROLINA			
Clyburn, J.	6th	D	C
Duncan, J.	3rd	R	F
Gowdy, T.	4th	R	F
Mulvaney, M.	5th	R	F*
Scott, T.	1st	R	F
Wilson, J.	2nd	R	F
SOUTH DAKOTA			
Noem, K.	At Large	R	F
TENNESSEE			
Black, D.	6th	R	F*
Blackburn, M.	7th	R	F
Cohen, S.	9th	D	C
Cooper, J.	5th	D	C

(continues)

State	District	Party	Grade
DesJarlais, S.	4th	R	F
Duncan, J.	2nd	R	F
Fincher, S.	8th	R	F
Fleischmann, C.	3rd	R	F
Roe, D.	1st	R	F
TEXAS			
Barton, J.	6th	R	F*
Brady, K.	8th	R	F
Burgess, M.	26th	R	F
Canseco, F.	23rd	R	F
Carter, J.	31st	R	F*
Conaway, K.	11th	R	F
Cuellar, H.	28th	D	C
Culberson, J.	7th	R	F
Doggett, L.	25th	D	B*
Farenthold, B.	27th	R	F
Flores, B.	17th	R	F
Gohmert, L.	1st	R	F
Gonzalez, C.	20th	D	C
Granger, K.	12th	R	F*
Green, A.	9th	D	C
Green, G.	29th	D	C
Hall, R.	4th	R	F
Hensarling, J.	5th	R	F
Hinojosa, R.	15th	D	C*
Jackson Lee, S.	18th	D	C
Johnson, E.	30th	D	C
Johnson, S.	3rd	R	F
Marchant, K.	24th	R	F*
McCaul, M.	10th	R	F*
Neugebauer, R.	19th	R	F
Olson, P.	22nd	R	F
Paul, R.	14th	R	F*
Poe, T.	2nd	R	F*
Reyes, S.	16th	D	C
Sessions, P.	32nd	R	F
Smith, L.	21st	R	F
Thornberry, M.	13th	R	F
UTAH			
Bishop, R.	1st	R	F
Chaffetz, J.	3rd	R	F
Matheson, J.	2nd	D	C
VERMONT			
Welch, P.	At Large	D	C

(continues)

State	District	Party	Grade
VIRGINIA			
Cantor, E.	7th	R	F
Connolly, G.	11th	D	C
Forbes, J.	4th	R	F*
Goodlatte, B.	6th	R	F
Griffith, H.	9th	R	D*
Hurt, R.	5th	R	F
Moran, J.	8th	D	C
Rigell, E.	2nd	R	F
Scott, R.	5th	D	A
Wittman, R.	1st	R	F
Wolf, F.	10th	R	F
WASHINGTON			
Dicks, N.	6th	D	B*
Hastings, D.	4th	R	F*
Herrera Beutler, J.	3rd	R	F
Inslee, J.	1st	D	C
Larsen, R.	2nd	D	C
McDermott, J.	7th	D	B*
McMorris Rodgers, C.	5th	R	F
Reichert, D.	8th	R	C
Smith, A.	9th	D	B*
WEST VIRGINIA			
Capito, S.	2nd	R	F
McKinley, D.	1st	R	F
Rahall, N.	3rd	D	F
WISCONSIN			
Baldwin, T.	2nd	D	C
Duffy, S.	7th	R	F
Kind, R.	3rd	D	C
Moore, G.	4th	D	C
Petri, T.	6th	R	F
Ribble, R.	8th	R	F
Ryan, P.	1st	R	F
Sensenbrenner, J.	5th	R	F
WYOMING			
Lummis, C.	At Large	R	F

ACKNOWLEDGMENTS

MY FRIEND HERB SILVERMAN—THE PRESIDENT OF THE SECULAR Coalition for America, the Jewish atheist who ran for governor of South Carolina, the man who is an inspiration to all in the modern secular movement—is the First Cause, if you will, behind this book. In several ways he is directly responsible for making this project possible, and for that I thank him. I am also deeply indebted to Leon Seltzer and Lybi Ma, without whom this work never would have been possible; my editor, Laura Lancaster, who has worked with me from the beginning on this book and whose assistance has been invaluable; and my friend and colleague Roy Speckhardt of the American Humanist Association, whose hard work is responsible for so much of the success of the AHA and the secular movement.

Maggie Ardiente, Jennifer Bardi, Rob Boston, Elizabeth Cornwell, Richard Dawkins, Sharon Fratepietro, Jesse Galef, Wendy Kaminer, Brian Magee, Hemant Mehta, Bill Nye, Steven Pinker, Michael Shermer, Julia Sweeney, and Tim van Leer each provided support in one way or another for this project. Bill Burgess and Monica Miller of the AHA's Appignani Humanist Legal Center have also provided assistance, as have many of my AHA board colleagues, including Lou Altman, Carl Coon, Becky Hale, Jennifer Kalmanson, Howard Katz, Amanda Knief, Mel Lipman, Raul Martinez, Susan Sackett, Jason Torpy, Mike Werner, and Kristen Wintermute. Also important have been my colleagues from the Secular Coalition for America: August Brunsman, Woody Kaplan, Eliza Kashinsky, Ron Solomon, and Todd Stiefel.

The leadership crew from Greater Worcester Humanists is a constant source of support for me and for much of the secular activism discussed in this book. This group includes Robyn Franke, Don Guyton, Ann and Steve Jasperson, Chris Lackey, Keith MacKinnon, David and Linda Miller, Chris Moran, Bruce Palmer, and Kara Wilson. Also important has been the Boston-Cambridge crew connected with Greater Boston Humanists and the Harvard Humanist Chaplaincy: Lenn and Jane Bernstein, Greg Epstein, Tom Ferrick, Jonathan Figdor (who is heading out to Stanford to start a humanist chaplaincy there), Joe Gerstein, Peter Denison, Dorothy Harrigan, and Stuart Wamsley.

I would be remiss if I did not mention Lou Franco, Ellery Schempp, Paul Groark, Steve Rade, Lou Appignani, as well as Rich, Bob, and Doug Mason, all of whom had an impact, direct or indirect, on this work. Also noteworthy is the assistance of the staff in my Fitchburg office: Melissa Guadalupe and Jessica Sambolin. I worked closely with Donna Cherry, Eric Nguyen, Siobhan Paganelli, Elisabeth Tone, Andrew Varhol, Surie Rudoff, Greg Abazorius, and David Ratner in the post-writing phase of the process.

The support of one's spouse is important in the undertaking of any big project, but an effort such as this—publicly advocating for nonbelievers—requires a spouse with a special kind of patience and understanding. Luckily for me, my wife Katy is just such a person. My kids—Rebecca, Nicholas, and Benjamin—are also a source of inspiration that has kept me on track throughout this project, as have been my parents. In fact, though in my extended family there are more believers than nonbelievers, it is the ability of all those within the family to live in harmony—despite our vastly differing views—that keeps me optimistic about the wider human family.

There are many others who deserve a mention—AHA chapter leaders around the country, AHA and SCA staff, secular activists who have done so much to raise public awareness, financial supporters of the movement, and many others—but unfortunately space limitations prohibit such a prolonged list. Suffice it to say that I'm very grateful to all of these individuals, however, and to all of those mentioned above. Viva secularity!

NOTES

INTRODUCTION: THE DECLINE OF THE AMERICAN DIALOGUE

1. Debs would again receive almost a million votes in the 1920 election, campaigning from his prison cell after being convicted of sedition for speaking out against the First World War, but that vote total translated to only about 3.5 percent. The difference was the Nineteenth Amendment, ratified before the election in 1920, which recognized the right of women to vote, thereby almost doubling voter turnout.
2. Woodrow Wilson to Winterton C. Curtis, August 29, 1922; Marvin Olasky and John Perry, *Monkey Business: The True Story of the Scopes Trial* (Nashville: Broadman and Holman Publishers, 2005), 77.
3. Michael Lind, "Fundamental Flaws," *Observer,* November 10, 2001, http://www.guardian.co.uk/world/2001/nov/11/afghanistan.religion1.
4. Theodore Roosevelt, "My Life as a Naturalist," *American Museum Journal,* May 1918, published by *Natural History Magazine,* http://naturalhistorymag.com/picks-from-the-past/12449/my-life-as-a-naturalist.
5. From a letter declining presidency of Yale University, Henry F. Pringle, *The Life and Times of William Howard Taft,* vol. 1 (New York: Farrar & Rinehart, 1939), 45.
6. Eugene Victor Debs, Bruce Rogers, and Stephen Marion Reynolds, *Debs: His Life, Writings and Speeches: With a Department of Appreciations* (Girard, KS: Appeal to Reason, 1908), 487.
7. ABC News, August 18, 2011, "NH mother uses child as prop to question Rick Perry on evolution," http://abcnews.go.com/blogs/politics/2011/08/nh-mother-uses-child-as-a-prop-to-question-rick-perry-on-evolution/#.
8. Lisa Miller, "Be Not Afraid of Evangelicals," *Washington Post,* August 18, 2011, http://www.washingtonpost.com/national/on-faith/dominionism-beliefs-among-conservative-christians-overblown/2011/08/17/gIQAb5eaNJ_story.html.

CHAPTER 1: THE WEDDING INVITATION

1. Definitions of the various secular identifiers—atheist, agnostic, humanist, and so forth—can vary, and there is no need here for a comprehensive analysis of all the optional definitions. An exhaustive discussion of all the various definitions of agnostic, for example, could go on for many pages but would serve little purpose here, where the main point is to note that Secular Americans identify in many different ways.
2. Since humanism can be called a religion, religious conservatives have sometimes argued that various principles of humanism, such as the acceptance of evolution, should not be taught in public schools. That argument overlooks the fact that the teaching of accurate science is always valid, regardless of whether it happens to be accepted by a religion. The teaching of science can never in itself be a governmental endorsement of religion.

3. Barry A. Kosmin and Ariela Keysar, American Religious Identity Survey (ARIS 2008), (Hartford, CT: Trinity College, 2009).
4. Ibid.
5. Ibid.
6. Ibid.
7. "Americans' Church Attendance Up in 2010," Gallup survey report, June 25, 2010, http:// www.gallup.com/poll/141044/americans-church-attendance-inches-2010.aspx.
8. Kosmin and Keysar, ARIS.
9. Thomas Paine, *The Age of Reason* (Mineola, NY: Dover Publications, 2004 ed.), 22.
10. John Dewey, *A Common Faith* (New Haven, CT: Yale University Press, 1934), 50–51.
11. Gustav Niebuhr, "U.S. 'Secular' Groups Set Tone for Terror Attacks, Falwell Says," *New York Times,* September 14, 2001, http://www.nytimes.com/2001/09/14/national/14FALW .html.
12. "What's Wrong with the Moral Majority," Richard Heffner's Open Mind, February 5, 1982, http://www.thirteen.org/openmind/public-affairs/whats-wrong-with-the-moral-majority /813/.
13. Joel D. Vaughan, *The Rise and Fall of the Christian Coalition* (Eugene, OR: Wipf and Stock / Resource Publications, 2009), 185. The Christian Coalition's church-based distribution of voter guides was also reported widely in mainstream media and by church-state watchdog groups.
14. "Focus on the Family's Foundational Values," Focus on the Family, accessed December 6, 2011, http://www.focusonthefamily.com/about_us/guiding-principles.aspx.
15. Jay Maeder, "Repealing the Abortion Law, May 1972, Chapter 397," *New York Daily News,* July 10, 2001, http://articles.nydailynews.com/2001-07-10/news/18369154_1_abortion -law-life-committee-repeal.
16. Michael Murphy, "Conservative Pioneer Became an Outcast," *Arizona Republic,* May 31, 1998, http://www.azcentral.com/specials/special25/articles/0531goldwater2.html.
17. Interview with Zinn at his Boston University office, March 17, 2003.
18. Diana Kendall, *Sociology in Our Times: The Essentials,* 6th ed. (Belmont, CA: Thomson Wadsworth, 2007), 367.
19. Thomas Jefferson, *Thomas Jefferson: Writings,* ed. Merrill D. Peterson (New York: Literary Classics of the United States, 1984), 1459.
20. Ronald Hayman, *Nietzsche* (New York: Routledge, 1999), 5.
21. Pew Research Center Publications, "Voting Religiously," November 5, 2008 (updated November 10, 2008), http://pewresearch.org/pubs/1022/exit-poll-analysis-religion.
22. Ibid.

CHAPTER 2: A RELIGIOUS PEOPLE?

1. Barack Obama, "My Spiritual Journey," *Time,* October 16, 2006, http://www.time.com /time/magazine/article/0,9171,1546579,00.html. This line is also repeated in Obama's book, *The Audacity of Hope.*
2. Al Gore, interview by Kevin Rose, November 2008, Current TV, Digg Dialogg, http:// tv.digg.com/diggdialogg/algore.
3. US Department of Justice, FBI Criminal Justice Information Services Division, Crime in the United States, 1990–2009, Table 1, http://www2.fbi.gov/ucr/cius2009/data/table_01 .html.
4. Mia Dauvergne and John Turner, "Police-reported crime statistics in Canada, 2009," Statistic Canada, Summer 2010 (Chart 5), http://www.statcan.gc.ca/pub/85-002-x/2010002 /article/11292-eng.htm#a6.
5. Eurostat, "Crime and Criminal Justice," 2010 report, 7, http://epp.eurostat.ec.europa.eu /cache/ITY_OFFPUB/KS-SF-10-058/EN/KS-SF-10-058-EN.PDF.
6. Steve Crabtree and Brett Pelham, "What Alabamians and Iranians Have in Common," Gallup, February 9, 2009, http://www.gallup.com/poll/114211/alabamians-iranians-common.aspx.

7. United Nations Office on Drugs and Crime provides comparative data on international homicide rates at http://www.unodc.org/unodc/en/data-and-analysis/homicide.html.

8. Gregory S. Paul, "Cross-National Correlations of Quantifiable Societal Health with Popular Religiosity and Secularism in the Prosperous Democracies," *Journal of Religion & Society* 7 (2005).

9. Ruth Gledhill, "Societies Worse Off 'When They Have God on Their Side,'" *Times*, September 27, 2005.

10. Phil Zuckerman, "Atheism, Secularity, and Well-Being: How the Findings of Social Science Counter Negative Stereotypes and Assumptions," *Sociology Compass* vol. 3, no. 6 (December 2009).

11. Ibid., 7-8.

12. Ibid.

13. Gary F. Jensen, "Religious Cosmologies and Homicide Rates among Nations," *Journal of Religion & Society* vol. 8 (2006).

14. Ibid., 11.

15. John Hechinger, "U.S. Teens Lag as China Soars in International Test," *Bloomberg*, December 7, 2010, http://www.bloomberg.com/news/2010-12-07/teens-in-u-s-rank-25th-on-math-test-trail-in-science-reading.html. The article discusses results of the 2009 report of the Program for International Student Assessment, a leading source on international student achievement.

16. Consistent with their image, the states of the so-called Bible Belt, America's Deep South and interior heartland, are indeed the most religious. In 2006 Gallup rankings of states according to church attendance, the top 15 states were Alabama, Louisiana, South Carolina, Mississippi, Utah, Arkansas, Nebraska, North Carolina, Tennessee, Georgia, Oklahoma, Texas, Kentucky, Kansas, and West Virginia. "Church or Synagogue Attendance by State," *San Diego Union-Tribune*, May 2, 2006, http://www.signonsandiego.com/union trib/20060502/news_lz1n2thelist.html.

17. Zuckerman, "Atheism, Secularity, and Well-Being," 955.

18. Ibid., 952-960.

19. The vast majority of red states carried by McCain in 2008 were from the Deep South and interior heartland, states with the highest rates of church attendance. "Church or Synagogue Attendance by State."

20. Eric Ostermeier, "Red States Have Higher Crime Rates than Blue States," Smart Politics, September 16, 2009, http://blog.lib.umn.edu/cspg/smartpolitics/2009/09/red_states_have_higher_crime_r.php.

21. "Teen Birth Rates Highest in Religious Red States," *Perspectives*, September 17, 2009, http://www.perrspectives.com/blog/archives/001621.htm.

22. "State Education Rankings: The Best and Worst For Math And Science," HuffPost Education, July 11, 2011, citing Science and Engineering Readiness Index, http://www.huffington post.com/2011/07/11/state-education-rankings-_n_894528.html.

23. Zuckerman, "Atheism, Secularity, and Well-Being," 953.

24. Ibid., 953-954.

25. "Atheists Identified as America's Most Distrusted Minority, According to New U of M Study," press release, University of Minnesota, University News Service, March 28, 2006, http://www1.umn.edu/news/news-releases/2006/UR_RELEASE_MIG_2816.html.

26. Clif LeBlanc and John O'Connor, "Sanford Admits Affair: 'I've Let down a Lot of People,'" thestate.com, June 25, 2009, http://www.thestate.com/2009/06/25/839231/sanford-admits-affair-ive-let.html.

27. Shailagh Murray, "Senator's Number on 'Madam' Phone List," *Washington Post*, July 10, 2007, http://www.washingtonpost.com/wp-dyn/content/article/2007/07/09/AR20070709 02030.html.

28. David Osborne, "Newt Gingrich: Shining Knight of the Post-Reagan Right," *Mother Jones*, November 1, 1984, http://motherjones.com/politics/1984/11/newt-gingrich-shining-knight-post-reagan-right.

29. David Brody, "Newt Gingrich Tells the Brody File He 'Felt Compelled to Seek God's Forgiveness,'" *The Brody File* (blog), March 8, 2011, http://blogs.cbn.com/thebrodyfile /archive/2011/03/08/newt-gingrich-tells-brody-file-he-felt-compelled-to-seek.aspx.

30. Kendra Marr, "Newt Talks Faith—Not Affairs—at Cornerstone Church in Texas," *Politico*, March 27, 2011, http://www.politico.com/news/stories/0311/52023.html.

31. Ibid.

32. Bill Forman, "The resurrection of Pastor Ted," *Colorado Springs Independent*, October 1, 2009.

33. Luisa Kroll, "Megachurches, Megabusinesses," *Forbes*, September 17, 2003, http://www .forbes.com/2003/09/17/cz_lk_0917megachurch.html.

34. "United States Has More Megachurches than Previously Thought," Faith Communities Today, Press release about FACT2005 Megachurch Project, http://faithcommunitiestoday .org/press-release-about-fact2005-megachurch-project.

35. Lydia Saad, "Churchgoing Among U.S. Catholics Slides to Tie Protestants," Gallup report, April 9, 2009, http://www.gallup.com/poll/117382/church-going-among-catholics-slides -tie-protestants.aspx.

36. "Somalia: Girl Stoned Was a Child of 13," press release, Amnesty International, October 31, 2008, http://www.amnesty.org/en/for-media/press-releases/somalia-girl-stoned-was -child-13-20081031.

37. Dan Harris, Katie Hinman, and Almin Karamehmedovic, "Anti-homosexual Bill in Uganda Causes Global Uproar," ABC News, March 10, 2010, http://abcnews.go.com/Nightline /anti-homosexuality-bill-uganda-global-uproar/story?id=10045436#.Tt6Q-GAx_Jw.

CHAPTER 3: A SECULAR HERITAGE

1. Kevin Sieff, "Ten Commandments in school stirs fight in Va. District," *Washington Post*, February 18, 2011, http://www.washingtonpost.com/local/in-rural-va-a-fight-to-keep-ten -commandments-in-schools/2011/02/17/ABGi7UH_story.html.

2. Ibid.

3. Garrett Epps, "Constitutional Myth #4: The Constitution Doesn't Separate Church and State," *Atlantic*, June 15, 2011, http://www.theatlantic.com/national/archive/2011/06 /constitutional-myth-4-the-constitution-doesnt-separate-church-and-state/240481/.

4. Teddy David and Matt Loffman, "Sarah Palin's 'Christian Nation' Remarks Spark Debate," ABC News, April 20, 2010, http://abcnews.go.com/Politics/sarah-palin-sparks-church -state-separation-debate/story?id=10419289&page=2#.Tt_iEGAx_Jw.

5. *The Congressional Prayer Caucus*, http://forbes.house.gov/PrayerCaucus/PastWork.aspx.

6. Andrew Romano, "How Dumb Are We?," *Daily Beast*, March 20, 2011, http: //www.thedailybeast.com/newsweek/2011/03/20/how-dumb-are-we.html; and Robert Holland and Don Soifer, "Americans Are Dangerously Ignorant of History," Lexington Institute, April 12, 2011, http://www.lexingtoninstitute.org/americans-are-dangerously -ignorant-of-history?a=1&c=1136.

7. "Independence Day: Seventeen Seventy When?" press release, Marist College Institute for Public Opinion, July 1, 2011, http://maristpoll.marist.edu/wp-content/misc/usapolls /US110615/July%204th/Complete%20July%201,%202011%20USA%20Marist%20 Poll%20Release%20and%20Tables.pdf.

8. Thomas Jefferson, *Thomas Jefferson: Writings*, ed. Merrill D. Peterson (New York: Literary Classics of the United States, 1984), 510.

9. The document can be found at the Library of Congress website, http://memory.loc.gov /cgi-bin/ampage?collId=llsp&fileName=002/llsp002.db&recNum=23.

10. Brooke Allen, "Our Godless Constitution," *Nation*, February 21, 2005. http://www.the nation.com/article/our-godless-constitution.

11. For more background on the treaty, see Ed Buckner, "Does the 1796–97 Treaty with Tripoli Matter to Church/State Separation?" speech given to Humanists of Georgia, June 22, 1997, available at http://www.stephenjaygould.org/ctrl/buckner_tripoli.html.

12. US Constitution, Article VI.

13. US Constitution, Article II, Section 1.

14. US Constitution, Article I, Section 7.

15. David Barton, "Is President Obama Correct? Is America No Longer a Christian Nation?" April 2009, *WallBuilders*, http://www.wallbuilders.com/libissuesarticles.asp?id=23909.

16. "Overview," *WallBuilders*, http://www.wallbuilders.com/ABTOverview.asp.

17. Siddhartha Mahanta, "The GOP's Favorite Fringe Historian," *Mother Jones*, April 27, 2011, http://motherjones.com/politics/2011/04/david-barton-gingrich-bachmann-huckabee.

18. Rob Boston, "David Barton Falsifies American History," *Church & State Magazine*, July-August 1996, http://www.yuricareport.com/Dominionism/BartonFalsifiesAmericanHistory.html. For more on Barton, see also Yoni Appelbaum, "American Scripture: How David Barton Won the Christian Right," *Atlantic*, May 10, 2011, http://www.theatlantic.com/politics/archive/2011/05/american-scripture-how-david-barton-won-the-christian-right/238603/; Erik Eckholm, "Using History to Mold Ideas on the Right," *New York Times*, May 4, 2011, http://www.nytimes.com/2011/05/05/us/politics/05barton.html; and Rob Boston, "Texas Tall Tale," *Church & State Magazine*, July-August 2009, http://au.org/church-state/julyaugust-2009-church-state/featured/texas-tall-tale.

19. Chris Vaughn, "A Man with a Message; Self-Taught Historian's Work on Church-State Rouses GOP," *Fort Worth Star-Telegram*, May 22, 2005, as reproduced by Baylor University, "Baylor in the News," http://www.baylor.edu/pr/bitn/news.php?action=story&story=34559.

20. See Boston, "David Barton Falsifies American History."

21. David Barton, May 4, 2011 appearance, video at http://www.thedailyshow.com/watch/wed-may-4-2011/exclusive—david-barton-extended-interview-pt—1.

22. David Barton, "An Historical Perspective on a Muslim Being Sworn into Congress on the Koran," *WallBuilders*, January 2007, http://www.wallbuilders.com/downloads/newsletter/Winter2006.pdf.

23. See Boston, "Texas Tall Tale."

24. Ibid.

25. Arlen Specter, "Defending the Wall: Maintaining Church/State Separation in America," *The Harvard Journal of Law and Public Policy* vol. 18, issue 2 (Spring 1995), quoted in People for the American Way, "David Barton: Propaganda Masquerading as History," special report, accessed December 7, 2011, http://67.192.238.60/media-center/publications/david-barton-propaganda-masquerading-history.

26. Michael Newdow, "Question to Justice Scalia: Does the Establishment Clause Permit the Disregard of Devout Catholics?" *Capital University Law Review* 38, no. 2 (Winter 2009): 72-73.

27. Ibid., 75.

28. Richard Middleton, *Colonial America* (Oxford: Blackwell Publishing, 2003), 95–100, 145, 158, 159, 349n.

29. H.R. 3908, 110th Cong., first session (2007).

30. Shawn Hendricks, "Demint Book Counters Socialism," *Baptist Press*, September 25, 2009, http://www.bpnews.net/bpnews.asp?id=31339.

31. Institute for Curriculum Service, *Jews in American History: A Teacher's Guide*, 4, http://www.icsresources.org/content/curricula/JewsInAmericanHistoryTeachersGuide.pdf.

32. Martin Luther, *On the Jews and Their Lies*, trans. Martin H. Bertram, AAARGH Internet 2009, 19-20, http://www.vho.org/aaargh/fran/livres9/Luthereng.pdf.

33. Robert Michael, *Holy Hatred: Christianity, Anti-Semitism, and the Holocaust* (New York: Palgrave Macmillan, 2006), 113.

34. Raymond Robert Fischer, *The Children of God: Messianic Jews and Gentile Christians Nourished by Common Jewish Roots*, 2nd ed. (Tiberias, Israel: Olim Publications, 2000), 239.

35. Michael, *Holy Hatred*, 82-84, 99-104.

36. Many fundamentalists believe that the restoration of the nation of Israel is a necessary contingency for the return of Jesus. See: Timothy P. Weber, *On the Road to Armageddon: How Evangelicals Became Israel's Best Friend* (Grand Rapids, Michigan: Baker Academic, 2004).

37. Benjamin Franklin to Ezra Stiles, March 9, 1790, http://www.beliefnet.com/resourcelib/docs/44/Letter_from_Benjamin_Franklin_to_Ezra_Stiles_1.html.

38. George Washington to Hebrew congregation of Newport, Rhode Island, August 18, 1790, Papers of George Washington, http://gwpapers.virginia.edu/documents/hebrew/reply.html.

39. George Washington to annual meeting of Quakers, October 1789, in *The Writings of George Washington*, ed. Jared Sparks (Boston: American Stationers' Company, 1837), 169.

40. See Newdow, "Question to Justice Scalia," 21-28.

41. Gary Wills, *Head and Heart: American Christianities* (New York: Penguin, 2007), 237.

42. Newdow, "Question to Justice Scalia," 41-46.

43. This was a May 6, 2009, headline at the Fox News website.

44. Jocelyn Fong, "FoxNews.com Invents Presidential Prayer Day Tradition to Claim Obama Broke It," *Media Matters for America,* May 7, 2010, http://mediamatters.org/blog/201005070023.

45. Joel Siegel, "Obama Leaves God out of Thanksgiving Speech, Riles Critics," ABC News, November 25, 2011.

46. Jefferson, *Writings,* 1469.

47. Ibid., 902.

48. William Herndon to Edward McPherson, clerk of the US House of Representatives, February 4, 1866. See: Emily Sohn, "Did President Lincoln Believe in God?" *Discovery News,* April 15, 2011, http://news.discovery.com/history/president-abraham-lincoln-religion-god-110415.html.

49. Jennifer Michael Hecht, *Doubt: A History* (New York: HarperCollins, 2003), 417.

50. Elizabeth Cady Stanton, *The Woman's Bible* (Project Gutenberg e-book edition), http://www.gutenberg.org/ebooks/9880, (Kindle edition, ebook #9880, release date February 2006).

51. Elizabeth Frost-Knoppman and Kathryn Cullen-Dupon, *Women's Suffrage in America,* updated ed. (New York: Facts on File, 2005), 233.

52. Robert Baird, *Religion in America* (New York: Harper & Brothers, 1844), 48.

53. See "Mark Twain's Autobiography Set for Unveiling, a Century after His Death," *PBS Newshour,* July 7, 2010, http://www.pbs.org/newshour/bb/entertainment/july-dec10/twain_07-07.html.

54. Hepburn quote is from *Ladies' Home Journal,* October 1991, cited at http://www.adherents.com/people/ph/Katharine_Hepburn.html.

55. The interview can be heard at http://www.youtube.com/watch?v=6y98E7q-XvA.

CHAPTER 4: SECULARITY AND MORALITY

1. Charles Darwin, *The Origin of Species: 150th Anniversary Edition* (Alachua, FL: Bridge-Logos, 2009). Comfort's "special introduction" appears on pages 1-54.

2. The Origin into Schools Project at http://www.livingwaters.com/index.php?id=383&option=com_content&task=view.

3. An organism with rudimentary light sensitivity, given millions of years, the right environmental evolutionary pressures, and a long series of mutations, can eventually evolve an eye as an adaptation that provides obvious survival advantages. The evolution of the eye is explained well for the nonscientist in *The Blind Watchmaker* by Richard Dawkins. Though Dawkins is best known by the general public for his promotion of atheism and his debunking of theistic beliefs, as an evolutionary biologist, he has several books that explain evolution in terms that nonscientists can understand—for example, *The Selfish Gene* and *The Greatest Show on Earth.*

4. Although the video was taken down from Cameron's website, it can still be found elsewhere online. It can be found with a transcript at http://www.rationalitynow.com/blog/2009/09/17/ray-comfort-and-charles-darwin/.

5. Sam Jones, John Hooper, and Tom Kington, "Pope Benedict XVI Goes to War with 'Atheist Extremism,'" *Guardian,* September 16, 2010, http://www.guardian.co.uk/world/2010/sep/16/pope-benedict-xvi-atheism-extremism.

6. Robert P. Ericksen and Susannah Heschel, *Betrayal: German Churches and the Holocaust* (Minneapolis, MN: Augsburg Fortress Publishers, 1999), 10.

7. Ibid.

8. Adolf Hitler, *Mein Kampf,* trans. James Murphy (Hurst and Blackett, 1939), online at http://www.archive.org/stream/MeinKampf_483/HitlerAdolf-MeinKampf-Volume IIi1939525P.#page/n0/mode/2up. Quotes can be found on pages 475 and 483, and references to God can be found throughout the text.

9. John Cornwell, *Hitler's Pope: The Secret History of Pius XII* (New York: Penguin Group,1999).

10. Edward Pentin, "John Paul II's 1979 'Novena,'" *National Catholic Register,* June 16, 2010, http://www.ncregister.com/daily-news/john_paul_iis_1979_novena/.

11. Alan Dershowitz, *Rights from Wrongs: A Secular Theory on the Origin of Rights* (New York: Basic Books, 2005).

12. Harvard professor and author Steven Pinker discusses human propensities toward both violence and altruism in great detail in *The Better Angels of Our Nature: Why Violence Has Declined* (New York: Viking, 2011).

13. Daniel C. Dennett, *Breaking the Spell: Religion as a Natural Phenomenon* (New York: Penguin Group, 2006).

14. Greg M. Epstein, *Good Without God: What a Billion Nonreligious People Do Believe* (New York: HarperCollins, 2009).

15. Leviticus 20:13.

16. Jesse McKinley and Kirk Johnson, "Mormons Tipped Scale in Ban on Gay Marriage," *New York Times,* November 15, 2008.

17. "My Coming out of the Atheist Closet Story," http://whywontgodhealamputees.com /forums/index.php?topic=11729.0.

CHAPTER 5: THE DISASTER OF THE RELIGIOUS RIGHT

1. The quoted text of Kennedy's speech is from http://www.npr.org/templates/story/story .php?storyId=16920600; the quoted text of Romney's is from http://www.theboston channel.com/politics/14789305/detail.html.

2. Rob Boston, "The 12 Worst (and Most Powerful) Christian Right Groups," Alter-Net, May 2, 2011, http://www.alternet.org/teaparty/150809/the_12_worst_(and_most _powerful)_christian_right_groups/.

3. A December 2010 Gallup poll found that four in ten Americans believe that God created humans in their present form within the last ten thousand years, http://www.gallup.com /poll/145286/four-americans-believe-strict-creationism.aspx.

4. See, for example, Jeffrey T. Kuhner, "Obama's Culture of Death," *Washington Times,* July 21, 2011, http://www.washingtontimes.com/news/2011/jul/21/obamas-culture-of-death/. Kuhner accuses Obama of trying to "destroy our Judeo-Christian culture and replace it with European-style radical secularism" because his administration is "seriously considering adding contraception to the list of services" that must be covered by health insurers. "Contraception violates the natural moral order," Kuhner says.

5. Testifying before a US Senate committee on June 7, 2007, on the issue of global warming, Religious Right leader David Barton explained views of religious conservatives that led to opposition to efforts to combat global warming and regulate exploitation of the environment. "God strongly warned against elevating nature and the environment over humans and their Creator," he told the Senate panel, adding, "God placed man and woman over creation, not under it." http://www.wallbuilders.com/libissuesarticles.asp?id=7586.

6. A Public Policy Polling survey in May 2011 found that 34 percent of Americans believe that the Rapture will happen in their lifetime or were "not sure." http://www.publicpolicy polling.com/pdf/PPP_Release_US_0526.pdf.

7. Phil Zuckerman, "Atheism, Secularity, and Well-Being: How the Findings of Social Science Counter Negative Stereotypes and Assumptions," *Sociology Compass* vol. 3, no. 6 (2009): 954.

8. Quoted sections are from the so-called Land letter at the website of the Ethics and Religious Liberty Commission of the Southern Baptist Convention, http://erlc.com/article/the-so-called-land-letter/.

9. "Poll: 70% Believe Saddam, 9-11 Link," *USA Today*, September 6, 2003, which reports the results of a *Washington Post* poll. A *Newsweek* poll from January 2004 found that 49 percent believed that the Iraq regime was responsible for the September 11 attacks.

10. The article was published in the *International Journal for the Psychology of Religion* vol. 2, no. 2 (1992): 113-133.

11. Ibid., 118.

12. Ibid., 123.

13. Ibid., 126-127.

14. For an informative description of the Creation Museum, see "A Trip to the Creation 'Science' Museum" by Scott Potter at http://eveloce.scienceblog.com/15/a-trip-to-the-creation-science-museum/.

15. Since nobody has ever proved that Noah or his ark ever existed, one must chuckle at the paper of record unquestioningly reporting that a religious group from Kentucky is building a "full-size replica," but no doubt they checked their sources.

16. "Crossing the Church-State Divide by Ark," editorial, *New York Times*, May 30, 2011, http://www.nytimes.com/2011/05/31/opinion/31tue4.html.

17. Ibid. See also "Biblical Theme Park Coming to Kentucky with Government Assistance," Fox News, May 20, 2011, http://www.foxnews.com/travel/2011/05/20/biblical-theme-park-coming-kentucky-government-assistance/.

18. Gallup report, February 11, 2009. http://www.gallup.com/poll/114544/darwin-birthday-believe-evolution.aspx.

19. Peter Montgomery, "New Religious Right Video: Secularism Means Doom for America," People for the American Way, October 13, 2011, http://www.rightwingwatch.org/content/new-religious-right-video-secularism-means-doom-america.

20. The Congressional Prayer Caucus, http://forbes.house.gov/PrayerCaucus/About.aspx.

21. H.R. Res. 121 and H.R. Res. 3477, 2009, 111th Cong.

22. Mark A. Noll, "The Bible and Slavery," in *Religion and the American Civil War*, ed. Randall M. Miller, Harry S. Stout, and Charles Reagan Wilson (New York: Oxford University Press, 1998), 45.

23. The Cornwall Alliance, http://www.cornwallalliance.org/.

24. The "Cornwall Declaration on Environmental Stewardship" is available in its entirety via http://www.cornwallalliance.org/articles/read/an-evangelical-declaration-on-global-warming/.

25. "Bi-Partisan Congressional Measures to Stop EPA Power Grab," press release, Cornwall Alliance, March 28, 2011, http://www.cornwallalliance.org/press/read/bi-partisan-congressional-measures-to-stop-epa-power-grab/.

26. See: "The Cornwall Declaration on Environmental Stewardship," http://www.cornwallalliance.org/docs/the-cornwall-declaration-on-environmental-stewardship.pdf.

27. "About the Cornwall Alliance," http://www.cornwallalliance.org/about/.

28. Lee Fang, "The Oily Operators behind the Religious Climate Change Denial Front Group, Cornwall Alliance," *Think Progress*, June 15, 2010, http://thinkprogress.org/green/2010/06/15/174718/cornwall-alliance-frontgroup/.

29. People for the American Way, "The 'Green Dragon' Slayers: How the Religious Right and Corporate Right Are Joining Forces to Fight Environmental Protection," April 22, 2011, http://www.pfaw.org/rww-in-focus/the-green-dragon-slayers-how-the-religious-right-and-the-corporate-right-are-joining-fo.

30. Michael O'Brien, "Boehner: CO_2 threat to environment 'almost comical'," The Hill's Blog Briefing Room, April 19, 2009. (Comment reportedly made when appearing on *The Week with George Stephanopoulos*, ABC News, April 19, 2009.)

31. Irin Carmon, "Rick Santorum Is Coming for Your Birth Control," *Salon.com*, January 4, 2012, http://www.salon.com/2012/01/04/rick_santorum_is_coming_for_your_birth_control/.

32. Hugh Kramer, "America Should Outlaw Blasphemy and Profanity Says AFA's Bryan Fischer," *LA Atheism Examiner,* May 28, 2011, http://www.examiner.com/atheism-in-los -angeles/america-should-outlaw-blasphemy-and-profanity-says-afa-s-bryan-fischer.

33. Kyle Mantyla, "Bush White House Visitor Log Reveals Revolving Door of Religious Right Leaders," People for the American Way, September 9, 2009, http://www.rightwing watch.org/content/bushs-white-house-visitor-log-reveals-revolving-door-religious-right -leaders.

34. Melinda Deslatte, "La. Senators Reject Repeal of Science Act," *Erie Times-News (AP),* May 26, 2011. http://www.goerie.com/apps/pbcs.dll/article?AID=/20110526/APN/1105260608.

35. The Wedge document is available in its entirety via www.antievolution.org/features/wedge .html.

36. *Kitzmiller, et al. v. Dover Area School District, et al.,* U.S. District Court, Middle District Penn., Case 04cv2688.

37. Manny Fernandez, "Perry Leads Prayer Rally for 'Nation in Crisis,'" *New York Times,* August 6, 2011. The Response website, http://theresponseusa.com/, has since removed Perry's speech and focused on subsequent events in other states.

38. Tim Murphy, "Rick Perry Ally: Statue of Liberty is a 'Demonic Idol,'" *Mother Jones,* July 12, 2011, http://motherjones.com/mojo/2011/07/rick-perry-ally-statue-liberty-demonic-idol.

CHAPTER 6: BETTER LATE THAN NEVER

1. "Our Mission and Vision," People for the American Way, http://www.pfaw.org/about-us /our-mission-and-vision·

2. "Falwell Attacked Lynn as 'About as Reverend as an Oak Tree'; Guest Host Asman Asked Permission to 'Repeat It at Some Point,'" Media Matters for America, December 2, 2005, http://mediamatters.org/mmtv/200512020015.

3. Human Rights Campaign, www.hrc.org.

4. 47 CFR 25.701.

5. Statement of Chairman William E. Kennard, In the Matter of Implementation of Section 25 of the Cable Television Consumer Protection and Competition Act of 1992, Direct Broadcast Public Interest Obligations, MM Docket 93-25.

6. Ibid.

7. Petitioner's Complaint, In the Matter of the Secular Coalition for America, FCC, DA 04-3989.

8. Adam Schreck, "Congressman Says He Doesn't Believe in God," *Los Angeles Times,* March 13, 2007.

9. Stark's entire floor statement can be found at http://www.stark.house.gov/index.php ?option=com_content&view=article&id=2211:floor-statement-supporting-the-national -day-of-reason&catid=81:floor-statements-2011&Itemid=84.

10. Obama's inaugural speech can be found at: http://articles.cnn.com/2009-01-20/politics /obama.politics_1_nation-generation-president-bush/4?_s=PM:POLITICS.

11. Paul Starobin, "The Rise of the Godless," *The National Journal,* March 2009.

12. James C. McKinley Jr., "Atheist Ads on Buses Rattle Fort Worth," *New York Times,* December 13, 2010, http://www.nytimes.com/2010/12/14/us/14atheist.html.

13. Adam Tuss, "New Metro Ads Likely to Stir Up Controversy," WTOP Radio, November 11, 2008, http://www.wtop.com/?nid=&sid=1515427.

14. Ibid.

15. This quote appears on the home page of outcampaign.org.

16. "Students Protest Pharmacist's Refusal to Give Rape Survivor EC," *Ms. Magazine* (citing the *Arizona Daily Star*), October 28, 2005, http://www.msmagazine.com/news/uswire story.asp?ID=9356. This incident is also described on the SCA website: www.secular.org /issues/pharmacists.

17. Video of the exchange can be found at http://secular.org/video/scas-amanda-knief-presses -president-obama-faith-based-policies-during-town-hall-meeting.

18. RFRA is codified federally at 42 U.S.C. § 2000bb-2000bb-4.

CHAPTER 7: REASON FOR HOPE AND HOPE FOR REASON

1. Franklin Bowditch Dexter, ed., *Documentary History of Yale University* (New Haven, CT: Yale University Press, 1916), 20-21.
2. "Campus Group List," Secular Student Alliance, http://secularstudents.org/affiliates.
3. Interview, March 16, 2011.
4. William M. Arkin, "The Pentagon Unleashes a Holy Warrior," *Los Angeles Times,* October 16, 2003, http://articles.latimes.com/2003/oct/16/opinion/oe-arkin16.
5. Ibid.
6. Kimberly Winston, Religion News Service, "At religious campuses, atheist groups operate underground," *USA Today,* November 4, 2011, http://www.usatoday.com/news/religion /story/2011-11-04/atheist-college-campus/51073822/1.
7. The McCollums' story is the subject of a 2011 documentary entitled *The Lord Is Not on Trial Here Today,* which aired in the United States on PBS.
8. Paul Davis, "Florist found in Connecticut to deliver roses to Cranston West prayer banner opponent," *Providence Journal,* January 19, 2012.
9. *Lee v. Weisman,* 505 U.S. 577, 592 (1992).
10. Greta Christina, "High School Student Stands Up against Prayer at Public School and Is Ostracized, Demeaned and Threatened," AlterNet, May 25, 2011, http://www.alternet .org/belief/151086/high_school_student_stands_up_against_prayer_at_public_school _and_is_ostracized,_demeaned_and_threatened?page=entire.
11. Rich Klindworth, "Laurens 55 Graduates Will Pray amid Controversy," WSPA, May 18, 2011, http://www2.wspa.com/news/2011/may/18/9/no-graduation-upstate-school -ar-1837419/.
12. Kathryn Kranjc, "Atheists Share Personal Reflections in USC Panel," *Daily Gamecock,* April 13, 2011, http://www.dailygamecock.com/mix/item/1271-atheists-share-personal -reflections-in-usc-panel.
13. Barry Kosmin and Ariela Keysar with Ryan Cragan and Juhem Navarro-Rivera, *American Nones: The Profile of the No Religion Population. A Report Based on the American Religious Identification Survey 2008* (Hartford, CT: Trinity College, 2009).
14. "Jeff Hawkins and Janet Strauss Pledge $100,000 Challenge to SSA," Secular Student Alliance, www.secularstudents.org/node/3594.
15. John L. Allen Jr., "Cardinal George's Plan to Evangelize America," *National Catholic Reporter,* October 7, 2009, http://ncronline.org/news/people/cardinal-georges-plan -evangelize-america.
16. Walker Bristol, "Peers, Parents and Popularity," *New Humanism,* May 11, 2011, http://www.thenewhumanism.org/authors/walker-bristol/articles/peers-parents-and -popularity.
17. The Harvard humanist chaplaincy's website is www.harvardhumanist.org.
18. Phil Zuckerman, "Secular Studies Arrives at Last," *Huffington Post,* May 17, 2011, http: //www.huffingtonpost.com/phil-zuckerman/secular-studies-arrives-a_b_862870.html. See also Laurie Goodstein, "Pitzer College in California Adds Major in Secularism," *New York Times,* May 7, 2011, http://www.nytimes.com/2011/05/08/us/08secular.html.
19. NSRN Online: Nonreligion and Secularity Research Network, http://nsrn.net/.
20. Zuckerman, "Secular Studies."

CHAPTER 8: WHEN "HAPPY HOLIDAYS" IS AN ACT OF HOSTILITY

1. Quoted material is from a watch list published at the Catholic League's website, www .catholicleague.org/black-christmas-is-vintage-weinstein/.
2. On its website (www.afa.net), the AFA publishes a "Naughty or Nice List" that declares whether companies are "for" or "against" Christmas.
3. "AFA Declares Another Victory in the War on Christmas," press release, AFA, November 22, 2010, http://www.afa.net/Media/PressRelease.aspx?id=2147500643.

4. "'Factor' Producer Jesse Watters Visits Massachusetts School That Won't Let Children Celebrate Christmas," FOXNews, December 7, 2009, http://www.foxnews.com /story/0,2933,579662,00.html; "Pennsylvania Town Removes Nativity Scene after Complaint," The Factor Online, December 8, 2010, http://www.billoreilly.com/b/Pennsylvania -town-removes-nativity-after-complaint/163807913350681450.html.

5. "Fox Betrays Christmas Crusade, Sells 'Holiday' Ornaments for Your 'Holiday Tree,'" Media Matters for America, November 30, 2005, http://mediamatters.org/research /200511300006.

6. The school-prayer case is *Engel v. Vitale,* 370 U.S. 421 (1962); the Bible-reading case is *Abington School District v. Schempp,* 374 U.S. 203 (1963).

7. *Engel v. Vitale,* 370 U.S. 421, at 442-443.

8. Gregory Kane, "Gregory Kane: Banning Prayer in Schools Hurts Public Morality," *Washington Examiner,* April 5, 2010, http://washingtonexaminer.com/node/102406.

9. Ibid.

10. Allan Parachini et al., *Prayer in Public Schools: An International Survey,* report by the ACLU of Southern California, May 1995. This report is available via the Education Resources Information Center (ERIC), http://www.eric.ed.gov/ERICWebPortal/search /detailmini.jsp?_nfpb=true&_&ERICExtSearch_SearchValue_0=ED393711&ERICExt Search_SearchType_0=no&accno=ED393711.

11. Programme for International Student Assessment of the Organisation for Economic Co -operation and Development, report, 2009. Detailed OECD information is available at http://www.oecd.org/document/61/0,3746,en_32252351_32235731_46567613_1_1_1 _1,00.html.

12. Edward J. Larson and Larry Witham, "Leading Scientists Still Reject God," *Nature,* July 23, 1998, http://www.stephenjaygould.org/ctrl/news/file002.html.

13. The "cult following" comment was reported in "Schools Should Not Limit Origins-of-Life Discussions to Evolution, Republican Legislators Say," *Stillwater Gazette,* September 27, 2005, http://www.stillwatergazette.com/articles/2003/10/02/export160.txt; see also: Kevin Allman, "Michelle Bachmann on Intelligent Design," *The Independent Weekly,* June 18, 2011, http://www.theind.com/news/8515-michele-bachmann-on-intelligent -design.

14. Ariel Hart, "Judge in Georgia Orders Anti-evolution Stickers Removed from Textbooks," *New York Times,* January 14, 2005, http://www.nytimes.com/2005/01/14 /national/14sticker.html.

15. James C. McKinley Jr., "Texas Conservatives Win Curriculum Change," *New York Times,* March 12, 2010, http://www.nytimes.com/2010/03/13/education/13texas.html.

16. Marx did not advocate for the forceful abolition of religion, but rather thought that an evolved society would simply result in the decline of religion. Nevertheless, even though most informed observers would agree that the Soviet Union was a poor reflection of the ideas of Karl Marx, the words "communism" and "Marxism" became synonymous with totalitarian government in postwar America.

17. "Mission," National Day of Prayer website, http://nationaldayofprayer.org/about/our -mission/.

18. Ibid.

19. National Legal Foundation, www.nlf.net.

20. All NLF quotes are from its mission statement, which can be found at http://www.nlf.net /About/mission.html.

21. Foundation for Moral Law, morallaw.org.

22. "About the Foundation for Moral Law," http://morallaw.org/about.

23. United States Justice Foundation, www.usjf.net.

24. Gary Kreep, "Obama's Birth Certificate Scandal," *Hawaii Reporter,* January 28, 2011, http://www.hawaiireporter.com/obamas-birth-certificate-scandal/123.

25. Liberty Council website, www.lc.org.

26. "Doctrinal Statement," Liberty Council, http://www.lc.org/index.cfm?PID=22102.

27. Thomas More Law Center website, www.thomasmore.org.

28. "About the Thomas More Law Center," http://www.thomasmore.org/qry/page.taf?id=23.
29. *Aronow v. United States,* 432 F.2d 242 (9th Cir. 1970).
30. Michelle Goldberg, "Bachmann's Unrivaled Extremism," *Daily Beast,* June 14, 2011, http://www.thedailybeast.com/articles/2011/06/14/michele-bachmanns-unrivaled-extremism-gay-rights-to-religion.html.
31. Pew Research Center / *Smithsonian* magazine survey, April 2011, http://www.people-press.org/2010/06/22/section-3-war-terrorism-and-global-trends/. Other surveys verify the predominance of such beliefs. A *Newsweek* poll from 1999 found that 71 percent of evangelicals believed that the world would end according to apocalyptic biblical prophecy, and about half who believe that said it would happen in their lifetime. http://www.prnewswire.com/news-releases/newsweek—forty-percent-of-americans-believe-the-world-will-end-as-the-bible-predicts—a-battle-between-jesus-and-the-antichrist-at-armageddon-76809152.html.
32. *Boy Scouts of America v. Dale,* 530 U.S. 640 (2000).
33. "BSA Lose Parents," http://www.bsa-discrimination.org/html/bsa_membership.html.
34. "List of Corporations Who Refuse to Fund the BSA," http://www.scoutingforall.org/data/layer02/wycd/corplist.html.
35. "Boy Scouts of America Kick Out 19-Year-Old Eagle Scout for Being an Atheist," press release, Scouting for All, October 26, 2002, http://www.scoutingforall.org/data/archives/aaic/2002102901.html.
36. "Kicked Out of the Boy Scouts for Being an Atheist," *The Friendly Atheist* (blog), June 25, 2009, http://www.patheos.com/blogs/friendlyatheist/2009/06/25/kicked-out-of-the-boy-scouts-for-being-an-atheist/.
37. William M. Arkin, "The Pentagon Unleashes a Holy Warrior," *Los Angeles Times,* October 16, 2003, http://articles.latimes.com/2003/oct/16/opinion/oe-arkin16.
38. Military Association of Atheists and Freethinkers website, www.militaryatheists.org.
39. Military Religious Freedom Foundation website, www.militaryreligiousfreedom.org.
40. See *Real Time with Bill Maher,* episode 190, September 24, 2010, http://www.hbo.com/real-time-with-bill-maher/episodes/0/190-episode/video/190-september-24-overtime.html.
41. Stan Goff, "Playing the Atheism Card against Pat Tillman's Family," *Truth Dig,* July 28, 2006, http://www.truthdig.com/report/item/20060728_worm_dirt/; see also Johanna Neuman, "Deceit Surrounding Death of Tillman Spawns Disgust," *Denver Post,* April 25, 2007, http://www.denverpost.com/broncos/ci_5743176.
42. "Report of Americans United for Separation of Church and State on Religious Coercion and Endorsement of Religion at the United States Air Force Academy," April 28, 2005. The full report can be found at members.au.org/pdf/050428AirForceReport.pdf.
43. Ibid.
44. Laurie Goodstein, "Air Force Academy Staff Found Promoting Religion," *New York Times,* June 23, 2005, http://www.nytimes.com/2005/06/23/politics/23academy.html?pagewanted=all.
45. T. R. Reid, "Air Force Removes Chaplain from Post," *Washington Post,* May 13, 2005, http://www.washingtonpost.com/wp-dyn/content/article/2005/05/12/AR2005051201740.html.
46. Military Association of Atheists and Freethinkers website, http://www.militaryatheists.org/spirituality.html.
47. James Dao, "Atheists Seek Chaplain Role in Military," *New York Times,* April 26, 2011, http://www.nytimes.com/2011/04/27/us/27atheists.html?pagewanted=all.
48. Military religious demographic studies are discussed in detail at http://www.militaryatheists.org/demographics.html.
49. Military Association of Atheists and Freethinkers website, http://militaryatheists.org/demographics.html.
50. "Chaplains Wanted for Atheists in Foxholes," NPR News, December 4, 2011. http://m.npr.org/news/front/143057431.

CHAPTER 9: A NEW PLAN OF ACTION

1. *Elk Grove Unified School District v. Newdow,* 542 U.S. 1 (2004).
2. Chris H. Sieroty, "Congress Reacts to 'under God' Ruling," United Press International, June 26, 2002, http://www.upi.com/Top_News/2002/06/26/Congress-reacts -to-under-God-ruling/UPI-91131025141383/.
3. *Newdow v. Rio Linda Union School District,* 05-17257 (9th Cir. 2010).
4. *Hein v. FFRF,* 551 U.S. 587 (2007).
5. Souter was quoting Justice Potter Stewart's concurring opinion in *Flast v. Cohen,* 392 U.S. 83 (1968)
6. *FFRF v. Obama,* 10-1973 (7th Cir. 2010).
7. *Griswold v. Connecticut,* 381 U.S. 479 (1965).
8. *Brown v. Board of Education,* 347 U.S. 483 (1954).
9. See, for example, Justice Thomas's concurring opinion in the *Elk Grove* case, sup.
10. For more detail on Scalia, see his biography by Joan Biskupic, *American Original: The Life and Constitution of Supreme Court Justice Antonin Scalia* (New York: Sarah Crichton Books, 2009).
11. *Goodridge v. Department of Public Health,* 440 Mass. 309 (2003).
12. Frank Newport, "For First Time, Majority of Americans Favor Legal Gay Marriage," Gallup, May 20, 2011, http://www.gallup.com/poll/147662/first-time-majority-americans -favor-legal-gay-marriage.aspx.
13. Buono was interviewed by Tim O'Brien on the PBS show, www.pbs.org/wnet /religionandethics/episodes/october-2-2009/mojave-cross/4424
14. *Doe v. Acton,* Middlesex Superior Court 10-4261.
15. "Voters Recall Pledge Objector," *Washington Times,* March 23, 2005, http://www .washingtontimes.com/news/2005/mar/23/20050323-110303-1711r/?page=all.
16. Ibid.

CHAPTER 10: A SECULAR FUTURE

1. Sagan was the AHA's Humanist of the Year in 1981; Roddenberry was the AHA's Humanist Arts Award recipient in 1991.
2. Adam Liptak, "U.S. Prison Population Dwarfs that of Other Nations," *New York Times,* April 23, 2008.
3. Sylvia A. Allegretto, "U.S. Workers Enjoy Far Fewer Vacation Days than Europeans," Economic Policy Institute, August 24, 2005, http://www.epi.org/publication/web features_snapshots_20050824/.
4. The exact ratio of CEO-to-worker pay will vary depending on the criteria used, but by any measure, the ratio has been increasing dramatically for over 30 years. According to one report, by no means the most liberal, CEOs earned about 35 times what average workers earned in 1978, but by 2006, CEOs earned 262 times more than average workers. See Lawrence Mishel, "CEO-to-Worker Pay Imbalance Grows," Economic Policy Institute, June 21, 2006, http://www.epi.org/publication/webfeatures_snapshots_2006 0621/.
5. Andrew Romano, "How Dumb Are We?" *Daily Beast,* March 20, 2011, http://www.the dailybeast.com/newsweek/2011/03/20/how-dumb-are-we.html.
6. Noam Chomsky, "Sports and Spectacle," *Nation,* August 15, 2011.
7. "Manufacture of consent" is wording that was first used by Walter Lippmann in his 1922 book, *Public Opinion,* but in recent years, it has been most closely associated with Chomsky.
8. Edward J. Larson and Larry Witham, "Leading Scientists Still Reject God," *Nature* vol. 394, no. 6691 (1998): 313.
9. Barack Obama, *Dreams from My Father: A Story of Race and Inheritance* (New York: Three Rivers Press, 2004 edition), xii.

10. Ibid., 50.
11. When Obama was inaugurated on January 20, 2009, the AHA ran a full-page ad in the *Washington Post* celebrating his humanist upbringing. The headline of the ad read, "President Obama: Living Proof that Nontheistic Family Values Build Character."
12. Barack Obama, *The Audacity of Hope: Thoughts on Reclaiming the American Dream* (New York: Crown Publishers, 2006), 202, 205.
13. Obama, *Dreams from My Father,* 348.
14. Ibid., 141.
15. Ibid., 163, 286-287.
16. Carl Coon, *One Planet, One People: Beyond "Us Vs. Them"* (Amherst, NY: Prometheus Books, 2004), 134.
17. Ibid., 139.

AFTERWORD: ANOTHER WEDDING

1. *Goodridge v. Department of Public Health,* 440 Mass. 309 at 349–350 (2003).

INDEX